ASSASSINS of DISOBEDIENCE!
Invoking the Power of the Most High Through Obedience, is the Key to
Living Your Best Life as the Supreme Ingredient!
Heaven or Hell?

CHILDREN OF THE MOST HIGH:
PRISTINE YOUTH AND FAMILY SOLUTIONS, LLC.
SONS AND DAUGHTERS OF THE MOST HIGH PUBLISHERS ®

Oh, Gracious Most High Heavenly father, Holy is your name,
Your Will Be Done Now and Forever!
Yashu'a (Jesus) said: *"Thou shalt love the Most High Heavenly Father,*
thy Sustainer with all thy heart, and with all thy soul,
and with all thy mind. Thou shalt love
thy neighbour as thyself."

By

Woodie Hughes Jr.
CEO & Founder of the Children of the Most High:
Pristine Youth and Family Solutions LLC.
Sons and Daughters of the Most High Publishers®
Mr. Hughes is a Servant of the Most High, and a Teacher
of the Most High's Doctrine.

I0154743

I

Yashu'a (Jesus) said: *"A new commandment I give unto*
you, that ye love one another; as I have loved you,
that ye also love one another."

ASSASSINS of DISOBEDIENCE:
Invoking the Power of the Most High Through Obedience, is the Key to Living Your Best Life as the Supreme Ingredient!
Heaven or Hell?

Editor: Sons and Daughters of the Most High Editors

ISBN: 978-1-948355-00-1

Library of Congress Control Number: 2020912010

FOR MORE INFORMATION CONTACT:

Woodie Hughes Jr., CEO & Founder of the Children of the Most High: Pristine Youth and Family Solutions, LLC.
Sons and Daughters of the Most High Publishers ®

Online ordering is available for all products at our Amazon Store Front on our website at: childrenofthemosthigh.com
Or, write to us at: Children of the Most High: Pristine Youth and Family Solutions, LLC. P.O. Box 6365, Warner Robins, Georgia 31095.

II

Yashu'a (Jesus) said: "A new commandment I give unto you, that ye love one another; as I have loved you, that ye also love one another."

Table of Contents

III

Yashu'a (Jesus) said: "A new commandment I give unto you, that ye love one another; as I have loved you, that ye also love one another."

Table of Contents

IV

Yashu'a (Jesus) said: "*A new commandment I give unto you, that ye love one another; as I have loved you, that ye also love one another.*"

Table of Contents

Yashu'a (Jesus) said: "A new commandment I give unto you, that ye love one another; as I have loved you, that ye also love one another."

CHILDREN OF THE MOST HIGH:
PRISTINE YOUTH AND FAMILY SOLUTIONS, LLC.
SONS AND DAUGHTERS OF THE MOST HIGH PUBLISHERS ®

Oh, Gracious Most High Heavenly father, Holy is your name, Your Will Be Done Now and Forever! **Yashu'a (Jesus) said:** *"Thou shalt love the Most High Heavenly Father, thy Sustainer with all thy heart, and with all thy soul, and with all thy mind. Thou shalt love thy neighbour as thyself."*

Greetings:

We greet all members of humanity in peace! Nothing would exist if you Oh Gracious Most High Heavenly Father, The Creator didn't create it. You are alone in Your Greatness; you have no partners that share in your grace. To you all sovereignty is due and you are all powerful over everything. We seek refuge in you, the ever watchful Most High who hears and knows all things! Glory be to you as many times as the number of things you have created! All gratitude is due to you oh gracious Most High Heavenly Father, you are the Creator and Sustainer of all the boundless universes. You are the Yielder, and the most Merciful. The Ruler of the Day of Judgement. It's you whom we worship and it is you alone whom we beseech for help.

Yashu'a (Jesus) said: "A new commandment I give unto you, that ye love one another; as I have loved you, that ye also love one another."

ASSASSINS of DISOBEDIENCE!
Invoking the Power of the Most High Through Obedience, is the Key to Living Your Best Life
as the Supreme Ingredient!
Heaven or Hell?

CHILDREN OF THE MOST HIGH:
PRISTINE YOUTH AND FAMILY SOLUTIONS, LLC.
SONS AND DAUGHTERS OF THE MOST HIGH PUBLISHERS ®

Oh, Gracious Most High Heavenly father, Holy is your name,
Your Will Be Done Now and Forever!
Yashu'a (Jesus) said: *"Thou shalt love the Most High Heavenly Father, thy Sustainer with all thy heart, and with all thy soul, and with all thy mind. Thou shalt love thy neighbour as thyself."*

Oh Guide, guide us to the narrow path **which reflects moral integrity and positive character traits in action** of the ones who stand straight, the narrow path of those who earned your grace not inclusive of those who brought an everlasting curse on themselves, those who conceal the facts of that which they know to be true in order to lead the **sincere-hearted seekers** of your truth astray. Amen

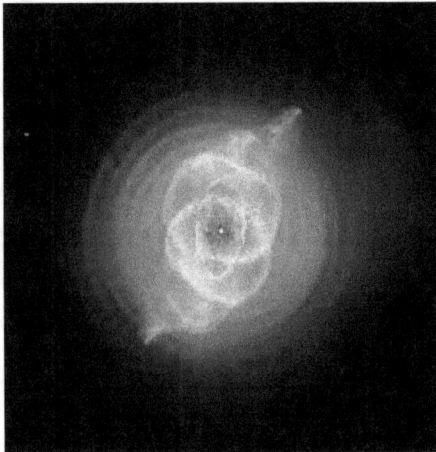

2

Yashu'a (Jesus) said: *"A new commandment I give unto you, that ye love one another; as I have loved you, that ye also love one another."*

ASSASSINS of DISOBEDIENCE!
Invoking the Power of the Most High Through Obedience, is the Key to Living Your Best Life
as the Supreme Ingredient!
Heaven or Hell?

CHILDREN OF THE MOST HIGH:
PRISTINE YOUTH AND FAMILY SOLUTIONS, LLC.
SONS AND DAUGHTERS OF THE MOST HIGH PUBLISHERS ®

Oh, Gracious Most High Heavenly father, Holy is your name,
Your Will Be Done Now and Forever!
Yashu'a (Jesus) said: *"Thou shalt love the Most High Heavenly Father, thy Sustainer with all*
thy heart, and with all thy soul, and with all thy mind. Thou shalt love
thy neighbour as thyself."

What does the phrase: "those who earned your grace" mean as oppose to saying "those who receive your grace?" The word: **"grace"** in the King James Version (KJV) bible book of Genesis chapter 6 verse 8 is: חֵן **Khane or chen** pronounced as **khān (KJV bible Hebrew Strong's Concordance#2580).** The word: **"חֵן Khane or chen"** means **"favor, kindness."** The word: **"grace"** in the KJV bible book of John chapter 1 verse 17 is: χάρις **Kharece or charis** pronounced as **khä'-rēs (KJV bible Greek Strong's Concordance#5485).** The word: **"χάρις Kharece or charis"** means **"joy, delight."** So, the phrase: **"those who earned your grace"** is in reference **to those people who are no longer physically alive that have transitioned to a higher life** such as: **Yashu'a (Jesus), John the Baptist, Yowkhanan Bar Zebedee (John Son of Zebedee who was Yashu'a (Jesus) beloved disciple), or Ab-Ra-Kham (Abraham).**

3

Yashu'a (Jesus) said: *"A new commandment I give unto you, that ye love one another; as I have loved you, that ye also love one another."*

ASSASSINS of DISOBEDIENCE!
Invoking the Power of the Most High Through Obedience, is the Key to Living Your Best Life
as the Supreme Ingredient!
Heaven or Hell?

CHILDREN OF THE MOST HIGH:
PRISTINE YOUTH AND FAMILY SOLUTIONS, LLC.
SONS AND DAUGHTERS OF THE MOST HIGH PUBLISHERS ®

Oh, Gracious Most High Heavenly father, Holy is your name,
Your Will Be Done Now and Forever!
Yashu'a (Jesus) said: "Thou shalt love the Most High Heavenly Father, thy Sustainer with all
thy heart, and with all thy soul, and with all thy mind. Thou shalt love
thy neighbour as thyself."

The phrase: **"those who receive your grace"** is in reference **to**

any person or people who the Most High Heavenly Father

bestows **favor** on by allowing them to still be physically alive,

and to have an opportunity to experience **joy** while still be

physically alive.

4

Yashu'a (Jesus) said: "A new commandment I give unto
you, that ye love one another; as I have loved you,
that ye also love one another."

ASSASSINS of DISOBEDIENCE!
Invoking the Power of the Most High Through Obedience, is the Key to Living Your Best Life
as the Supreme Ingredient!
Heaven or Hell?

CHILDREN OF THE MOST HIGH:
PRISTINE YOUTH AND FAMILY SOLUTIONS, LLC.
SONS AND DAUGHTERS OF THE MOST HIGH PUBLISHERS ®

Oh, Gracious Most High Heavenly father, Holy is your name,
Your Will Be Done Now and Forever!
Yashu'a (Jesus) said: "Thou shalt love the Most High Heavenly Father, thy Sustainer with all
thy heart, and with all thy soul, and with all thy mind. Thou shalt love
thy neighbour as thyself."

Dedication

The "ASSASSINS of DISOBEDIENCE! Invoking the Power of the Most High Through Obedience, is the Key to Living Your Best Life as the Supreme Ingredient! Heaven or Hell?" book is dedicated to all youth and all adults who are children of the Most High that want to learn the doctrine of the **Most High (ELYOWN עֶלְיוֹן) God (EL אֵל)** in a way that reflects the original languages of the bible before being translated into the English language, and that reflects the original Most High Heavenly Father's doctrine that Yashu'a Ha Mashiakh (Jesus the Messiah) taught. In the KJV bible book of Genesis chapter 14 verse 18 states: "And Melchizedek king of Salem brought forth bread and wine: and he *was* the priest of the **Most High** God."

Yashu'a (Jesus) said: "A new commandment I give unto
you, that ye love one another; as I have loved you,
that ye also love one another."

ASSASSINS of DISOBEDIENCE!
Invoking the Power of the Most High Through Obedience, is the Key to Living Your Best Life
as the Supreme Ingredient!
Heaven or Hell?

CHILDREN OF THE MOST HIGH:
PRISTINE YOUTH AND FAMILY SOLUTIONS, LLC.
SONS AND DAUGHTERS OF THE MOST HIGH PUBLISHERS ®

Oh, Gracious Most High Heavenly father, Holy is your name,
Your Will Be Done Now and Forever!
Yashu'a (Jesus) said: "Thou shalt love the Most High Heavenly Father, thy Sustainer with all
thy heart, and with all thy soul, and with all thy mind. Thou shalt love
thy neighbour as thyself."

The title: "**Most High**" is: the KJV bible Hebrew Strong's Concordance#**5945** for the title: "**Most High**" (ELYOWN עֶלְיוֹן EL אֵל), which means: "Highest, Most High, <u>Name of God</u>, as title, <u>The Supreme</u>:—(Most, on) high(-er, -est), upper(-most)." The title: "**God'** <u>in this verse</u> is the KJV bible Hebrew Strong's Concordance#**5945** for the title: "**God**" (EL אֵל), which means: "God, god, power, mighty, goodly, great, idols, might, strong, god, god-like one, mighty one, mighty men, men of rank, mighty heroes, angels, god, false god, (demons, imaginations), and mighty things in nature."

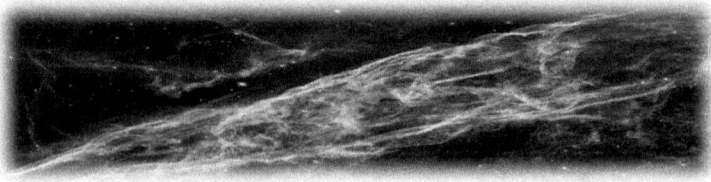

6

Yashu'a (Jesus) said: "A new commandment I give unto
you, that ye love one another; as I have loved you,
that ye also love one another."

CHILDREN OF THE MOST HIGH:
PRISTINE YOUTH AND FAMILY SOLUTIONS, LLC.
SONS AND DAUGHTERS OF THE MOST HIGH PUBLISHERS ®

Oh, Gracious Most High Heavenly father, Holy is your name,
Your Will Be Done Now and Forever!
Yashu'a (Jesus) said: "Thou shalt love the Most High Heavenly Father, thy Sustainer with all thy heart, and with all thy soul, and with all thy mind. Thou shalt love thy neighbour as thyself."

Acknowledgements

We thank the Most High Heavenly Father who is: The Most High Heavenly One, the Sustainer, the Nourisher, the Provider of Life, and the Creator of the boundless universes, thank you for sending the Messiah Yashu'a (Jesus) who was a willing sacrifice, and for your angelic-beings that protect us, inspire us and guide us to obey you, inclusive of the **Sun of Righteousness** (the word for "**Sun**" is **Shemesh** צְדָקָה pronounced **Sheh'·mesh**, the word for "**Righteousness**" is **Tsĕdaqah** שֶׁמֶשׁ pronounced **Tsed·ä·kä'**) who arises with healing in his wings as stated in the King James Version (KJV) bible book of **Malachi chapter 4 verse 2**, and we thank the Most High Heavenly One for life, for health and for everything else!

7

Yashu'a (Jesus) said: "A new commandment I give unto you, that ye love one another; as I have loved you, that ye also love one another."

ASSASSINS of DISOBEDIENCE!
*Invoking the Power of the Most High Through Obedience, is the Key to Living Your Best Life
as the Supreme Ingredient!*
Heaven or Hell?

CHILDREN OF THE MOST HIGH:
PRISTINE YOUTH AND FAMILY SOLUTIONS, LLC.
SONS AND DAUGHTERS OF THE MOST HIGH PUBLISHERS ®

*Oh, Gracious Most High Heavenly father, Holy is your name,
Your Will Be Done Now and Forever!*
Yashu'a (Jesus) said: *"Thou shalt love the Most High Heavenly Father, thy Sustainer with all
thy heart, and with all thy soul, and with all thy mind. Thou shalt love
thy neighbour as thyself."*

A Special Thank You to: My Dad (The Honorable: Mr. Woodie
Hughes Sr.), and Mom (the Noble: Mrs. Annette Hughes) for
accepting the Messiah Yashu'a (Jesus) and raising me and my
brothers in a Godly home filled with love as they like the
Messiah Yashu'a (Jesus); willingly sacrificed their youth and
many worldly possessions to ensure that my brothers and I had
the greatest opportunity to achieve the maximum levels of
success in all areas of our lives; **thank you Mom and Dad**!

8

*Yashu'a (Jesus) said: "A new commandment I give unto
you, that ye love one another; as I have loved you,
that ye also love one another."*

ASSASSINS of DISOBEDIENCE!
Invoking the Power of the Most High Through Obedience, is the Key to Living Your Best Life
as the Supreme Ingredient!
Heaven or Hell?

CHILDREN OF THE MOST HIGH:
PRISTINE YOUTH AND FAMILY SOLUTIONS, LLC.
SONS AND DAUGHTERS OF THE MOST HIGH PUBLISHERS ®

Oh, Gracious Most High Heavenly father, Holy is your name,
Your Will Be Done Now and Forever!
Yashu'a (Jesus) said: "Thou shalt love the Most High Heavenly Father, thy Sustainer with all
thy heart, and with all thy soul, and with all thy mind. Thou shalt love
thy neighbour as thyself."

A Special Thank You to: My Beloved Wife and best friend (Mrs. Tonya L. Hughes) who sacrificed her health and well-being to give birth to our children. Our children inspire me every day to keep working hard for our family and to continuously work hard to help uplift members of humanity so that we can work together to help people and the planet earth to maintain, and sustain positive health and balance for that great day, when: "Thy kingdom will come to earth as it is in heaven." We also thank the many other family members, friends, colleagues, mentors, and global spiritual family who are the children of the Most High and who are in the body of Christ.

9

Yashu'a (Jesus) said: "A new commandment I give unto
you, that ye love one another; as I have loved you,
that ye also love one another."

ASSASSINS of DISOBEDIENCE!
Invoking the Power of the Most High Through Obedience, is the Key to Living Your Best Life
as the Supreme Ingredient!
Heaven or Hell?

CHILDREN OF THE MOST HIGH:
PRISTINE YOUTH AND FAMILY SOLUTIONS, LLC.
SONS AND DAUGHTERS OF THE MOST HIGH PUBLISHERS ®

Oh, Gracious Most High Heavenly father, Holy is your name,
Your Will Be Done Now and Forever!
Yashu'a (Jesus) said: "Thou shalt love the Most High Heavenly Father, thy Sustainer with all
thy heart, and with all thy soul, and with all thy mind. Thou shalt love
thy neighbour as thyself."

Who are the Children of the Most High Pristine Youth and Family Solutions, LLC.?

We are teachers of the doctrine of the Most High; the doctrine that the real Messiah Yashu'a (Jesus) taught. In the KJV bible book of John chapter 7 verse 16; the Messiah Yashu'a (Jesus) stated: "My doctrine isn't mine, but his that sent me." The Children of the Most High, Pristine Youth and Family Solutions, LLC. purpose is to do the Most High Heavenly Father's will only! We exist and work under the authority of the Most High Heavenly Father, who is the Creator and the Ruler of all of the boundless universes!

Yashu'a (Jesus) said: "A new commandment I give unto
you, that ye love one another; as I have loved you,
that ye also love one another."

ASSASSINS of DISOBEDIENCE!
Invoking the Power of the Most High Through Obedience, is the Key to Living Your Best Life
as the Supreme Ingredient!
Heaven or Hell?

CHILDREN OF THE MOST HIGH:
PRISTINE YOUTH AND FAMILY SOLUTIONS, LLC.
SONS AND DAUGHTERS OF THE MOST HIGH PUBLISHERS ®

Oh, Gracious Most High Heavenly father, Holy is your name,
Your Will Be Done Now and Forever!
Yashu'a (Jesus) said: "Thou shalt love the Most High Heavenly Father, thy Sustainer with all
thy heart, and with all thy soul, and with all thy mind. Thou shalt love
thy neighbour as thyself."

We acknowledge the Messiah Jesus as our Savior who **we refer to** in his original Judean/Galilean Aramic (Hebrew) language birth name **Yasu'a** or **Yashu'a** (ישוע) meaning "**Savior**" and **Jesus,** who is **the Son of God** in English. **We have accepted the Lord Jesus Christ (Yashu'a Ha Mashiakh – Jesus the Messiah or Yehoshu'a, which means Yahayyu is Salvation or Yahayyu Saves) as our Savior and we are in the Body of Christ!**

CHILDREN OF THE MOST HIGH:
PRISTINE YOUTH AND FAMILY SOLUTIONS, LLC.
SONS AND DAUGHTERS OF THE MOST HIGH PUBLISHERS ®

Yashu'a (Jesus) said: "A new commandment I give unto you, that ye love one another; as I have loved you, that ye also love one another."

ASSASSINS of DISOBEDIENCE!
Invoking the Power of the Most High Through Obedience, is the Key to Living Your Best Life
as the Supreme Ingredient!
Heaven or Hell?

CHILDREN OF THE MOST HIGH:
PRISTINE YOUTH AND FAMILY SOLUTIONS, LLC.
SONS AND DAUGHTERS OF THE MOST HIGH PUBLISHERS ®

Oh, Gracious Most High Heavenly father, Holy is your name,
Your Will Be Done Now and Forever!
Yashu'a (Jesus) said: "Thou shalt love the Most High Heavenly Father, thy Sustainer with all thy heart, and with all thy soul, and with all thy mind. Thou shalt love thy neighbour as thyself."

What is the Mission, Vision, and Motto of the Children of the Most High; Pristine Youth and Family Solutions, LLC?

The Mission is: To inspire and empower all children of the Most High to pristinely make the world a safe and healthy place for all members of humanity. **The Vision is**: To create a world that is ruled by Love and the "**Will**" of the Most High, void of negative emotions, greed, lusts and love of money. According to the KJV bible book of Matthew chapter 19 verse 26, the Messiah Yashu'a (Jesus) said unto them, "With men this is impossible; but with God all things are possible." According to the KJV bible book of Philippians chapter 4 verse 13; it states: "I can do all things through Christ which strengthened me."

12

ASSASSINS of DISOBEDIENCE!
Invoking the Power of the Most High Through Obedience, is the Key to Living Your Best Life
as the Supreme Ingredient!
Heaven or Hell?

CHILDREN OF THE MOST HIGH:
PRISTINE YOUTH AND FAMILY SOLUTIONS, LLC.
SONS AND DAUGHTERS OF THE MOST HIGH PUBLISHERS ®

Oh, Gracious Most High Heavenly father, Holy is your name,
Your Will Be Done Now and Forever!
Yashu'a (Jesus) said: *"Thou shalt love the Most High Heavenly Father, thy Sustainer with all*
thy heart, and with all thy soul, and with all thy mind. Thou shalt love
thy neighbour as thyself."

Therefore; with God and through Christ, the children of the Most High Pristine Youth and Family Solutions, LLC. Mission and Vision can become a reality for the children of the Most High!

Motto: There is no right way to do the wrong thing!

13

Yashu'a (Jesus) said: *"A new commandment I give unto you, that ye love one another; as I have loved you, that ye also love one another."*

ASSASSINS of DISOBEDIENCE!
Invoking the Power of the Most High Through Obedience, is the Key to Living Your Best Life
as the Supreme Ingredient!
Heaven or Hell?

CHILDREN OF THE MOST HIGH:
PRISTINE YOUTH AND FAMILY SOLUTIONS, LLC.
SONS AND DAUGHTERS OF THE MOST HIGH PUBLISHERS ®

Oh, Gracious Most High Heavenly father, Holy is your name,
Your Will Be Done Now and Forever!
Yashu'a (Jesus) said: "Thou shalt love the Most High Heavenly Father, thy Sustainer with all
thy heart, and with all thy soul, and with all thy mind. Thou shalt love
thy neighbour as thyself."

Who is the Most High to the Children of the Most High Pristine Youth and Family Solutions, LLC.?

The Most High Heavenly Father is Love, the Sustainer, the Nourisher, the Provider of all Life, and the Omnipotent and the Omnipresent Creator of the boundless universes. The Most High Heavenly Father encompasses and interpenetrates all existence inclusive of every part of nature both visible as well as invisible. Oh, Most High Heavenly Father, you are all, and there is nothing nearer to us than you; for you encompass all things! Glory be to you alone!

14

Yashu'a (Jesus) said: "A new commandment I give unto
you, that ye love one another; as I have loved you,
that ye also love one another."

ASSASSINS of DISOBEDIENCE!
Invoking the Power of the Most High Through Obedience, is the Key to Living Your Best Life
as the Supreme Ingredient!
Heaven or Hell?

CHILDREN OF THE MOST HIGH:
PRISTINE YOUTH AND FAMILY SOLUTIONS, LLC.
SONS AND DAUGHTERS OF THE MOST HIGH PUBLISHERS ®

Oh, Gracious Most High Heavenly father, Holy is your name,
Your Will Be Done Now and Forever!
Yashu'a (Jesus) said: "Thou shalt love the Most High Heavenly Father, thy Sustainer with all
thy heart, and with all thy soul, and with all thy mind. Thou shalt love
thy neighbour as thyself."

In the KJV bible book of John chapter 4 verse 23, the Messiah Yashu'a (Jesus) said: "God is a Spirit: and they that worship him must worship him in spirit and in truth." In the KJV bible book of Genesis, chapter 14 verse 18 states: "And Melchizedek (**Malkiy-Tsedeq**, מַלְכִּי־צֶדֶק) king of Salem brought forth bread and wine: and he was the priest of the **Most High** (ELYOWN עֶלְיוֹן) **God** (EL אֵל)."

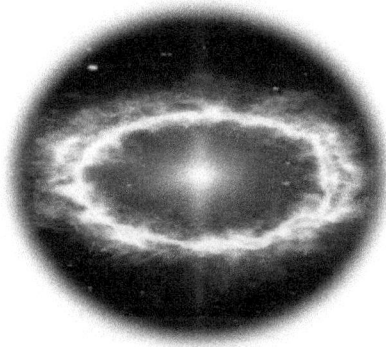

15

Yashu'a (Jesus) said: "A new commandment I give unto you, that ye love one another; as I have loved you, that ye also love one another."

ASSASSINS of DISOBEDIENCE!
Invoking the Power of the Most High Through Obedience, is the Key to Living Your Best Life
as the Supreme Ingredient!
Heaven or Hell?

CHILDREN OF THE MOST HIGH:
PRISTINE YOUTH AND FAMILY SOLUTIONS, LLC.
SONS AND DAUGHTERS OF THE MOST HIGH PUBLISHERS ®

Oh, Gracious Most High Heavenly father, Holy is your name,
Your Will Be Done Now and Forever!
Yashu'a (Jesus) said: *"Thou shalt love the Most High Heavenly Father, thy Sustainer with all*
thy heart, and with all thy soul, and with all thy mind. Thou shalt love
thy neighbour as thyself."

Who is the Real Messiah Jesus to the Children of the Most High Pristine Youth and Family Solutions, LLC.?

The Children of the Most High, Pristine Youth and Family Solutions, LLC., acknowledges the Real Messiah Jesus as our Savior who **we refer to** in his original Galilean/Judean Aramic (Hebrew) language, original birth name **Yasu'a (يسوع)** or **Yashu'a (ישוע)** meaning "**Savior**" also spelled Yeshua or Yehoshu'a, **Iesous** ('Iησοῦς) in the Greek translation and as **Kurios** (Greek word for Lord), and **Issa** or **Isa** in Ashuric Syriac (Arabic). Now when **Yehoshu'a** is translated in the Hebrew language it translates as **Yahayyu Saves** or simply **Joshua**, and in the Galilean language as Yashu'a or **Yasu'a** Inar **Rab** (which translates as **Jesus Son of the Sustainer**), **Yashu'a**

Yashu'a (Jesus) said: "A new commandment I give unto you, that ye love one another; as I have loved you, that ye also love one another."

ASSASSINS of DISOBEDIENCE!
Invoking the Power of the Most High Through Obedience, is the Key to Living Your Best Life
as the Supreme Ingredient!
Heaven or Hell?

CHILDREN OF THE MOST HIGH:
PRISTINE YOUTH AND FAMILY SOLUTIONS, LLC.
SONS AND DAUGHTERS OF THE MOST HIGH PUBLISHERS ®

Oh, Gracious Most High Heavenly father, Holy is your name,
Your Will Be Done Now and Forever!
Yashu'a (Jesus) said: "Thou shalt love the Most High Heavenly Father, thy Sustainer with all
thy heart, and with all thy soul, and with all thy mind. Thou shalt love
thy neighbour as thyself."

Bar Yahayyu (بَ حـِ بَ, **Existing One**). In Modern Hebrew translates as **Savior Son of the Everliving** or **Savior Son of the Existing One** or **Living One**, **Yasu'** and **Haru** as **Karast** **"Christ"** to the **Ancient** original indigenous Egyptian people of what is called: "Egypt" today, not to be confused with the Egyptians who are the nonindigenous people who migrated to what is now known as Egypt. Yashu'a called **Jesus,** is **the Son of God** in English. Yashu'a (Jesus), **the Son of the Most High God** is the way back to the Most High. In the KJV bible book of John chapter 14 verse 6; the Messiah Yashu'a (Jesus) said: "I am the way, the truth, and the life: no man (the words: "no man" is not in the original language that this verse was revealed in.

Yashu'a (Jesus) said: "A new commandment I give unto
you, that ye love one another; as I have loved you,
that ye also love one another."

ASSASSINS of DISOBEDIENCE!
Invoking the Power of the Most High Through Obedience, is the Key to Living Your Best Life
as the Supreme Ingredient!
Heaven or Hell?

CHILDREN OF THE MOST HIGH:
PRISTINE YOUTH AND FAMILY SOLUTIONS, LLC.
SONS AND DAUGHTERS OF THE MOST HIGH PUBLISHERS ®

Oh, Gracious Most High Heavenly father, Holy is your name,
Your Will Be Done Now and Forever!
Yashu'a (Jesus) said: "Thou shalt love the Most High Heavenly Father, thy Sustainer with all
thy heart, and with all thy soul, and with all thy mind. Thou shalt love
thy neighbour as thyself."

The original word for "no man" in the Greek KJV bible translation is: "**Oudeis**" (οὐδείς, Oudeis (is the KJV bible Greek Strong's Concordance#**3762**) means: *not one; no one, nothing*. So, this phrase is inclusive of males and females, not just males) cometh unto the Father, but by me."

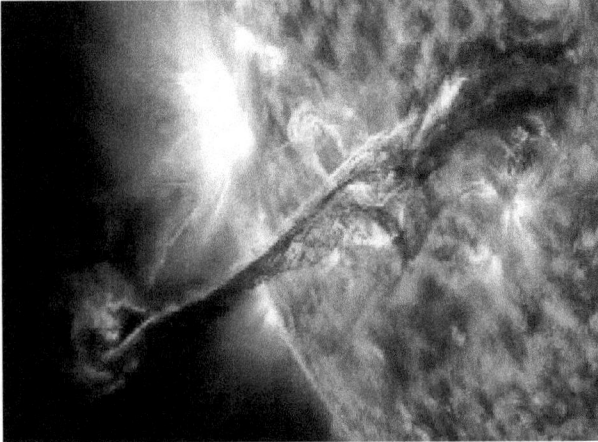

18

Yashu'a (Jesus) said: "A new commandment I give unto you, that ye love one another; as I have loved you, that ye also love one another."

ASSASSINS of DISOBEDIENCE!
Invoking the Power of the Most High Through Obedience, is the Key to Living Your Best Life
as the Supreme Ingredient!
Heaven or Hell?

CHILDREN OF THE MOST HIGH:
PRISTINE YOUTH AND FAMILY SOLUTIONS, LLC.
SONS AND DAUGHTERS OF THE MOST HIGH PUBLISHERS ®

Oh, Gracious Most High Heavenly father, Holy is your name,
Your Will Be Done Now and Forever!
Yashu'a (Jesus) said: *"Thou shalt love the Most High Heavenly Father, thy Sustainer with all*
thy heart, and with all thy soul, and with all thy mind. Thou shalt love
thy neighbour as thyself."

However, according to the Messiah Yashu'a (Jesus), no one can come to him unless the Most High Heavenly Father sends them to him. Yashu'a (Jesus) said in the KJV bible book of John chapter 6 verse 44: "No man (οὐδείς **oudeis**) can (δύναμαι **dynamai**) come (ἔρχομαι **erchomai**) to (πρός **pros**) me (μέ **mé, meh**), except (ἐὰν μή **ean mē**; KJV bible Greek Strong's Concordance#**3362** meaning: **if not, unless, whoever... not**) the Father which hath sent me draw (ἕλκω **helkō**; KJV bible Greek Strong's Concordance#**1670** meaning: **to draw by inward power, lead, impel; to drag (literally or figuratively)** him: and I will raise him up at the last day." Again, in the aforementioned verse, the words: "<u>no man</u>" is not in the original language that this verse was revealed in.

19

Yashu'a (Jesus) said: "A new commandment I give unto
you, that ye love one another; as I have loved you,
that ye also love one another."

ASSASSINS of DISOBEDIENCE!
Invoking the Power of the Most High Through Obedience, is the Key to Living Your Best Life
as the Supreme Ingredient!
Heaven or Hell?

CHILDREN OF THE MOST HIGH:
PRISTINE YOUTH AND FAMILY SOLUTIONS, LLC.
SONS AND DAUGHTERS OF THE MOST HIGH PUBLISHERS ®

Oh, Gracious Most High Heavenly father, Holy is your name,
Your Will Be Done Now and Forever!
Yashu'a (Jesus) said: "Thou shalt love the Most High Heavenly Father, thy Sustainer with all
thy heart, and with all thy soul, and with all thy mind. Thou shalt love
thy neighbour as thyself."

The original word for "no man" is: "**Oudeis**" (οὐδείς, Oudeis
(KJV bible Greek Strong's Concordance#**3762**) means: *not
one; no one, nothing*.

**What does the Children of the Most High Pristine Youth
and Family Solutions, LLC. do?**

The Children of the Most High; Pristine Youth and Family
Solutions LLC. does the will of the Most High Heavenly Father.
We are **Teachers** and **Administrators** of the Most High
Doctrine and work diligently to teach youth and adults how to
solve problems, and how to successfully work through difficult
problems or issues or situations by utilizing the **Children of the
Most High Pristine Youth and Family Solutions, LLC. 9X9
True Vine "Yashu'a" (Jesus) B.A. (Soul) K.A. (Spirit)**

*Yashu'a (Jesus) said: "A new commandment I give unto
you, that ye love one another; as I have loved you,
that ye also love one another."*

ASSASSINS of DISOBEDIENCE!
Invoking the Power of the Most High Through Obedience, is the Key to Living Your Best Life
as the Supreme Ingredient!
Heaven or Hell?

CHILDREN OF THE MOST HIGH:
PRISTINE YOUTH AND FAMILY SOLUTIONS, LLC.
SONS AND DAUGHTERS OF THE MOST HIGH PUBLISHERS ®

Oh, Gracious Most High Heavenly father, Holy is your name,
Your Will Be Done Now and Forever!
Yashu'a (Jesus) said: "Thou shalt love the Most High Heavenly Father, thy Sustainer with all
thy heart, and with all thy soul, and with all thy mind. Thou shalt love
thy neighbour as thyself."

R.E. (Sun) ("RE" is pronounced as "RAY") Sequential Order of Learning. More information about the True Vine "Yashu'a" (Jesus) B.A.-K.A.-R.E. Sequential Order of Learning will be expounded on in chapter 3. Our targeted audiences are youth (who are between the 5th and 12th grades) and adults who are children of the Most High. So, we teach in an effort to make the doctrine of the Most High clear in the minds of people who want to learn the original message or messages of the scriptures before they were translated into other languages, and we teach in an effort to create an opportunity for them to learn how to apply the doctrine of the Most High in all that they aspire to do!

21

Yashu'a (Jesus) said: "A new commandment I give unto
you, that ye love one another; as I have loved you,
that ye also love one another."

ASSASSINS of DISOBEDIENCE!
Invoking the Power of the Most High Through Obedience, is the Key to Living Your Best Life
as the Supreme Ingredient!
Heaven or Hell?

CHILDREN OF THE MOST HIGH:
PRISTINE YOUTH AND FAMILY SOLUTIONS, LLC.
SONS AND DAUGHTERS OF THE MOST HIGH PUBLISHERS ®

Oh, Gracious Most High Heavenly father, Holy is your name,
Your Will Be Done Now and Forever!
Yashu'a (Jesus) said: *"Thou shalt love the Most High Heavenly Father, thy Sustainer with all*
thy heart, and with all thy soul, and with all thy mind. Thou shalt love
thy neighbour as thyself."

Why does the Children of the Most High Pristine Youth and Family Solutions, LLC. refer to themselves as <u>T</u>eachers / <u>A</u>dministers of the Most High Heavenly Father's Doctrine instead of <u>P</u>reachers?

The Children of the Most High Pristine Youth and Family Solutions, LLC. refer to themselves as <u>T</u>eachers and **<u>A</u>dministers of the Most High Heavenly Father's Doctrine** that Yashu'a (Jesus) taught instead of <u>P</u>reachers because the Most High inspired and endowed them with the knowledge and with the ability to teach with the True-Vine (Yashu'a, Jesus) Spirit of the Word of Knowledge in the KJV bible book of 1st Corinthians chapter 12 verse 8 to teach the Most High's Doctrine as mentioned in the KJV bible book of John chapter 7 verse 16.

Yashu'a (Jesus) said: *"A new commandment I give unto you, that ye love one another; as I have loved you, that ye also love one another."*

ASSASSINS of DISOBEDIENCE!
Invoking the Power of the Most High Through Obedience, is the Key to Living Your Best Life
as the Supreme Ingredient!
Heaven or Hell?

CHILDREN OF THE MOST HIGH:
PRISTINE YOUTH AND FAMILY SOLUTIONS, LLC.
SONS AND DAUGHTERS OF THE MOST HIGH PUBLISHERS ®

Oh, Gracious Most High Heavenly father, Holy is your name,
Your Will Be Done Now and Forever!
Yashu'a (Jesus) said: "Thou shalt love the Most High Heavenly Father, thy Sustainer with all
thy heart, and with all thy soul, and with all thy mind. Thou shalt love
thy neighbour as thyself."

In the KJV bible book of Matthews chapter 28 verses 19-20, the Messiah Yashu'a (Jesus) said: "Go ye therefore, and teach all nations, baptizing them in the name of the Father, and of the Son, and of the Holy Ghost. Teaching them to observe all things whatsoever I have commanded you: and, lo, I am with you always, even unto the end of the world. Amen." The word in the aforementioned KJV bible book of Matthews chapter 28 verse 19 for *teach* is: the **KJV bible Greek Strong's Concordance#3100 mathēteuō (μαθητεύω) which means: teach, instruct, be disciple**.

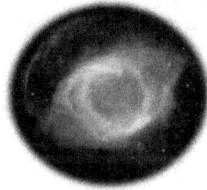

23

Yashu'a (Jesus) said: "A new commandment I give unto
you, that ye love one another; as I have loved you,
that ye also love one another."

ASSASSINS of DISOBEDIENCE!
Invoking the Power of the Most High Through Obedience, is the Key to Living Your Best Life
as the Supreme Ingredient!
Heaven or Hell?

CHILDREN OF THE MOST HIGH:
PRISTINE YOUTH AND FAMILY SOLUTIONS, LLC.
SONS AND DAUGHTERS OF THE MOST HIGH PUBLISHERS ®

Oh, Gracious Most High Heavenly father, Holy is your name,
Your Will Be Done Now and Forever!
Yashu'a (Jesus) said: *"Thou shalt love the Most High Heavenly Father, thy Sustainer with all*
thy heart, and with all thy soul, and with all thy mind. Thou shalt love
thy neighbour as thyself."

The word in the book of Matthews chapter 28 verse 20 for *Teaching* is: the **KJV bible Greek Strong's Concordance#1321 didaskō (διδάσκω) which means: to teach, to hold discourse with others in order to instruct them, deliver didactic discourses, to be a teacher, to discharge the office of a teacher, conduct one's self as a teacher, to teach one, to impart instruction, instill doctrine into one, the thing taught or enjoined, to explain or expound a thing, to teach one something.**

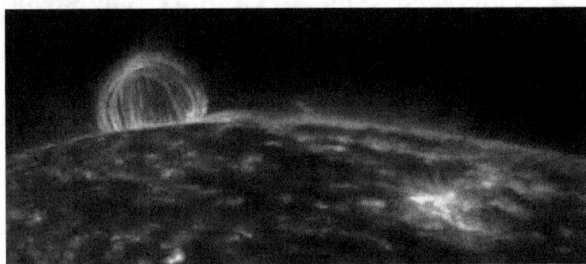

24

Yashu'a (Jesus) said: "A new commandment I give unto you, that ye love one another; as I have loved you, that ye also love one another."

CHILDREN OF THE MOST HIGH:
PRISTINE YOUTH AND FAMILY SOLUTIONS, LLC.
SONS AND DAUGHTERS OF THE MOST HIGH PUBLISHERS ®

Oh, Gracious Most High Heavenly father, Holy is your name,
Your Will Be Done Now and Forever!
Yashu'a (Jesus) said: *"Thou shalt love the Most High Heavenly Father, thy Sustainer with all thy heart, and with all thy soul, and with all thy mind. Thou shalt love thy neighbour as thyself."*

The word for **"Preach" in the KJV bible book of Matthew chapter 11 verse 1** is: the **KJV bible Greek Strong's Concordance#2784 kēryssō (κηρύσσω) which means to: preach, publish, and proclaim.** In the KJV bible book of Matthew chapter 11 verse 1; it states: "And it came to pass, when Jesus had made an end of commanding his twelve disciples, he departed thence to **teach** and to **preach** in their cities. The plural noun of "**teach**" is "**Teachers**": the **KJV bible Greek Strong's Concordance#1320 didaskalos** (διδάσκαλος, meaning one who teaches or teachers) and has the same root foundation as the word for "**Teach**" (the **KJV bible Greek Strong's Concordance#1321 didaskō** (διδάσκω) in the book of Acts chapter 13 verse 1; and states:

25

Yashu'a (Jesus) said: *"A new commandment I give unto you, that ye love one another; as I have loved you, that ye also love one another."*

ASSASSINS of DISOBEDIENCE!
Invoking the Power of the Most High Through Obedience, is the Key to Living Your Best Life
as the Supreme Ingredient!
Heaven or Hell?

CHILDREN OF THE MOST HIGH:
PRISTINE YOUTH AND FAMILY SOLUTIONS, LLC.
SONS AND DAUGHTERS OF THE MOST HIGH PUBLISHERS ®

Oh, Gracious Most High Heavenly father, Holy is your name,
Your Will Be Done Now and Forever!
Yashu'a (Jesus) said: *"Thou shalt love the Most High Heavenly Father, thy Sustainer with all thy heart, and with all thy soul, and with all thy mind. Thou shalt love thy neighbour as thyself."*

"Now there were in the church that was at Antioch certain prophets and **teachers**; as Barnabas, and Simeon that was called **Niger**, and Lucius of Cyrene, and Manaen, which had been brought up with Herod the tetrarch, and Saul." In the aforementioned verse, the word: "**Niger**" is the **KJV Bible Greek Strong's Concordance#3526 Νίγερ (Niger)** which means: **Νίγερ Níger, neeg'-er; of Latin origin; black; Niger, a Christian**: Niger. According to the African American Registry (2019): "The history of the word **nigger is often traced to the Latin word Niger**, **meaning Black**. This word became the noun, Negro (Black person) in English."

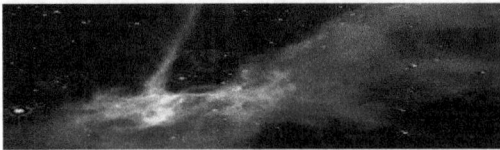

26

Yashu'a (Jesus) said: *"A new commandment I give unto you, that ye love one another; as I have loved you, that ye also love one another."*

ASSASSINS of DISOBEDIENCE!
Invoking the Power of the Most High Through Obedience, is the Key to Living Your Best Life
as the Supreme Ingredient!
Heaven or Hell?

CHILDREN OF THE MOST HIGH:
PRISTINE YOUTH AND FAMILY SOLUTIONS, LLC.
SONS AND DAUGHTERS OF THE MOST HIGH PUBLISHERS ®

Oh, Gracious Most High Heavenly father, Holy is your name,
Your Will Be Done Now and Forever!
Yashu'a (Jesus) said: "Thou shalt love the Most High Heavenly Father, thy Sustainer with all
thy heart, and with all thy soul, and with all thy mind. Thou shalt love
thy neighbour as thyself."

The KJV bible book of Hosea, chapter 4 verse 6; states: "My people are destroyed for lack of knowledge: because thou hast rejected knowledge, I will also reject thee, that thou shalt be no priest to me: seeing thou hast forgotten the law of thy God, I will also forget thy children." The KJV bible book of Isaiah, chapter 5 verse 13; states: "Therefore my people are gone into captivity, because they have no knowledge: and their honorable men are famished, and their multitude dried up with thirst."

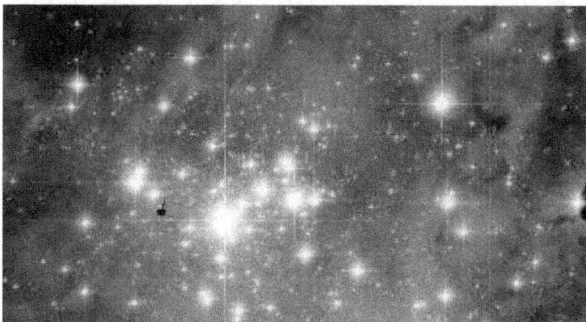

27

Yashu'a (Jesus) said: "A new commandment I give unto you, that ye love one another; as I have loved you, that ye also love one another."

ASSASSINS of DISOBEDIENCE!
Invoking the Power of the Most High Through Obedience, is the Key to Living Your Best Life
as the Supreme Ingredient!
Heaven or Hell?

CHILDREN OF THE MOST HIGH:
PRISTINE YOUTH AND FAMILY SOLUTIONS, LLC.
SONS AND DAUGHTERS OF THE MOST HIGH PUBLISHERS ®

Oh, Gracious Most High Heavenly father, Holy is your name,
Your Will Be Done Now and Forever!
Yashu'a (Jesus) said: *"Thou shalt love the Most High Heavenly Father, thy Sustainer with all*
thy heart, and with all thy soul, and with all thy mind. Thou shalt love
thy neighbour as thyself."

So, the Children of the Most High Pristine Youth and Family Solutions, LLC. refer to themselves as **Teachers** instead of **Preachers** because after over 25 years of teaching and studying the scriptures in the languages that they were originally revealed in, the children of the Most High don't find themselves **preaching**, they found themselves **teaching**. According to the Online American Heritage Dictionary, **teaching means; instructing, explaining, and elaborating**. So, we **teach** in an effort to ensure that the children of the Most High do their best to make the doctrine of the Most High clear in the minds of people who want to learn the original message or messages of the scriptures before they were translated into other languages.

Yashu'a (Jesus) said: "A new commandment I give unto you, that ye love one another; as I have loved you, that ye also love one another."

CHILDREN OF THE MOST HIGH:
PRISTINE YOUTH AND FAMILY SOLUTIONS, LLC.
SONS AND DAUGHTERS OF THE MOST HIGH PUBLISHERS ®

Oh, Gracious Most High Heavenly father, Holy is your name,
Your Will Be Done Now and Forever!
Yashu'a (Jesus) said: "Thou shalt love the Most High Heavenly Father, thy Sustainer with all thy heart, and with all thy soul, and with all thy mind. Thou shalt love thy neighbour as thyself."

According to the Online American Heritage Dictionary (2020),

Administer is defined as:

ad·min·is·ter (ăd-mĭn☐ĭ-stər)

v. **ad·min·is·tered**, **ad·min·is·ter·ing**, **ad·min·is·ters**

v.tr.

1. To have charge of; manage.

2.a. To apply as a remedy: *administer a sedative.* **1.** To manage as an administrator. **2.** To minister: *administering to their every whim.* [Middle English *administren,* from Old French *administrer,* from Latin *administrāre* : *ad,* ad- + *ministrāre,* to manage (from *minister, ministr-,* servant; see <u>MINISTER</u>).]

29

CHILDREN OF THE MOST HIGH:
PRISTINE YOUTH AND FAMILY SOLUTIONS, LLC.
SONS AND DAUGHTERS OF THE MOST HIGH PUBLISHERS ®

Oh, Gracious Most High Heavenly father, Holy is your name,
Your Will Be Done Now and Forever!
Yashu'a (Jesus) said: *"Thou shalt love the Most High Heavenly Father, thy Sustainer with all thy heart, and with all thy soul, and with all thy mind. Thou shalt love thy neighbour as thyself."*

So, we are "**Administers of the Most High's Doctrine**" by way of the Most High Heavenly Father giving the Children of the Most High: Pristine Youth and Family Solutions, LLC. **charge of managing the administering** of his Doctrine to inspire and empower all children of the Most High to pristinely make the world a safe and healthy place for all members of humanity. Which occurs by **applying** the Doctrine of the Most High **as a remedy** to create a world that is ruled by Love and the "Will" of the Most High, void of negative emotions, greed, lusts and love of money.

30

Yashu'a (Jesus) said: *"A new commandment I give unto you, that ye love one another; as I have loved you, that ye also love one another."*

ASSASSINS of DISOBEDIENCE!
Invoking the Power of the Most High Through Obedience, is the Key to Living Your Best Life
as the Supreme Ingredient!
Heaven or Hell?

CHILDREN OF THE MOST HIGH:
PRISTINE YOUTH AND FAMILY SOLUTIONS, LLC.
SONS AND DAUGHTERS OF THE MOST HIGH PUBLISHERS ®

Oh, Gracious Most High Heavenly father, Holy is your name,
Your Will Be Done Now and Forever!
Yashu'a (Jesus) said: *"Thou shalt love the Most High Heavenly Father, thy Sustainer with all thy heart, and with all thy soul, and with all thy mind. Thou shalt love thy neighbour as thyself."*

Why does the work that the Children of the Most High Pristine Youth and Family Solutions, LLC. do Matter? In order for the Children of the Most High; Pristine Youth and Family Solutions LLC. to be obedient to the Most High Heavenly Father, we seek to be positive difference makers who helps and teach youth and adults how to apply the doctrine of the Most High through the **True Vine "Yashu'a" (Jesus) B.A.-K.A.-R.E. Sequential Order of Learning** to teach them how to create positive predetermined goals, how to achieve positive success according to what positive success means to them, how to achieve positive happiness according to what positive happiness means to them, and how to learn to work together with members of humanity to create a world where all youth and all adults are happy, healthy, and balanced mentally, spiritually, physically, emotionally,

31

Yashu'a (Jesus) said: "A new commandment I give unto you, that ye love one another; as I have loved you, that ye also love one another."

ASSASSINS of DISOBEDIENCE!
Invoking the Power of the Most High Through Obedience, is the Key to Living Your Best Life
as the Supreme Ingredient!
Heaven or Hell?

CHILDREN OF THE MOST HIGH:
PRISTINE YOUTH AND FAMILY SOLUTIONS, LLC.
SONS AND DAUGHTERS OF THE MOST HIGH PUBLISHERS ®

Oh, Gracious Most High Heavenly father, Holy is your name,
Your Will Be Done Now and Forever!
Yashu'a (Jesus) said: "Thou shalt love the Most High Heavenly Father, thy Sustainer with all
thy heart, and with all thy soul, and with all thy mind. Thou shalt love
thy neighbour as thyself."

financially, personally, professionally, and socially. "Happiness is associated with and precedes numerous successful outcomes, as well as behaviors paralleling success, Lyubomirsky, King, & Diener, (2005). Furthermore, the evidence suggests that positive affect is the hallmark of well-being and may be the cause of many of the desirable characteristics, resources, and successes correlated with happiness, (Lyubomirsky, King, & Diener, (2005)." It also matters for our youth to receive the protection from the Most High Heavenly Father from all harm during the pre-adult years and beyond, in order to have an opportunity to become adults that can continue to create a world where all youth and all adults are happy, healthy, and balanced mentally, spiritually, physically, emotionally, financially, personally, professionally, and socially.

32

Yashu'a (Jesus) said: "A new commandment I give unto you, that ye love one another; as I have loved you, that ye also love one another."

ASSASSINS of DISOBEDIENCE!
Invoking the Power of the Most High Through Obedience, is the Key to Living Your Best Life
as the Supreme Ingredient!
Heaven or Hell?

CHILDREN OF THE MOST HIGH:
PRISTINE YOUTH AND FAMILY SOLUTIONS, LLC.
SONS AND DAUGHTERS OF THE MOST HIGH PUBLISHERS ®

Oh, Gracious Most High Heavenly father, Holy is your name,
Your Will Be Done Now and Forever!
Yashu'a (Jesus) said: "Thou shalt love the Most High Heavenly Father, thy Sustainer with all
thy heart, and with all thy soul, and with all thy mind. Thou shalt love
thy neighbour as thyself."

According the bible, this can only occur if our youth learn God's knowledge and obey God's laws. In the KJV bible book of Hosea chapter 4 verse 6, the LORD states: "**My people are destroyed for lack of knowledge**: because thou hast rejected knowledge, I will also reject thee, that thou shalt be no priest to me: <u>**seeing thou hast forgotten the law of thy God, I will also forget thy children**</u>." So, according to the aforementioned verse, in order to best prepare today's youth to survive and thrive until adulthood and beyond, they need to learn **God's (אלהים Elôhîym) knowledge (Elôhîym, אלהים is the original word for "God" before being translated as the word: "God" in the KJV bible book of Genesis chapter 1 verse 1)**, and **God's (אלהים Elôhîym) laws to be eligible to receive God's (אלהים Elôhîym) protection from all harm.**

33

Yashu'a (Jesus) said: "A new commandment I give unto
you, that ye love one another; as I have loved you,
that ye also love one another."

ASSASSINS of DISOBEDIENCE!
Invoking the Power of the Most High Through Obedience, is the Key to Living Your Best Life
as the Supreme Ingredient!
Heaven or Hell?

CHILDREN OF THE MOST HIGH:
PRISTINE YOUTH AND FAMILY SOLUTIONS, LLC.
SONS AND DAUGHTERS OF THE MOST HIGH PUBLISHERS ®

Oh, Gracious Most High Heavenly father, Holy is your name,
Your Will Be Done Now and Forever!
Yashu'a (Jesus) said: "Thou shalt love the Most High Heavenly Father, thy Sustainer with all
thy heart, and with all thy soul, and with all thy mind. Thou shalt love
thy neighbour as thyself."

Therefore, today's youth must be informed with **God's** (אלהים
Elôhîym) **A**ll, **W**ise, **A**bundant, **R**ight, **E**xact (A.W.A.R.E.)
Knowledge. How do you know? Because God's **A.W.A.R.E.**
knowledge is **bes**t, **accurate**, **correct** (**right, healthy**) and
exact and best to guide and protect all of the global children of
the Most High from all harm. For this reason, **God's** (אלהים
Elôhîym) **A.W.A.R.E. Knowledge** gives the children of the
Most High the ability to develop the habit of **positive thinking**
or correct (**right, healthy**) **thinking** as oppose to **negative
thinking** or **wrong thinking**.

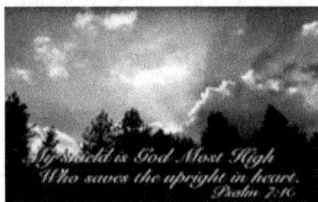

34

Yashu'a (Jesus) said: "A new commandment I give unto
you, that ye love one another; as I have loved you,
that ye also love one another."

ASSASSINS of DISOBEDIENCE!
Invoking the Power of the Most High Through Obedience, is the Key to Living Your Best Life
as the Supreme Ingredient!
Heaven or Hell?

CHILDREN OF THE MOST HIGH:
PRISTINE YOUTH AND FAMILY SOLUTIONS, LLC.
SONS AND DAUGHTERS OF THE MOST HIGH PUBLISHERS ®

Oh, Gracious Most High Heavenly father, Holy is your name,
Your Will Be Done Now and Forever!
Yashu'a (Jesus) said: "Thou shalt love the Most High Heavenly Father, thy Sustainer with all
thy heart, and with all thy soul, and with all thy mind. Thou shalt love
thy neighbour as thyself."

A person with **wrong knowledge** thinks negatively by having **wrong I. D. E. A. S. (I**mpure **D**esires **E**motionally **A**ctivated **S**equentially) or negative thoughts continuously, which leads to negative thinking, negative speaking, negative actions, and negative character. <u>**Learning, applying and obeying the laws of Elohiym (God), activates the will of the Most High Heavenly Father in the mind which initiates all thoughts, and a person acts and speaks, as he or she thinks!**</u> This is why in the KJV bible book of Hebrews chapter 8 verse 10; it states: "For this is the covenant that I will make with the house of Israel after those days, saith the Lord; <u>**I will put my laws into their mind, and write them in their hearts**</u>: and I will be to them a God, and they shall be to me a people."

Yashu'a (Jesus) said: "A new commandment I give unto
you, that ye love one another; as I have loved you,
that ye also love one another."

ASSASSINS of DISOBEDIENCE!
Invoking the Power of the Most High Through Obedience, is the Key to Living Your Best Life
as the Supreme Ingredient!
Heaven or Hell?

CHILDREN OF THE MOST HIGH:
PRISTINE YOUTH AND FAMILY SOLUTIONS, LLC.
SONS AND DAUGHTERS OF THE MOST HIGH PUBLISHERS ®

Oh, Gracious Most High Heavenly father, Holy is your name,
Your Will Be Done Now and Forever!
Yashu'a (Jesus) said: "Thou shalt love the Most High Heavenly Father, thy Sustainer with all
thy heart, and with all thy soul, and with all thy mind. Thou shalt love
thy neighbour as thyself."

In the KJV bible book of Revelation chapter 22 verses 12-16; Yashu'a (Jesus) stated: "**And, behold, I come quickly; and my reward is with me, to give every man according as his work shall be. I am Alpha and Omega, the beginning and the end, the first and the last. Blessed are they that do his** [the Most High, Heavenly Father's, **ELYOWN** עֶלְיוֹן **EL** אֵל] **commandments, that they may have right to the tree of life, and may enter in through the gates into the city. For without are dogs, and sorcerers, and whoremongers, and murderers, and idolaters, and whosoever loveth and maketh a lie. "I Jesus [Yashu'a] have sent mine angel to testify unto you these things in the churches. I am the root and the offspring of David, and the bright and morning star.**"

Yashu'a (Jesus) said: "A new commandment I give unto you, that ye love one another; as I have loved you, that ye also love one another."

ASSASSINS of DISOBEDIENCE!
Invoking the Power of the Most High Through Obedience, is the Key to Living Your Best Life
as the Supreme Ingredient!
Heaven or Hell?

CHILDREN OF THE MOST HIGH:
PRISTINE YOUTH AND FAMILY SOLUTIONS, LLC.
SONS AND DAUGHTERS OF THE MOST HIGH PUBLISHERS ®

Oh, Gracious Most High Heavenly father, Holy is your name,
Your Will Be Done Now and Forever!
Yashu'a (Jesus) said: "Thou shalt love the Most High Heavenly Father, thy Sustainer with all
thy heart, and with all thy soul, and with all thy mind. Thou shalt love
thy neighbour as thyself."

Hence, **God's (אלהים Elôhîym) A.W.A.R.E. Knowledge** is the **best knowledge** for our youth to be taught in order for them to have the best opportunity to be recipients of **Elohiym** (God's) protection, and to help ensure that our youth will become the future positive leaders of tomorrow, today!

37

Yashu'a (Jesus) said: "A new commandment I give unto you, that ye love one another; as I have loved you, that ye also love one another."

ASSASSINS of DISOBEDIENCE!
Invoking the Power of the Most High Through Obedience, is the Key to Living Your Best Life
as the Supreme Ingredient!
Heaven or Hell?

CHILDREN OF THE MOST HIGH:
PRISTINE YOUTH AND FAMILY SOLUTIONS, LLC.
SONS AND DAUGHTERS OF THE MOST HIGH PUBLISHERS ®

Oh, Gracious Most High Heavenly father, Holy is your name,
Your Will Be Done Now and Forever!
Yashu'a (Jesus) said: *"Thou shalt love the Most High Heavenly Father, thy Sustainer with all*
thy heart, and with all thy soul, and with all thy mind. Thou shalt love
thy neighbour as thyself."

The Children of the Most High: Pristine Youth and Family Solutions, LLC. is putting forth this book entitled: "**ASSASSINS of DISOBEDIENCE! Invoking the Power of the Most High Through Obedience, is the Key to Living Your Best Life as the Supreme Ingredient! Heaven or Hell?**" By the will of the Most High Heavenly Father to **inspire ALL youth and ALL adults who are children of the Most High** to obey the Most High Commandments now and forever, and to become empowered, inspired, and guided by the "WILL" of the Most High ONLY!!!

38

Yashu'a (Jesus) said: *"A new commandment I give unto you, that ye love one another; as I have loved you, that ye also love one another."*

ASSASSINS of DISOBEDIENCE!
Invoking the Power of the Most High Through Obedience, is the Key to Living Your Best Life
as the Supreme Ingredient!
Heaven or Hell?

CHILDREN OF THE MOST HIGH:
PRISTINE YOUTH AND FAMILY SOLUTIONS, LLC.
SONS AND DAUGHTERS OF THE MOST HIGH PUBLISHERS ®

Oh, Gracious Most High Heavenly father, Holy is your name,
Your Will Be Done Now and Forever!
Yashu'a (Jesus) said: *"Thou shalt love the Most High Heavenly Father, thy Sustainer with all*
thy heart, and with all thy soul, and with all thy mind. Thou shalt love
thy neighbour as thyself."

All gratitude is due to you oh gracious Most High Heavenly Father, you are the Creator and Sustainer of all the boundless universes. You are the Yielder, and the most Merciful. The Ruler of the Day of Judgement. It's you whom we worship and it is you alone whom we beseech for help, oh Guide, guide us to the **narrow path** **which reflects moral integrity and positive character traits in action** of the ones who stand straight, the narrow path of those who earned your grace not inclusive of those who brought an everlasting curse on themselves, those who conceal the facts of that which they know to be true in order to lead the **sincere-hearted seekers** of your truth astray, **Amen.**

Yashu'a (Jesus) said: "A new commandment I give unto you, that ye love one another; as I have loved you, that ye also love one another."

ASSASSINS of DISOBEDIENCE!
Invoking the Power of the Most High Through Obedience, is the Key to Living Your Best Life
as the Supreme Ingredient!
Heaven or Hell?

CHILDREN OF THE MOST HIGH:
PRISTINE YOUTH AND FAMILY SOLUTIONS, LLC.
SONS AND DAUGHTERS OF THE MOST HIGH PUBLISHERS ®

Oh, Gracious Most High Heavenly father, Holy is your name,
Your Will Be Done Now and Forever!
Yashu'a (Jesus) said: *"Thou shalt love the Most High Heavenly Father, thy Sustainer with all*
thy heart, and with all thy soul, and with all thy mind. Thou shalt love
thy neighbour as thyself."

What does the phrase: "those who earned your grace" mean as oppose to saying "those who receive your grace?"

The word: "**grace**" in the King James Version (KJV) bible book of Genesis chapter 6 verse 8 is: חֵן **Khane** or **chen** pronounced as **khān (KJV bible Hebrew Strong's Concordance#2580)**. The word: "חֵן **Khane** or **chen**" means "**favor, kindness**." The word: "**grace**" in the KJV bible book of John chapter 1 verse 17 is: χάρις **Kharece** or **charis** pronounced as **khä'-rēs (KJV bible Greek Strong's Concordance#5485)**. The word: "χάρις **Kharece** or **charis**" means "**joy, delight**." So, the phrase: "**those who earned your grace**" is in reference **to those people who are no longer physically alive that have transitioned to a higher life** such as: **Yashu'a (Jesus), John the Baptist,**

40

ASSASSINS of DISOBEDIENCE!
Invoking the Power of the Most High Through Obedience, is the Key to Living Your Best Life
as the Supreme Ingredient!
Heaven or Hell?

CHILDREN OF THE MOST HIGH:
PRISTINE YOUTH AND FAMILY SOLUTIONS, LLC.
SONS AND DAUGHTERS OF THE MOST HIGH PUBLISHERS ®

Oh, Gracious Most High Heavenly father, Holy is your name,
Your Will Be Done Now and Forever!
Yashu'a (Jesus) said: "Thou shalt love the Most High Heavenly Father, thy Sustainer with all
thy heart, and with all thy soul, and with all thy mind. Thou shalt love
thy neighbour as thyself."

Yowkhanan Bar Zebedee (John Son of Zebedee who was Yashu'a (Jesus) beloved disciple), or **Ab-Ra-Kham (Abraham)**. The phrase: **"those who receive your grace"** is in reference **to any person or people** who the Most High Heavenly Father bestows **favor** on by allowing them to still be physically alive, and to have an opportunity to experience **joy** while still be physically alive. In KJV bible book of Matthew chapter 7 verses 13-14; Yashu'a **(Jesus) said**: "Enter ye in at the strait gate: for wide is the gate, and broad is the way, that leadeth to destruction, and many there be which go in thereat (διά diá, dee-ah'; and means "**through**"): "Because strait *is* the gate, and narrow *is* the way, which leadeth unto life, and few there be that find it."

41

ASSASSINS of DISOBEDIENCE!
Invoking the Power of the Most High Through Obedience, is the Key to Living Your Best Life
as the Supreme Ingredient!
Heaven or Hell?

CHILDREN OF THE MOST HIGH:
PRISTINE YOUTH AND FAMILY SOLUTIONS, LLC.
SONS AND DAUGHTERS OF THE MOST HIGH PUBLISHERS ®

Oh, Gracious Most High Heavenly father, Holy is your name,
Your Will Be Done Now and Forever!
Yashu'a (Jesus) said: "Thou shalt love the Most High Heavenly Father, thy Sustainer with all
thy heart, and with all thy soul, and with all thy mind. Thou shalt love
thy neighbour as thyself."

In KJV bible book of Revelation chapter 2 verses 26-29; Yashu'a **(Jesus) said**: "And he [or she] that overcometh, and keepeth my works unto the end, to him [or her] will I give power over the nations. And he shall rule them with a rod of iron; as the vessels of a potter shall they be broken to shivers: even as I received of my Father. And I will give him the morning star. He [or she] that hath an ear, let him hear what the Spirit saith unto the churches."

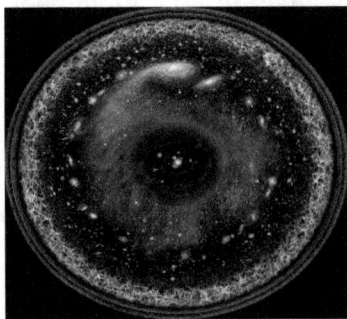

42

Yashu'a (Jesus) said: "A new commandment I give unto you, that ye love one another; as I have loved you, that ye also love one another."

ASSASSINS of DISOBEDIENCE!
Invoking the Power of the Most High Through Obedience, is the Key to Living Your Best Life
as the Supreme Ingredient!
Heaven or Hell?

CHILDREN OF THE MOST HIGH:
PRISTINE YOUTH AND FAMILY SOLUTIONS, LLC.
SONS AND DAUGHTERS OF THE MOST HIGH PUBLISHERS ®

Oh, Gracious Most High Heavenly father, Holy is your name,
Your Will Be Done Now and Forever!
Yashu'a (Jesus) said: "Thou shalt love the Most High Heavenly Father, thy Sustainer with all
thy heart, and with all thy soul, and with all thy mind. Thou shalt love
thy neighbour as thyself."

Chapter 1: According to the Messiah Yashu'a (Jesus), does being Obedient to the Most High Heavenly Father Matter?

The Most High Heavenly Father is
"The Life Giver and The Yielder."

In the KJV bible book of 2nd Chronicles chapter 30 verse 8; it states:
"Now be ye not stiff necked, as your fathers were, but yield yourselves
unto the LORD, and enter into his sanctuary, which he hath sanctified
forever: and serve the LORD your God, that the fierceness
of his wrath may turn away from you."

43

Yashu'a (Jesus) said: "A new commandment I give unto
you, that ye love one another; as I have loved you,
that ye also love one another."

ASSASSINS of DISOBEDIENCE!
Invoking the Power of the Most High Through Obedience, is the Key to Living Your Best Life
as the Supreme Ingredient!
Heaven or Hell?

CHILDREN OF THE MOST HIGH:
PRISTINE YOUTH AND FAMILY SOLUTIONS, LLC.
SONS AND DAUGHTERS OF THE MOST HIGH PUBLISHERS ®

Oh, Gracious Most High Heavenly father, Holy is your name,
Your Will Be Done Now and Forever!
Yashu'a (Jesus) said: "Thou shalt love the Most High Heavenly Father, thy Sustainer with all
thy heart, and with all thy soul, and with all thy mind. Thou shalt love
thy neighbour as thyself."

The Messiah Yashu'a (Jesus) said: "I am Alpha and Omega, the beginning and the end, the first and the last. **Blessed *are* they that do his commandments**, that they may have right to the tree of life, and may enter in through the gates into the city. For without *are* dogs, and sorcerers, and whoremongers, and murderers, and idolaters, and whosoever loveth and maketh a lie. **I Yashu'a (Jesus) have sent mine angel to testify unto you these things in the churches**. I am the root and the offspring of David, *and* the bright and morning star, **KJV bible, Revelation 22:13-16."**

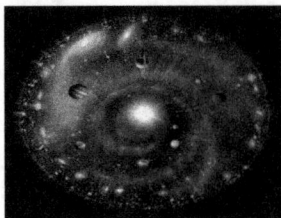

44

Yashu'a (Jesus) said: "A new commandment I give unto you, that ye love one another; as I have loved you, that ye also love one another."

ASSASSINS of DISOBEDIENCE!
Invoking the Power of the Most High Through Obedience, is the Key to Living Your Best Life
as the Supreme Ingredient!
Heaven or Hell?

CHILDREN OF THE MOST HIGH:
PRISTINE YOUTH AND FAMILY SOLUTIONS, LLC.
SONS AND DAUGHTERS OF THE MOST HIGH PUBLISHERS ®

Oh, Gracious Most High Heavenly father, Holy is your name,
Your Will Be Done Now and Forever!
Yashu'a (Jesus) said: "Thou shalt love the Most High Heavenly Father, thy Sustainer with all
thy heart, and with all thy soul, and with all thy mind. Thou shalt love
thy neighbour as thyself."

According to Yashu'a (Jesus), does being obedient to the Most High Heavenly Father matter?

In the KJV **bible book of Revelation** chapter 22 verse 14; it states; **"Blessed are they that do his commandments, that they may have right to the tree of life, and may enter in through the gates into the city."** In the **KJV bible Greek Strong's Concordance**, the word for **commandments is** "#1785, "ἐντολὰς ἐντολή **entole (en-tol-ay')**; which means: **injunction,** i.e., **an authoritative prescription:** — **commandment,** precept. Often for מִצְוָה, in the Psalms the plural ἐντολαί also for פִּקּוּדִים; an **order, command,** charge, precept; 1. universally, a charge, injunction." The same word for **commandment** (ἐντολὰς ἐντολή **entole (en-tol-ay')**; is used in the KJV bible book of John chapter 12 verses 49-50.

45

Yashu'a (Jesus) said: "A new commandment I give unto
you, that ye love one another; as I have loved you,
that ye also love one another."

ASSASSINS of DISOBEDIENCE!
Invoking the Power of the Most High Through Obedience, is the Key to Living Your Best Life
as the Supreme Ingredient!
Heaven or Hell?

CHILDREN OF THE MOST HIGH:
PRISTINE YOUTH AND FAMILY SOLUTIONS, LLC.
SONS AND DAUGHTERS OF THE MOST HIGH PUBLISHERS ®

Oh, Gracious Most High Heavenly father, Holy is your name,
Your Will Be Done Now and Forever!
Yashu'a (Jesus) said: *"Thou shalt love the Most High Heavenly Father, thy Sustainer with all*
thy heart, and with all thy soul, and with all thy mind. Thou shalt love
thy neighbour as thyself."

In these verses; the Messiah Yashu'a said: "For I have not spoken of myself; but the Father which sent me, he gave me a commandment (ἐντολὰς ἐντολή entole (en-tol-ay'), what I should say, and what I should speak. And I know that his commandment (ἐντολὰς ἐντολή entole (en-tol-ay') is life everlasting: whatsoever I speak therefore, even as the Father said unto me, so I speak."

46

Yashu'a (Jesus) said: *"A new commandment I give unto*
you, that ye love one another; as I have loved you,
that ye also love one another."

CHILDREN OF THE MOST HIGH:
PRISTINE YOUTH AND FAMILY SOLUTIONS, LLC.
SONS AND DAUGHTERS OF THE MOST HIGH PUBLISHERS ®

Oh, Gracious Most High Heavenly father, Holy is your name,
Your Will Be Done Now and Forever!
Yashu'a (Jesus) said: "Thou shalt love the Most High Heavenly Father, thy Sustainer with all thy heart, and with all thy soul, and with all thy mind. Thou shalt love thy neighbour as thyself."

In the aforementioned KJV bible book of Revelation chapter 22 verse 14, it states: **"Blessed are they that do his commandments."** Why? Because those who are obedient to Elôhîym (אלהים – God) commandments, **"may have right to the tree of life."** **What is the tree of life**? According to the **KJV bible Greek Strong's Concordance** word for **"the tree"** is **#3586, "ξύλον xylon (xoo'-lon)**; which means: tree, timber or other wooden article or substance. The word for **of life is #1785, "ζωή zōē, (dzo-ay')**; which means: chiefly for חיים; life; 1. universally, life, i. e. the state of one who is possessed of vitality or is animate."

47

ASSASSINS of DISOBEDIENCE!
Invoking the Power of the Most High Through Obedience, is the Key to Living Your Best Life
as the Supreme Ingredient!
Heaven or Hell?

CHILDREN OF THE MOST HIGH:
PRISTINE YOUTH AND FAMILY SOLUTIONS, LLC.
SONS AND DAUGHTERS OF THE MOST HIGH PUBLISHERS ®

Oh, Gracious Most High Heavenly father, Holy is your name,
Your Will Be Done Now and Forever!
Yashu'a (Jesus) said: "Thou shalt love the Most High Heavenly Father, thy Sustainer with all
thy heart, and with all thy soul, and with all thy mind. Thou shalt love
thy neighbour as thyself."

What does this verse mean to the children of the Most High who have accepted the Messiah Yashu'a (Jesus) as their Savior? It means, blessed are they who <u>**symbolically**</u> wash their robes in the blood of the Lamb (Yashu'a, Jesus), by <u>**being persecuted for righteousness namesake**</u> so that there may exist, their authority over the **tree of life**. These beings will have the right to partake of the **tree of life** and may enter into the city, **New Jerusalem (Jeru-Salem is also Haru-Salaam (Jeru/Haru City of Peace)** by way of its doors. This is why in the KJV bible book of Matthew chapter 5 verse 10; Yashu'a (Jesus) said: "Blessed are they which are persecuted for righteousness' sake: for theirs is the kingdom of heaven."

Yashu'a (Jesus) said: "A new commandment I give unto you, that ye love one another; as I have loved you, that ye also love one another."

ASSASSINS of DISOBEDIENCE!
Invoking the Power of the Most High Through Obedience, is the Key to Living Your Best Life
as the Supreme Ingredient!
Heaven or Hell?

CHILDREN OF THE MOST HIGH:
PRISTINE YOUTH AND FAMILY SOLUTIONS, LLC.
SONS AND DAUGHTERS OF THE MOST HIGH PUBLISHERS ®

Oh, Gracious Most High Heavenly father, Holy is your name,
Your Will Be Done Now and Forever!
Yashu'a (Jesus) said: "Thou shalt love the Most High Heavenly Father, thy Sustainer with all
thy heart, and with all thy soul, and with all thy mind. Thou shalt love
thy neighbour as thyself."

When you said: "In the Messiah Yashu'a (Jesus) bible book of Revelation," are you saying that Jesus has his own book in the bible? In the KJV bible book of Revelation chapter 1 verses 1-3; it states: **"The Revelation of Jesus Christ, which God ($\theta\varepsilon\acute{o}\varsigma$ Theos) gave unto him**, to shew unto his servants' things which must shortly come to pass; and **he sent and signified *it* by his angel** unto his servant John." Who bare record of the word of God, and of the testimony of Jesus Christ, and of all things that he saw. "Blessed *is* he [or she] that readeth, and they that hear the words of this prophecy, and keep those things which are written therein: **for the time *is* at hand**."

49

Yashu'a (Jesus) said: "A new commandment I give unto
you, that ye love one another; as I have loved you,
that ye also love one another."

ASSASSINS of DISOBEDIENCE!
Invoking the Power of the Most High Through Obedience, is the Key to Living Your Best Life
as the Supreme Ingredient!
Heaven or Hell?

CHILDREN OF THE MOST HIGH:
PRISTINE YOUTH AND FAMILY SOLUTIONS, LLC.
SONS AND DAUGHTERS OF THE MOST HIGH PUBLISHERS ®

Oh, Gracious Most High Heavenly father, Holy is your name,
Your Will Be Done Now and Forever!
Yashu'a (Jesus) said: "Thou shalt love the Most High Heavenly Father, thy Sustainer with all
thy heart, and with all thy soul, and with all thy mind. Thou shalt love
thy neighbour as thyself."

Therefore; according to the KJV book of Revelation chapter 1 verse 1; the KJV book of Revelation is "**The Revelation of Jesus Christ, which God gave unto him**." So, in response to the question, **YES**, **according the word of God** ($\theta\varepsilon\delta\varsigma$ Theos), **God** ($\theta\varepsilon\delta\varsigma$ Theos) **gave the book of Revelation to the Messiah Yashu'a (Jesus)**; to shew unto his servants' things which must shortly come to pass; and **he sent and signified *it* by his angel** unto his servant John." Who bare record of the word of God, and of the testimony of Jesus Christ, and of all things that he saw."

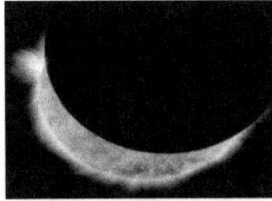

50

Yashu'a (Jesus) said: "A new commandment I give unto you, that ye love one another; as I have loved you, that ye also love one another."

ASSASSINS of DISOBEDIENCE!
Invoking the Power of the Most High Through Obedience, is the Key to Living Your Best Life
as the Supreme Ingredient!
Heaven or Hell?

CHILDREN OF THE MOST HIGH:
PRISTINE YOUTH AND FAMILY SOLUTIONS, LLC.
SONS AND DAUGHTERS OF THE MOST HIGH PUBLISHERS ®

Oh, Gracious Most High Heavenly father, Holy is your name,
Your Will Be Done Now and Forever!
Yashu'a (Jesus) said: *"Thou shalt love the Most High Heavenly Father, thy Sustainer with all*
thy heart, and with all thy soul, and with all thy mind. Thou shalt love
thy neighbour as thyself."

The aforementioned verse also mentioned that the Messiah Yashu'a (Jesus) will send **his angel** or if the **Messiah Yashu'a (Jesus)** made the statement in the first person, it would be "**My Angel**" instead of being said in the second person as "**His Angel**." What does the phrase "**My Angel**" mean in the Messiah Yashu'a (Jesus) **Galilean** or **Judean tongue** "(language שָׂפָה **Saphah (Saw-faw')**)? In the **Galilean** or **Judean language**, the phrase "**My Angel**" means "**Malachi**" ⟨𝘮𝘢𝘭𝘢𝘤𝘩𝘪⟩ מלאכי which corresponds with the KJV bible Hebrew Strong's Concordance **#4397**, **Aramic (Hebrew)** word "מַלְאָךְ **Mal'awk**, which means **angel, king, priest, messenger** and **Galilean Ashuric/Syriac (Arabic)** word **Malaakehe** (according to the Arabic Lanes Dictionary (2003), means "**Angelic-Being**").

51

Yashu'a (Jesus) said: "A new commandment I give unto
you, that ye love one another; as I have loved you,
that ye also love one another."

ASSASSINS of DISOBEDIENCE!
Invoking the Power of the Most High Through Obedience, is the Key to Living Your Best Life
as the Supreme Ingredient!
Heaven or Hell?

CHILDREN OF THE MOST HIGH:
PRISTINE YOUTH AND FAMILY SOLUTIONS, LLC.
SONS AND DAUGHTERS OF THE MOST HIGH PUBLISHERS ®

Oh, Gracious Most High Heavenly father, Holy is your name,
Your Will Be Done Now and Forever!
Yashu'a (Jesus) said: *"Thou shalt love the Most High Heavenly Father, thy Sustainer with all*
thy heart, and with all thy soul, and with all thy mind. Thou shalt love
thy neighbour as thyself."

מַלְאָךְ m. (from the root לָאַךְ to depute which see).

(1) *one sent, a messenger*, whether from a private person, Job 1:14, or of a king, 1 Sa. 16:19; 19:11, 14, 20; 1 Ki. 19:2, etc. (Syr. ܡܠܐܟܐ, Arab. ملاك id.)

(2) *a messenger of God*, i. e.—(*a*) *an angel*, Ex. 23:20; 33:2; 2 Sam. 24:16; Job 33:23 (see לִיץ); Zec. 1:9, seq.; 2:2, 7; 4:1, seq.; more fully מַלְאַךְ יְיָ Gen. 16:7; 21:17; 22:11, 15; Num. 22:22, seqq.; Jud. 6:11, seqq.; Cf. De Angelologia V. T., De Wettii Bibl. Dogm. § 171, seqq. edit. 2.—(*b*) *a prophet*, Hag. 1:13; Mal. 3:1.—(*c*) *a priest*, Ecc. 5:5; Mal.

1:1: Malachi 2:6; Malachi 2:7; Malachi 3:1; Malachi 4:1;"

Malachi 4:2; Malachi 4:3; Malachi 4:1; Malachi 4:2:

Malachi 4:3, Malachi 4:4, Malachi 4:5, Malachi 4:6."

52

Yashu'a (Jesus) said: *"A new commandment I give unto*
you, that ye love one another; as I have loved you,
that ye also love one another."

ASSASSINS of DISOBEDIENCE!
Invoking the Power of the Most High Through Obedience, is the Key to Living Your Best Life
as the Supreme Ingredient!
Heaven or Hell?

CHILDREN OF THE MOST HIGH:
PRISTINE YOUTH AND FAMILY SOLUTIONS, LLC.
SONS AND DAUGHTERS OF THE MOST HIGH PUBLISHERS ®

Oh, Gracious Most High Heavenly father, Holy is your name,
Your Will Be Done Now and Forever!
Yashu'a (Jesus) said: "Thou shalt love the Most High Heavenly Father, thy Sustainer with all
thy heart, and with all thy soul, and with all thy mind. Thou shalt love
thy neighbour as thyself."

In the KJV bible book of Exodus chapter 23 verses 23-24; it states: "For mine **Angel** (the KJV bible Hebrew Strong's Concordance **#4397**, **Aramic (Hebrew)** word "מַלְאָךְ Mal'awk, which means **angel, king, priest, messenger**) shall go before thee, and bring thee in unto **the Amorites**, and **the Hittites**, and **the Perizzites**, and **the Canaanites**, **the Hivites**, and **the Jebusites: and I will cut them off. Thou shalt not bow down to their gods, nor serve them, nor do after their works**: but thou shalt utterly overthrow them, and quite **break down their images**."

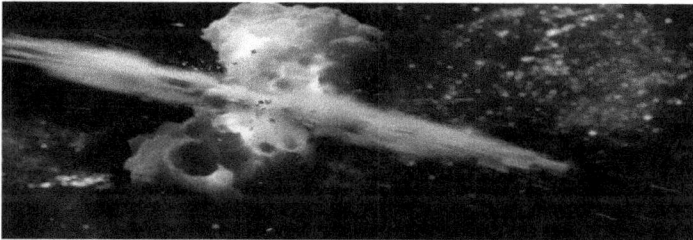

53

Yashu'a (Jesus) said: "A new commandment I give unto you, that ye love one another; as I have loved you, that ye also love one another."

ASSASSINS of DISOBEDIENCE!
Invoking the Power of the Most High Through Obedience, is the Key to Living Your Best Life
as the Supreme Ingredient!
Heaven or Hell?

CHILDREN OF THE MOST HIGH:
PRISTINE YOUTH AND FAMILY SOLUTIONS, LLC.
SONS AND DAUGHTERS OF THE MOST HIGH PUBLISHERS ®

Oh, Gracious Most High Heavenly father, Holy is your name,
Your Will Be Done Now and Forever!
Yashu'a (Jesus) said: *"Thou shalt love the Most High Heavenly Father, thy Sustainer with all*
thy heart, and with all thy soul, and with all thy mind. Thou shalt love
thy neighbour as thyself."

In the KJV bible book of Haggai chapter 1 verse 13; it states:
"Then spake **Haggai the LORD'S messenger** (the KJV bible
Hebrew Strong's Concordance **#4397**, **Aramic (Hebrew)** word
מַלְאָךְ **Mal'awk**, which means **angel**, **king**, **priest**, **messenger**;
in the Galilean Ashuric/Syriac **(Arabic)** is known as **Al**

Khidr (الـخـضـر) "**The Green One**" in reference to

sustaining and healing; For example: many healthy
vegetation is the **color green**. Healthy (Heal-Thy), or **the first
4 letters of the word heal**thy, spell the word **heal**.

54

Yashu'a (Jesus) said: "A new commandment I give unto
you, that ye love one another; as I have loved you,
that ye also love one another."

ASSASSINS of DISOBEDIENCE!
Invoking the Power of the Most High Through Obedience, is the Key to Living Your Best Life
as the Supreme Ingredient!
Heaven or Hell?

CHILDREN OF THE MOST HIGH:
PRISTINE YOUTH AND FAMILY SOLUTIONS, LLC.
SONS AND DAUGHTERS OF THE MOST HIGH PUBLISHERS ®

Oh, Gracious Most High Heavenly father, Holy is your name,
Your Will Be Done Now and Forever!
Yashu'a (Jesus) said: "Thou shalt love the Most High Heavenly Father, thy Sustainer with all
thy heart, and with all thy soul, and with all thy mind. Thou shalt love
thy neighbour as thyself."

Malachi is also the name Malachite, a dark green mineral carbonate of copper) in the LORD'S message (the KJV bible Hebrew Strong's Concordance "#4397, Aramic (Hebrew) word (מַלְאָכוּת MAL-AK-OOTH, Mal'akuwth, means message) unto the people, saying, I am with you, saith the LORD." In the KJV bible book of Genesis chapter 14 verse 13; it states: "And Melchizedek (is the KJV bible Hebrew Strong's Concordance #4442, Aramic (Hebrew) word "מַלְכִּי־צֶדֶק Malkiy-Tsedeq (Mal·ke·tseh'·dek), means justice, righteousness) king of Salem (Salem is the KJV bible Hebrew Strong's Concordance#8004 word "שָׁלֵם Sha-Lomé, Sha-Lom, Shâlêm, Shaw-lame, and means Peace; brought forth bread and wine: and he *was* the priest of the Most High God (עֶלְיוֹן 'Elyown אֵל 'EL)."

Yashu'a (Jesus) said: "A new commandment I give unto
you, that ye love one another; as I have loved you,
that ye also love one another."

ASSASSINS of DISOBEDIENCE!
*Invoking the Power of the Most High Through Obedience, is the Key to Living Your Best Life
as the Supreme Ingredient!
Heaven or Hell?*

CHILDREN OF THE MOST HIGH:
PRISTINE YOUTH AND FAMILY SOLUTIONS, LLC.
SONS AND DAUGHTERS OF THE MOST HIGH PUBLISHERS ®

*Oh, Gracious Most High Heavenly father, Holy is your name,
Your Will Be Done Now and Forever!*
Yashu'a (Jesus) said: *"Thou shalt love the Most High Heavenly Father, thy Sustainer with all
thy heart, and with all thy soul, and with all thy mind. Thou shalt love
thy neighbour as thyself."*

In the KJV bible book of Matthew chapter 5 verse 9; the Messiah Yashu'a said: "Blessed are the peacemakers: for they shall be called the children of God." In the KJV bible book of Malachi chapter 4 verse 2; it states: "But unto you that fear **my name** shall **the Sun of righteousness** (the KJV bible Hebrew Strong's Concordance **#8121**, is the **Aramic (Hebrew)** word for "**Sun**" שֶׁמֶשׁ **Shemesh** pronounced **Sheh'·mesh**, and the word for "**Righteousness**" is **Tsĕdaqah** שְׁמֶשׁ pronounced **Tsed-aw-kaw'**) arise with healing in his wings; and ye shall go forth, and grow up as calves of the stall."

56

Yashu'a (Jesus) said: "A new commandment I give unto you, that ye love one another; as I have loved you, that ye also love one another."

ASSASSINS of DISOBEDIENCE!
Invoking the Power of the Most High Through Obedience, is the Key to Living Your Best Life
as the Supreme Ingredient!
Heaven or Hell?

CHILDREN OF THE MOST HIGH:
PRISTINE YOUTH AND FAMILY SOLUTIONS, LLC.
SONS AND DAUGHTERS OF THE MOST HIGH PUBLISHERS

Oh, Gracious Most High Heavenly father, Holy is your name,
Your Will Be Done Now and Forever!
Yashu'a (Jesus) said: "Thou shalt love the Most High Heavenly Father, thy Sustainer with all
thy heart, and with all thy soul, and with all thy mind. Thou shalt love
thy neighbour as thyself."

The Word **Tsedeq** (צדיק) Or **Sodoq** (צדיק) Meaning *"Justice Or Righteousness"* Is Spelled Zodoq When Translated. In The Ashuric/Syriac (Arabic) The Word **Zodoq** Is **Sodoq** (صدق) From The Root Word **Sadaqa** (صدق) Meaning *"Righteous."* The Koran Uses Different Forms Of The Word Sodoq Such As **El Saddiqiyn, El Saddiquwn** (الصدقين And الصدقون) Meaning *"The Righteous"*, In Plural *(Koran 4:69)* And **Musaddiqiyn** (مصدقين) Meaning *"Ones Who Are Of Righteous"* *(Koran 57:18)*. The Word **Saddiyq** (صديق) Was Also Used For Joseph *(Koran 12:46)*, ENOCH (ADAFA) Who Was Known As Idris *(Koran 19:56)*, And Abraham *(Koran 19:41)*.

57

Yashu'a (Jesus) said: "A new commandment I give unto
you, that ye love one another; as I have loved you,
that ye also love one another."

ASSASSINS of DISOBEDIENCE!
Invoking the Power of the Most High Through Obedience, is the Key to Living Your Best Life
as the Supreme Ingredient!
Heaven or Hell?

CHILDREN OF THE MOST HIGH:
PRISTINE YOUTH AND FAMILY SOLUTIONS, LLC.
SONS AND DAUGHTERS OF THE MOST HIGH PUBLISHERS ®

Oh, Gracious Most High Heavenly father, Holy is your name,
Your Will Be Done Now and Forever!
Yashu'a (Jesus) said: "Thou shalt love the Most High Heavenly Father, thy Sustainer with all
thy heart, and with all thy soul, and with all thy mind. Thou shalt love
thy neighbour as thyself."

In the KJV bible book of Daniel chapter 12 verse 1; it states: "And **at that time** shall **Michael** (the KJV bible Hebrew Strong's Concordance **#4317**, is the **Aramic (Hebrew)** word for "**Michael**" is מִיכָאֵל **Miyka'el, pronounced as "Me·Kä·Al" which means "who dares to be like the Most High Heavenly Father (ELYOWN עֶלְיוֹן EL אֵל),** or "**Who is like God**") stand up, the great prince **which standeth for the children of thy people: and there shall be a time of trouble, such as never was since there was a nation even to that same time: and at that time thy people shall be delivered, every one that shall be found written in the book**."

58

ASSASSINS of DISOBEDIENCE!
Invoking the Power of the Most High Through Obedience, is the Key to Living Your Best Life
as the Supreme Ingredient!
Heaven or Hell?

CHILDREN OF THE MOST HIGH:
PRISTINE YOUTH AND FAMILY SOLUTIONS, LLC.
SONS AND DAUGHTERS OF THE MOST HIGH PUBLISHERS ®

Oh, Gracious Most High Heavenly father, Holy is your name,
Your Will Be Done Now and Forever!
Yashu'a (Jesus) said: *"Thou shalt love the Most High Heavenly Father, thy Sustainer with all*
thy heart, and with all thy soul, and with all thy mind. Thou shalt love
thy neighbour as thyself."

In the KJV bible book of Revelation chapter 12 verses 7-9; it states: "And there was war in heaven: **Michael and his angels** (ἄγγελος **Angelos, meaning Messengers** according to the **KJV bible Greek Strong's Concordance #32**) fought against the **dragon**; and **the dragon fought and his angels** (ἄγγελος **Angelos, meaning Messengers**, according to the KJV bible Greek **Strong's Concordance #32**, And prevailed not; neither was their place found any more in heaven. And the **great dragon** was cast out, that **old serpent, called the Devil, and Satan, which deceiveth the whole world: he was cast out into the earth, and his angels** (ἄγγελος Angelos, meaning Messengers) **were cast out with him**."

Yashu'a (Jesus) said: *"A new commandment I give unto you, that ye love one another; as I have loved you, that ye also love one another."*

ASSASSINS of DISOBEDIENCE!
Invoking the Power of the Most High Through Obedience, is the Key to Living Your Best Life
as the Supreme Ingredient!
Heaven or Hell?

CHILDREN OF THE MOST HIGH:
PRISTINE YOUTH AND FAMILY SOLUTIONS, LLC.
SONS AND DAUGHTERS OF THE MOST HIGH PUBLISHERS ®

Oh, Gracious Most High Heavenly father, Holy is your name,
Your Will Be Done Now and Forever!
Yashu'a (Jesus) said: "Thou shalt love the Most High Heavenly Father, thy Sustainer with all
thy heart, and with all thy soul, and with all thy mind. Thou shalt love
thy neighbour as thyself."

In the KJV bible book of Hebrews chapter 7 verses 1-4; it states: "For this **Melchisedec** (Μελχισέδεκ Melchisedek), **king of Salem** (Σαλήμ Salēm from the KJV bible Hebrew Strong's Concordance #8004 word "שָׁלֵם Sha-Lomé, Sha-Lom, Shâlêm, Shaw-lame, and means Peace), Priest of the Most High God**, who met Abraham returning from the slaughter of the kings, and blessed him; to whom also Abraham gave a tenth part of all; first being by interpretation **King of Righteousness**, and after that also **King of Salem ("שָׁלֵם Sha-Lomé)**, which is, **King of Peace**; **without father, without mother, without descent, having neither beginning of days, nor end of life; but made like unto the Son of God; abideth a priest continually**. Now consider how great this man *was*, unto whom even the patriarch Abraham gave the tenth of the spoils."

Yashu'a (Jesus) said: "A new commandment I give unto
you, that ye love one another; as I have loved you,
that ye also love one another."

CHILDREN OF THE MOST HIGH:
PRISTINE YOUTH AND FAMILY SOLUTIONS, LLC.
SONS AND DAUGHTERS OF THE MOST HIGH PUBLISHERS ®

Oh, Gracious Most High Heavenly father, Holy is your name,
Your Will Be Done Now and Forever!
Yashu'a (Jesus) said: *"Thou shalt love the Most High Heavenly Father, thy Sustainer with all thy heart, and with all thy soul, and with all thy mind. Thou shalt love thy neighbour as thyself."*

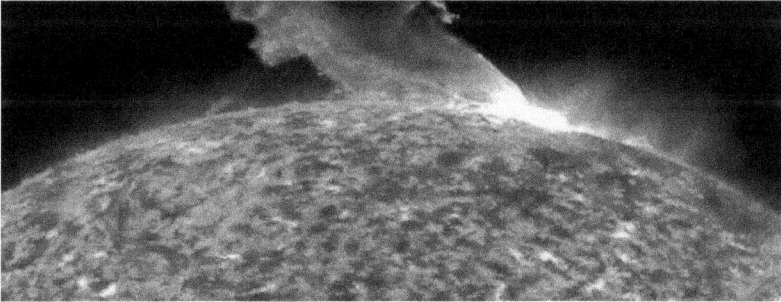

Is Yashua's (Jesus) Melchizedek? **NO**! In the KJV bible book of Hebrews chapter 5 verses 5-10; it states: "So, also Christ glorified not himself to be made a high priest; but he that said unto him, thou art my Son, today have I begotten thee. As he saith also in another place, **Thou art a priest for ever after the order of Melchisedec**. **Who in the days of his flesh, when he had offered up prayers and supplications with strong crying and tears unto him that was able to save him from death, and was heard in that he feared**."

61

Yashu'a (Jesus) said: "A new commandment I give unto you, that ye love one another; as I have loved you, that ye also love one another."

ASSASSINS of DISOBEDIENCE!
Invoking the Power of the Most High Through Obedience, is the Key to Living Your Best Life
as the Supreme Ingredient!
Heaven or Hell?

CHILDREN OF THE MOST HIGH:
PRISTINE YOUTH AND FAMILY SOLUTIONS, LLC.
SONS AND DAUGHTERS OF THE MOST HIGH PUBLISHERS ®

Oh, Gracious Most High Heavenly father, Holy is your name,
Your Will Be Done Now and Forever!
Yashu'a (Jesus) said: *"Thou shalt love the Most High Heavenly Father, thy Sustainer with all*
thy heart, and with all thy soul, and with all thy mind. Thou shalt love
thy neighbour as thyself."

"Though he were a Son, yet learned he obedience by the things which he suffered; And being made perfect, **he became the author of eternal salvation unto all them that obey him**; **Called of God a high priest after the order of Melchisedec**."

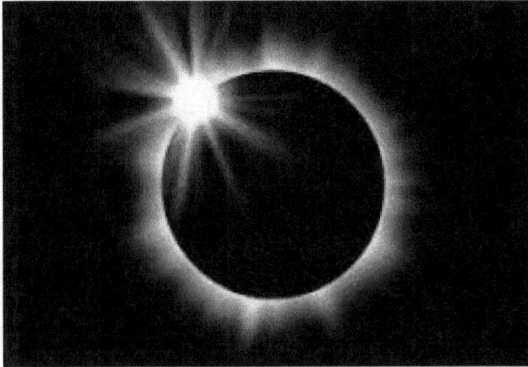

62

Yashu'a (Jesus) said: "A new commandment I give unto you, that ye love one another; as I have loved you, that ye also love one another."

ASSASSINS of DISOBEDIENCE!
Invoking the Power of the Most High Through Obedience, is the Key to Living Your Best Life
as the Supreme Ingredient!
Heaven or Hell?

CHILDREN OF THE MOST HIGH:
PRISTINE YOUTH AND FAMILY SOLUTIONS, LLC.
SONS AND DAUGHTERS OF THE MOST HIGH PUBLISHERS ®

Oh, Gracious Most High Heavenly father, Holy is your name,
Your Will Be Done Now and Forever!
Yashu'a (Jesus) said: *"Thou shalt love the Most High Heavenly Father, thy Sustainer with all*
thy heart, and with all thy soul, and with all thy mind. Thou shalt love
thy neighbour as thyself."

So, from the aforementioned verses; the **Messiah** Yashu'a

(Jesus) **is after the Order of Melchizedek, and is not the**

Angelic-Being "מַלְכִּי-צֶדֶק" **Malkiy-Tsedeq (Malachi, Al**

Khidr, or Melchizedek) which are various titles of the same

Arch Angelic-Being מִיכָאֵל **Miyka'el (Michael).**

63

Yashu'a (Jesus) said: "A new commandment I give unto
you, that ye love one another; as I have loved you,
that ye also love one another."

ASSASSINS of DISOBEDIENCE!
Invoking the Power of the Most High Through Obedience, is the Key to Living Your Best Life
as the Supreme Ingredient!
Heaven or Hell?

CHILDREN OF THE MOST HIGH:
PRISTINE YOUTH AND FAMILY SOLUTIONS, LLC.
SONS AND DAUGHTERS OF THE MOST HIGH PUBLISHERS ®

Oh, Gracious Most High Heavenly father, Holy is your name,
Your Will Be Done Now and Forever!
Yashu'a (Jesus) said: *"Thou shalt love the Most High Heavenly Father, thy Sustainer with all*
thy heart, and with all thy soul, and with all thy mind. Thou shalt love
thy neighbour as thyself."

So, when the KJV bible book of Revelation chapter 1 verse 1 mentions that the **Messiah Yashu'a (Jesus)** will send **his angel** or if the **Messiah Yashu'a (Jesus)** made the statement in the first person, it would be "**My Angel**". In the **Messiah Yashu'a (Jesus) Galilean** or **Judean tongue (language)**, the phrase "My Angel" means "**Malachi**" מלאכי, who, **is none other than the Arch Angelic-Being "Michael"**, מִיכָאֵל **Miyka'el, pronounced as "Me·Kä·Al" which means "who dares to be like the Most High Heavenly Father (ELYOWN עֶלְיוֹן EL אֵל), or "Who is like God").**

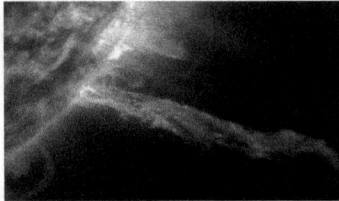

64

ASSASSINS of DISOBEDIENCE!
Invoking the Power of the Most High Through Obedience, is the Key to Living Your Best Life
as the Supreme Ingredient!
Heaven or Hell?

CHILDREN OF THE MOST HIGH:
PRISTINE YOUTH AND FAMILY SOLUTIONS, LLC.
SONS AND DAUGHTERS OF THE MOST HIGH PUBLISHERS ®

Oh, Gracious Most High Heavenly father, Holy is your name,
Your Will Be Done Now and Forever!
Yashu'a (Jesus) said: "Thou shalt love the Most High Heavenly Father, thy Sustainer with all
thy heart, and with all thy soul, and with all thy mind. Thou shalt love
thy neighbour as thyself."

Chapter 2: What does the title "Assassins, Disobedience, Invoking, Power, Obedience, Key, Living, Best, Life, Supreme, and Ingredient! Heaven and Hell?" mean?

The Most High Heavenly Father is "The Most Merciful."

In the KJV bible book of Exodus chapter 34 verse 6; it states:
"And the LORD passed by before him, and proclaimed,
The LORD, The LORD God, merciful and gracious, longsuffering, and
abundant in goodness and truth."

65

Yashu'a (Jesus) said: "A new commandment I give unto
you, that ye love one another; as I have loved you,
that ye also love one another."

ASSASSINS of DISOBEDIENCE!
Invoking the Power of the Most High Through Obedience, is the Key to Living Your Best Life
as the Supreme Ingredient!
Heaven or Hell?

CHILDREN OF THE MOST HIGH:
PRISTINE YOUTH AND FAMILY SOLUTIONS, LLC.
SONS AND DAUGHTERS OF THE MOST HIGH PUBLISHERS ®

Oh, Gracious Most High Heavenly father, Holy is your name,
Your Will Be Done Now and Forever!
Yashu'a (Jesus) said: "Thou shalt love the Most High Heavenly Father, thy Sustainer with all
thy heart, and with all thy soul, and with all thy mind. Thou shalt love
thy neighbour as thyself."

Define the words: Assassins, Disobedience, Invoking, Power, Obedience, Key, Living, Best, Life, Supreme, and Ingredient? Heaven and Hell?

According to the Online American Heritage Dictionary (2020), **Assassin** is defined as: "1. **One who murders** by surprise attack, especially **one who carries out a plot to kill** a prominent person. 2. **Assassin**, a member of a militant subgroup of Ismailis that in the 11th, 12th, and 13th centuries carried out political assassinations directed especially against Seljuk rule. 3. A game in which players eliminate other players by tagging them with an innocuous object, as a sock, rubber band, or pellet from a paintball gun, until only one player remains."

66

Yashu'a (Jesus) said: "A new commandment I give unto you, that ye love one another; as I have loved you, that ye also love one another."

ASSASSINS of DISOBEDIENCE!
Invoking the Power of the Most High Through Obedience, is the Key to Living Your Best Life
as the Supreme Ingredient!
Heaven or Hell?

CHILDREN OF THE MOST HIGH:
PRISTINE YOUTH AND FAMILY SOLUTIONS, LLC.
SONS AND DAUGHTERS OF THE MOST HIGH PUBLISHERS ®

Oh, Gracious Most High Heavenly father, Holy is your name,
Your Will Be Done Now and Forever!
Yashu'a (Jesus) said: *"Thou shalt love the Most High Heavenly Father, thy Sustainer with all thy heart, and with all thy soul, and with all thy mind. Thou shalt love thy neighbour as thyself."*

"[French, from Medieval Latin **assassīnus**, which **originated from the Arabic word Haššāsīn. Haššāsīn** or Ḥashshāshīn – a word that was modified in European languages as the **Assassins**." In the KJV bible book of **2ⁿᵈ Kings chapter 14 verse 6**; it states: "But the children **of the murderers** he slew not: **according unto that which is written in the book of the law of Moses, wherein the LORD commanded, saying, The fathers shall not be put to death for the children, nor the children be put to death for the fathers; but every man shall be put to death for his own sin.**" "The KJV bible Hebrew Strong's Concordance phrase: "**of the murderers**" is **#5221** נָכָה **nakah (nä·kä')** and means **to smite, kill, slay**."

ASSASSINS of DISOBEDIENCE!
Invoking the Power of the Most High Through Obedience, is the Key to Living Your Best Life
as the Supreme Ingredient!
Heaven or Hell?

CHILDREN OF THE MOST HIGH:
PRISTINE YOUTH AND FAMILY SOLUTIONS, LLC.
SONS AND DAUGHTERS OF THE MOST HIGH PUBLISHERS ®

Oh, Gracious Most High Heavenly father, Holy is your name,
Your Will Be Done Now and Forever!
Yashu'a (Jesus) said: "Thou shalt love the Most High Heavenly Father, thy Sustainer with all
thy heart, and with all thy soul, and with all thy mind. Thou shalt love
thy neighbour as thyself."

According to the Online American Heritage Dictionary (2020), the word **disobedience** is defined as: "**refusal or failure to obey.**" In the KJV bible book of John chapter 14 verses 15 and 21; the Messiah Yashu'a (Jesus) said: "**If ye love me, keep my commandments. He that hath my commandments, and keepeth them, he it is that loveth me: and he that loveth me shall be loved of my Father, and I will love him, and will manifest myself to him.**"

68

Yashu'a (Jesus) said: "A new commandment I give unto you, that ye love one another; as I have loved you, that ye also love one another."

ASSASSINS of DISOBEDIENCE!
Invoking the Power of the Most High Through Obedience, is the Key to Living Your Best Life
as the Supreme Ingredient!
Heaven or Hell?

CHILDREN OF THE MOST HIGH:
PRISTINE YOUTH AND FAMILY SOLUTIONS, LLC.
SONS AND DAUGHTERS OF THE MOST HIGH PUBLISHERS ®

Oh, Gracious Most High Heavenly father, Holy is your name,
Your Will Be Done Now and Forever!
Yashu'a (Jesus) said: "Thou shalt love the Most High Heavenly Father, thy Sustainer with all
thy heart, and with all thy soul, and with all thy mind. Thou shalt love
thy neighbour as thyself."

In the KJV bible book of Matthew chapter 7 verses 21-23; the Messiah Yashu'a (Jesus) said: "Not everyone that saith unto me, Lord, Lord, shall enter into the kingdom of heaven; but he that doeth the will of my Father which is in heaven. Many will say to me in that day, Lord, Lord, have we not prophesied in thy name? and in thy name have cast out devils? and in thy name done many wonderful works? And then will I profess unto them, I never knew you: depart from me, ye that work iniquity."

69

Yashu'a (Jesus) said: "A new commandment I give unto
you, that ye love one another; as I have loved you,
that ye also love one another."

ASSASSINS of DISOBEDIENCE!
Invoking the Power of the Most High Through Obedience, is the Key to Living Your Best Life
as the Supreme Ingredient!
Heaven or Hell?

CHILDREN OF THE MOST HIGH:
PRISTINE YOUTH AND FAMILY SOLUTIONS, LLC.
SONS AND DAUGHTERS OF THE MOST HIGH PUBLISHERS ®

Oh, Gracious Most High Heavenly father, Holy is your name,
Your Will Be Done Now and Forever!
Yashu'a (Jesus) said: *"Thou shalt love the Most High Heavenly Father, thy Sustainer with all*
thy heart, and with all thy soul, and with all thy mind. Thou shalt love
thy neighbour as thyself."

In the KJV bible book of Deuteronomy chapter 28 verse 1; it states: "And it shall come to pass, **if** thou shalt hearken diligently unto the voice of the LORD thy God, **to observe [and] to do all his commandments** which I command thee this day, that **the LORD thy God will set thee on high above all nations of the earth**." According to the Online American Heritage Dictionary (2020), the word **invoking** is defined as: "to call on (a higher power) for assistance, support, or inspiration." In the KJV bible book of John chapter 15 verse 7; the Messiah Yashu'a (Jesus) said: "If ye abide in me, and my words abide in you, ye shall ask what ye will, and it shall be done unto you."

70

ASSASSINS of DISOBEDIENCE!
Invoking the Power of the Most High Through Obedience, is the Key to Living Your Best Life
as the Supreme Ingredient!
Heaven or Hell?

CHILDREN OF THE MOST HIGH:
PRISTINE YOUTH AND FAMILY SOLUTIONS, LLC.
SONS AND DAUGHTERS OF THE MOST HIGH PUBLISHERS ®

Oh, Gracious Most High Heavenly father, Holy is your name,
Your Will Be Done Now and Forever!
Yashu'a (Jesus) said: *"Thou shalt love the Most High Heavenly Father, thy Sustainer with all*
thy heart, and with all thy soul, and with all thy mind. Thou shalt love
thy neighbour as thyself."

In the KJV bible book of Psalms chapter 19 verses 7-12; it states: "**The law** of the LORD [is] perfect, converting the soul: **the testimony** of the LORD [is] sure, making wise the simple. **The statutes** of the LORD [are] right, rejoicing the heart: **the commandment** of the LORD [is] pure, enlightening the eyes." "**The fear** of the LORD [is] clean, enduring forever: the judgments of the LORD [are] true [and] righteous altogether. More to be desired [are they] than gold, yea, than much fine gold: sweeter also than honey and the honeycomb. **Moreover, by them is thy servant warned: [and] in keeping of them [there is] great reward**."

Yashu'a (Jesus) said: "A new commandment I give unto
you, that ye love one another; as I have loved you,
that ye also love one another."

ASSASSINS of DISOBEDIENCE!
Invoking the Power of the Most High Through Obedience, is the Key to Living Your Best Life
as the Supreme Ingredient!
Heaven or Hell?

CHILDREN OF THE MOST HIGH:
PRISTINE YOUTH AND FAMILY SOLUTIONS, LLC.
SONS AND DAUGHTERS OF THE MOST HIGH PUBLISHERS ®

Oh, Gracious Most High Heavenly father, Holy is your name,
Your Will Be Done Now and Forever!
Yashu'a (Jesus) said: *"Thou shalt love the Most High Heavenly Father, thy Sustainer with all*
thy heart, and with all thy soul, and with all thy mind. Thou shalt love
thy neighbour as thyself."

According to the Online American Heritage Dictionary (2020), the word **power** is defined as: "1. a. **The ability or capacity to act or do something effectively**: b. **A specific capacity, faculty, or aptitude: her powers of concentration.** 2. a. **Physical strength or force exerted or capable of being exerted.** b. **Effectiveness at moving one's emotions or changing how one thinks: a novel of great power.** 3. a. **The ability or official capacity to exercise control; authority**: Middle English, from Old French **pooir, to be able, power,** from Vulgar Latin ***potēre, to be able,** from Latin **potis, able, powerful**; see **poti-** in the Appendix of Indo-European roots]."

ASSASSINS of DISOBEDIENCE!
Invoking the Power of the Most High Through Obedience, is the Key to Living Your Best Life
as the Supreme Ingredient!
Heaven or Hell?

CHILDREN OF THE MOST HIGH:
PRISTINE YOUTH AND FAMILY SOLUTIONS, LLC.
SONS AND DAUGHTERS OF THE MOST HIGH PUBLISHERS ®

Oh, Gracious Most High Heavenly father, Holy is your name,
Your Will Be Done Now and Forever!
Yashu'a (Jesus) said: *"Thou shalt love the Most High Heavenly Father, thy Sustainer with all thy heart, and with all thy soul, and with all thy mind. Thou shalt love thy neighbour as thyself."*

According to the Online American Heritage Dictionary (2020), the word **obedience** is defined as: "**The quality or condition of being obedient. b. The act of obeying**." In the KJV bible book of Revelation chapter 22 verses 14; it states: "**Blessed are they that do his commandments**, that they may have right to the tree of life, and may enter in through the gates into the city." According to the Online American Heritage Dictionary (2020), the word **key** is defined as: "**A determining factor in accomplishing or achieving something**."

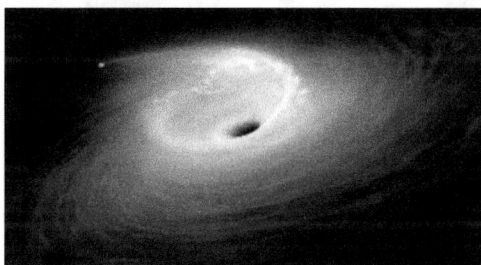

73

Yashu'a (Jesus) said: *"A new commandment I give unto you, that ye love one another; as I have loved you, that ye also love one another."*

ASSASSINS of DISOBEDIENCE!
Invoking the Power of the Most High Through Obedience, is the Key to Living Your Best Life
as the Supreme Ingredient!
Heaven or Hell?

CHILDREN OF THE MOST HIGH:
PRISTINE YOUTH AND FAMILY SOLUTIONS, LLC.
SONS AND DAUGHTERS OF THE MOST HIGH PUBLISHERS ®

Oh, Gracious Most High Heavenly father, Holy is your name,
Your Will Be Done Now and Forever!
Yashu'a (Jesus) said: "Thou shalt love the Most High Heavenly Father, thy Sustainer with all
thy heart, and with all thy soul, and with all thy mind. Thou shalt love
thy neighbour as thyself."

In the KJV bible book of Isaiah chapter 22 verse 22; it states: "And **the key** of the house of David will I lay upon his shoulder; so, he shall open, and none shall shut; and he shall shut, and none shall open." In the KJV bible book of Matthew chapter 16 verses 19; the Messiah Yashu'a (Jesus) said: "And I will give unto thee the keys of the kingdom of heaven: and whatsoever thou shalt bind on earth shall be bound in heaven: and whatsoever thou shalt loose on earth shall be loosed in heaven."

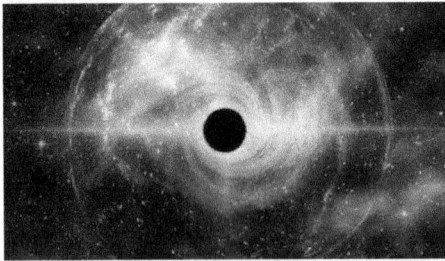

74

Yashu'a (Jesus) said: "A new commandment I give unto you, that ye love one another; as I have loved you, that ye also love one another."

ASSASSINS of DISOBEDIENCE!
Invoking the Power of the Most High Through Obedience, is the Key to Living Your Best Life
as the Supreme Ingredient!
Heaven or Hell?

CHILDREN OF THE MOST HIGH:
PRISTINE YOUTH AND FAMILY SOLUTIONS, LLC.
SONS AND DAUGHTERS OF THE MOST HIGH PUBLISHERS ®

Oh, Gracious Most High Heavenly father, Holy is your name,
Your Will Be Done Now and Forever!
Yashu'a (Jesus) said: *"Thou shalt love the Most High Heavenly Father, thy Sustainer with all*
thy heart, and with all thy soul, and with all thy mind. Thou shalt love
thy neighbour as thyself."

According to the Online American Heritage Dictionary (2020), the word **living** is defined as: **"of persons who are alive: relating to the routine conduct or maintenance of life**: **improved living conditions in the city. 5. Full of life, interest, or vitality**." In the KJV bible book of Genesis chapter 2 verse 7; it states: "And the LORD God formed man of the dust of the ground, and **breathed into his nostrils the breath of life**; **and man became a living soul**." According to the Online American Heritage Dictionary (2020), the word **life** is defined as: **"The interval of time between birth and death**."

75

Yashu'a (Jesus) said: "A new commandment I give unto
you, that ye love one another; as I have loved you,
that ye also love one another."

CHILDREN OF THE MOST HIGH:
PRISTINE YOUTH AND FAMILY SOLUTIONS, LLC.
SONS AND DAUGHTERS OF THE MOST HIGH PUBLISHERS ®

Oh, Gracious Most High Heavenly father, Holy is your name,
Your Will Be Done Now and Forever!
Yashu'a (Jesus) said: "Thou shalt love the Most High Heavenly Father, thy Sustainer with all thy heart, and with all thy soul, and with all thy mind. Thou shalt love thy neighbour as thyself."

According to the Online American Heritage Dictionary (2020), the word **best** is defined as: "**In a most excellent way; most advantageously.**" According to the Online American Heritage Dictionary (2020), the word **supreme** is defined as: "**Greatest in importance, degree, significance, character, or achievement.**" According to the Online American Heritage Dictionary (2020), the word **ingredient** is defined as: "**An element or component of something.**"

76

Yashu'a (Jesus) said: "A new commandment I give unto you, that ye love one another; as I have loved you, that ye also love one another."

ASSASSINS of DISOBEDIENCE!
Invoking the Power of the Most High Through Obedience, is the Key to Living Your Best Life
as the Supreme Ingredient!
Heaven or Hell?

CHILDREN OF THE MOST HIGH:
PRISTINE YOUTH AND FAMILY SOLUTIONS, LLC.
SONS AND DAUGHTERS OF THE MOST HIGH PUBLISHERS ®

Oh, Gracious Most High Heavenly father, Holy is your name,
Your Will Be Done Now and Forever!
Yashu'a (Jesus) said: "Thou shalt love the Most High Heavenly Father, thy Sustainer with all
thy heart, and with all thy soul, and with all thy mind. Thou shalt love
thy neighbour as thyself."

According to the Online American Heritage Dictionary (2020), the word **hell** is defined as: "a. **Often Hell the place of eternal punishment for the wicked after death, often imagined as being presided over by Satan and his devils. b. A state of separation from God; exclusion from God's presence. 2. The abode of the dead in any of various religious traditions, such as the Hebrew Sheol or the Greek Hades; the underworld. 3. a. A situation or place of evil, misery, discord, or destruction: "War is hell" (William Tecumseh Sherman). b. An extremely difficult experience; torment or anguish: went through hell on the job."**

77

Yashu'a (Jesus) said: "A new commandment I give unto
you, that ye love one another; as I have loved you,
that ye also love one another."

ASSASSINS of DISOBEDIENCE!
Invoking the Power of the Most High Through Obedience, is the Key to Living Your Best Life
as the Supreme Ingredient!
Heaven or Hell?

CHILDREN OF THE MOST HIGH:
PRISTINE YOUTH AND FAMILY SOLUTIONS, LLC.
SONS AND DAUGHTERS OF THE MOST HIGH PUBLISHERS ®

Oh, Gracious Most High Heavenly father, Holy is your name,
Your Will Be Done Now and Forever!
Yashu'a (Jesus) said: *"Thou shalt love the Most High Heavenly Father, thy Sustainer with all*
thy heart, and with all thy soul, and with all thy mind. Thou shalt love
thy neighbour as thyself."

In the KJV bible book of Revelation chapter 17 verse 8; it states: "The beast that thou sawest was, and is not; and shall ascend out of the bottomless pit, and go into perdition: **and they that dwell on the earth shall wonder, whose names were not written in the book of life from the foundation of the world**, when they behold the beast that was, and is not, and yet is." In the KJV bible book of Revelation chapter 19 verse 20; it states: "And the beast was taken, and with him the false prophet that wrought miracles before him, with which he deceived them that had received the mark of the beast, and them that worshipped his image. These both were cast alive into a lake of fire burning with brimstone."

78

Yashu'a (Jesus) said: *"A new commandment I give unto you, that ye love one another; as I have loved you, that ye also love one another."*

ASSASSINS of DISOBEDIENCE!
Invoking the Power of the Most High Through Obedience, is the Key to Living Your Best Life
as the Supreme Ingredient!
Heaven or Hell?

CHILDREN OF THE MOST HIGH:
PRISTINE YOUTH AND FAMILY SOLUTIONS, LLC.
SONS AND DAUGHTERS OF THE MOST HIGH PUBLISHERS ®

Oh, Gracious Most High Heavenly father, Holy is your name,
Your Will Be Done Now and Forever!
Yashu'a (Jesus) said: "Thou shalt love the Most High Heavenly Father, thy Sustainer with all
thy heart, and with all thy soul, and with all thy mind. Thou shalt love
thy neighbour as thyself."

In the KJV bible book of Revelation chapter 20 verse 10; it states: "And the devil that deceived them was cast into the lake of fire and brimstone, where the beast and the false prophet are, and shall be tormented day and night for ever and ever." In the KJV bible book of Revelation chapter 20 verse 15; it states: "And whosoever was not found written in the book of life was cast into the lake of fire."

SO, WHERE IS HELL?
HELL IS WHEREVER HEAVEN IS NOT!!!

79

Yashu'a (Jesus) said: "A new commandment I give unto you, that ye love one another; as I have loved you, that ye also love one another."

ASSASSINS of DISOBEDIENCE!
Invoking the Power of the Most High Through Obedience, is the Key to Living Your Best Life
as the Supreme Ingredient!
Heaven or Hell?

CHILDREN OF THE MOST HIGH:
PRISTINE YOUTH AND FAMILY SOLUTIONS, LLC.
SONS AND DAUGHTERS OF THE MOST HIGH PUBLISHERS ®

Oh, Gracious Most High Heavenly father, Holy is your name,
Your Will Be Done Now and Forever!
Yashu'a (Jesus) said: "Thou shalt love the Most High Heavenly Father, thy Sustainer with all
thy heart, and with all thy soul, and with all thy mind. Thou shalt love
thy neighbour as thyself."

According to the Online American Heritage Dictionary (2020), the word **heaven** is defined as: "**The abode of God, the angels, and the souls of those who are granted salvation.** b. **An eternal state of communion with God; everlasting bliss.** 3. **Any of the places in or beyond the sky conceived of as domains of divine beings in various religions.** 4. **A condition or place of great happiness, delight, or pleasure.**"

80

Yashu'a (Jesus) said: "A new commandment I give unto you, that ye love one another; as I have loved you, that ye also love one another."

CHILDREN OF THE MOST HIGH:
PRISTINE YOUTH AND FAMILY SOLUTIONS, LLC.
SONS AND DAUGHTERS OF THE MOST HIGH PUBLISHERS ®

Oh, Gracious Most High Heavenly father, Holy is your name,
Your Will Be Done Now and Forever!
Yashu'a (Jesus) said: "Thou shalt love the Most High Heavenly Father, thy Sustainer with all thy heart, and with all thy soul, and with all thy mind. Thou shalt love thy neighbour as thyself."

In the KJV bible book of Matthew chapter 6 verses 9-13; the Messiah Yashu'a (Jesus) said: "After this manner therefore pray ye: Our Father which art in heaven, Hallowed be thy name. Thy kingdom come. Thy will be done in earth, as it is in heaven. Give us this day our daily bread. And forgive us our debts, as we forgive our debtors. And lead us not into temptation, but deliver us from evil: For thine is the kingdom, and the power, and the glory, forever. Amen." In the aforementioned verse, the word for "**heaven**" is the KJV bible Greek Strong's Concordance **#3772** word: οὐρανός *ouranos*. **Ouranos** is the **Greek word** for the **English word "Orion" in reference to the Orion Star Constellation**. **Not to be mistaken for the Kingdom of God. Heaven (Ouranos) is** in the **Kingdom of God, (Hughes 2019)**.

81

Yashu'a (Jesus) said: "A new commandment I give unto you, that ye love one another; as I have loved you, that ye also love one another."

ASSASSINS of DISOBEDIENCE!
Invoking the Power of the Most High Through Obedience, is the Key to Living Your Best Life
as the Supreme Ingredient!
Heaven or Hell?

CHILDREN OF THE MOST HIGH:
PRISTINE YOUTH AND FAMILY SOLUTIONS, LLC.
SONS AND DAUGHTERS OF THE MOST HIGH PUBLISHERS ®

Oh, Gracious Most High Heavenly father, Holy is your name,
Your Will Be Done Now and Forever!
Yashu'a (Jesus) said: "Thou shalt love the Most High Heavenly Father, thy Sustainer with all
thy heart, and with all thy soul, and with all thy mind. Thou shalt love
thy neighbour as thyself."

In the **KJV bible book of Job chapter 9 verse 9**; it states: "Which maketh **Arcturus**, **Orion**, and **Pleiades**, and the **chambers of the south**." <u>These are Star Constellations</u> created by the Most High Heavenly Father. That's why in the KJV bible book of John chapter 14 verse 2; Yashu'a (Jesus) said: "In my Father's house [**throughout the boundless universes** and **outside the boundless universes**] are many mansions (the KJV bible Greek Strong's Concordance word for **"mansions"** is the word: **μονή monē** which means: **a staying, abiding, dwelling, abode**): if it were not so, I would have told you. I go to prepare a place for you, **(Hughes 2019)**."

82

Yashu'a (Jesus) said: "A new commandment I give unto you, that ye love one another; as I have loved you, that ye also love one another."

CHILDREN OF THE MOST HIGH:
PRISTINE YOUTH AND FAMILY SOLUTIONS, LLC.
SONS AND DAUGHTERS OF THE MOST HIGH PUBLISHERS ®

Oh, Gracious Most High Heavenly father, Holy is your name,
Your Will Be Done Now and Forever!
Yashu'a (Jesus) said: "Thou shalt love the Most High Heavenly Father, thy Sustainer with all thy heart, and with all thy soul, and with all thy mind. Thou shalt love thy neighbour as thyself."

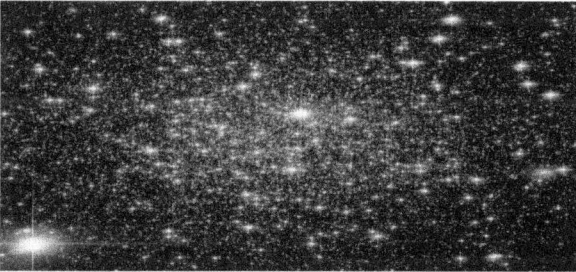

What do you mean when you say: "outside the boundless universes?" We mean that **Existence predates Creation**. In order for the Most High Heavenly Father to have **created the boundless universes, the Most High Heavenly Father had to exist before the creation of all that was created**. The Most High Heavenly Father is the **Creator of all creators** and **existed outside of creation** during the time that the **sum of things** or that which **adds up to something** were being created, **(Hughes 2019)**.

83

Yashu'a (Jesus) said: "A new commandment I give unto you, that ye love one another; as I have loved you, that ye also love one another."

ASSASSINS of DISOBEDIENCE!
Invoking the Power of the Most High Through Obedience, is the Key to Living Your Best Life
as the Supreme Ingredient!
Heaven or Hell?

CHILDREN OF THE MOST HIGH:
PRISTINE YOUTH AND FAMILY SOLUTIONS, LLC.
SONS AND DAUGHTERS OF THE MOST HIGH PUBLISHERS ®

Oh, Gracious Most High Heavenly father, Holy is your name,
Your Will Be Done Now and Forever!
Yashu'a (Jesus) said: *"Thou shalt love the Most High Heavenly Father, thy Sustainer with all*
thy heart, and with all thy soul, and with all thy mind. Thou shalt love
thy neighbour as thyself."

This is further discussed in the: "**2020 Mind Gardening in the Creative Garden of Will (Your Mind) to Grow a Living Water Mentality**" Book, **authored by: Woodie Hughes Jr**.

84

Yashu'a (Jesus) said: *"A new commandment I give unto you, that ye love one another; as I have loved you, that ye also love one another."*

ASSASSINS of DISOBEDIENCE!
Invoking the Power of the Most High Through Obedience, is the Key to Living Your Best Life
as the Supreme Ingredient!
Heaven or Hell?

CHILDREN OF THE MOST HIGH:
PRISTINE YOUTH AND FAMILY SOLUTIONS, LLC.
SONS AND DAUGHTERS OF THE MOST HIGH PUBLISHERS ®

Oh, Gracious Most High Heavenly father, Holy is your name,
Your Will Be Done Now and Forever!
Yashu'a (Jesus) said: *"Thou shalt love the Most High Heavenly Father, thy Sustainer with all thy heart, and with all thy soul, and with all thy mind. Thou shalt love thy neighbour as thyself."*

85

Yashu'a (Jesus) said: *"A new commandment I give unto you, that ye love one another; as I have loved you, that ye also love one another."*

ASSASSINS of DISOBEDIENCE!
Invoking the Power of the Most High Through Obedience, is the Key to Living Your Best Life
as the Supreme Ingredient!
Heaven or Hell?

CHILDREN OF THE MOST HIGH:
PRISTINE YOUTH AND FAMILY SOLUTIONS, LLC.
SONS AND DAUGHTERS OF THE MOST HIGH PUBLISHERS ®

Oh, Gracious Most High Heavenly father, Holy is your name,
Your Will Be Done Now and Forever!
Yashu'a (Jesus) said: *"Thou shalt love the Most High Heavenly Father, thy Sustainer with all*
thy heart, and with all thy soul, and with all thy mind. Thou shalt love
thy neighbour as thyself."

In the KJV bible book of Revelation chapter 13 verse 18; it states: "**Here is wisdom**. Let him that hath understanding count the number of the beast: **for it is the number of a man** (the KJV bible Greek Strong's Concordance#444 for the word "man" is ἄνθρωπος **anthrōpos** and means a person or human being, whether male or female); and his (or her or their) number is Six hundred threescore and six (**666**)."

86

Yashu'a (Jesus) said: "A new commandment I give unto
you, that ye love one another; as I have loved you,
that ye also love one another."

ASSASSINS of DISOBEDIENCE!
Invoking the Power of the Most High Through Obedience, is the Key to Living Your Best Life
as the Supreme Ingredient!
Heaven or Hell?

CHILDREN OF THE MOST HIGH:
PRISTINE YOUTH AND FAMILY SOLUTIONS, LLC.
SONS AND DAUGHTERS OF THE MOST HIGH PUBLISHERS ®

Oh, Gracious Most High Heavenly father, Holy is your name,
Your Will Be Done Now and Forever!
Yashu'a (Jesus) said: "Thou shalt love the Most High Heavenly Father, thy Sustainer with all
thy heart, and with all thy soul, and with all thy mind. Thou shalt love
thy neighbour as thyself."

So, for the Children of the Most High: Pristine Youth and Family Solutions, LLC., the title of this book: "**ASSASSINS of DISOBEDIENCE! Invoking the Power of the Most High Through Obedience, is the Key to Living Your Best Life as the Supreme Ingredient! Heaven or Hell?**" means the children of the Most High (**the peacemakers**) in KJV Matthew 5:9) will rigorously work on improving their character through the Messiah Yashu'a (Jesus) by **eliminating (assassinating) disobedience** to **God's (אֱלֹהִים 'Elohiym), commandments**. This is done through the Messiah Yashu'a (Jesus) by **Invoking the Power of the Most High Through Obedience** (being obedient to **the Most High Heavenly Father (ELYOWN עֶלְיוֹן EL אֵל**) and the Messiah Yashu'a (Jesus) commandments which is **the KEY ingredient** to the children of the Most High living their best life!

87

Yashu'a (Jesus) said: "A new commandment I give unto
you, that ye love one another; as I have loved you,
that ye also love one another."

ASSASSINS of DISOBEDIENCE!
Invoking the Power of the Most High Through Obedience, is the Key to Living Your Best Life
as the Supreme Ingredient!
Heaven or Hell?

CHILDREN OF THE MOST HIGH:
PRISTINE YOUTH AND FAMILY SOLUTIONS, LLC.
SONS AND DAUGHTERS OF THE MOST HIGH PUBLISHERS ®

Oh, Gracious Most High Heavenly father, Holy is your name,
Your Will Be Done Now and Forever!
Yashu'a (Jesus) said: "Thou shalt love the Most High Heavenly Father, thy Sustainer with all
thy heart, and with all thy soul, and with all thy mind. Thou shalt love
thy neighbour as thyself."

Chapter 3: According to the KJV bible, are Laws and Commandments the same?

The Messiah Yashu'a (Jesus) said: "He [or she] that hath my commandments, and keepeth them, he [or she] it is that loveth me: and he [or she] that loveth me shall be loved of my Father, and I will love him [or her], and will manifest myself to him [or her]."
John 14:21; KJV Bible."

The Most High Heavenly Father is "The King."

In the KJV bible book of Revelation chapter 22 verse 14; it states:
"The kingdom of heaven is like unto a certain King,
which made a marriage for his son."

88

Yashu'a (Jesus) said: "A new commandment I give unto
you, that ye love one another; as I have loved you,
that ye also love one another."

ASSASSINS of DISOBEDIENCE!
Invoking the Power of the Most High Through Obedience, is the Key to Living Your Best Life
as the Supreme Ingredient!
Heaven or Hell?

CHILDREN OF THE MOST HIGH:
PRISTINE YOUTH AND FAMILY SOLUTIONS, LLC.
SONS AND DAUGHTERS OF THE MOST HIGH PUBLISHERS ®

Oh, Gracious Most High Heavenly father, Holy is your name,
Your Will Be Done Now and Forever!
Yashu'a (Jesus) said: "Thou shalt love the Most High Heavenly Father, thy Sustainer with all
thy heart, and with all thy soul, and with all thy mind. Thou shalt love
thy neighbour as thyself."

In the KJV bible book of Isaiah chapter 9 verse 6; it states that **the Messiah Yashu'a (Jesus)** will be called "**The Prince of Peace**", and in the KJV bible book of Hebrews chapter 7 verse 2; it states: that **Melchizedek is the King of Peace**. However; the **Messiah Yashu'a (Jesus)** commanded the children of the Most High to keep his commandments. This is done by learning and practicing becoming "**Assassins of Disobedience**" from moment to moment in our **thoughts**, **actions** and **words**.

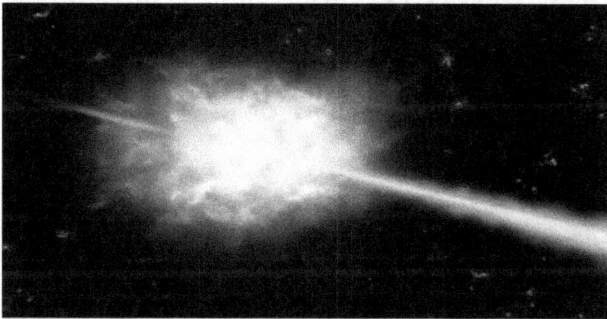

89

Yashu'a (Jesus) said: "A new commandment I give unto
you, that ye love one another; as I have loved you,
that ye also love one another."

ASSASSINS of DISOBEDIENCE!
Invoking the Power of the Most High Through Obedience, is the Key to Living Your Best Life
as the Supreme Ingredient!
Heaven or Hell?

CHILDREN OF THE MOST HIGH:
PRISTINE YOUTH AND FAMILY SOLUTIONS, LLC.
SONS AND DAUGHTERS OF THE MOST HIGH PUBLISHERS ®

Oh, Gracious Most High Heavenly father, Holy is your name,
Your Will Be Done Now and Forever!
Yashu'a (Jesus) said: *"Thou shalt love the Most High Heavenly Father, thy Sustainer with all*
thy heart, and with all thy soul, and with all thy mind. Thou shalt love
thy neighbour as thyself."

According to the KJV bible, are Laws and Commandments the same?

In the KJV bible book of Exodus chapter 22 verse 12 with Aramic (Hebrew) Excerpts:

24:12 וַיֹּאמֶר יְהֹוָה אֶל־מֹשֶׁה עֲלֵה אֵלַי הָהָרָה וֶהְיֵה־שָׁם וְאֶתְּנָה לְךָ אֶת־
לֻחֹת הָאֶבֶן וְהַתּוֹרָה וְהַמִּצְוָה אֲשֶׁר כָּתַבְתִּי לְהוֹרֹתָם:

And the LORD (יְהֹוָה Yahayyu, Yahuwa, Yehovah) said (אָמַר 'amar) unto Moses (מֹשֶׁה Mosheh), Come up (עָלָה `Alah) to me into the mount (הַר Har), and be there: and I will give (נָתַן Nathan) thee tables (לוּחַ Luwach) of stone (אֶבֶן 'Eben), and a <u>law</u> (תּוֹרָה <u>Towrah or Torah</u>), and <u>commandments</u> (מִצְוָה <u>Mits-waw or Mitsvah</u>) which I have written (כָּתַב Kathab); that thou mayest teach (יָרָה Yarah) them, (Safrai, Stern, Flusser, & Van Unnik, 1976)."

90

Yashu'a (Jesus) said: *"A new commandment I give unto you, that ye love one another; as I have loved you, that ye also love one another."*

ASSASSINS of DISOBEDIENCE!
Invoking the Power of the Most High Through Obedience, is the Key to Living Your Best Life
as the Supreme Ingredient!
Heaven or Hell?

CHILDREN OF THE MOST HIGH:
PRISTINE YOUTH AND FAMILY SOLUTIONS, LLC.
SONS AND DAUGHTERS OF THE MOST HIGH PUBLISHERS ®

Oh, Gracious Most High Heavenly father, Holy is your name,
Your Will Be Done Now and Forever!
Yashu'a (Jesus) said: *"Thou shalt love the Most High Heavenly Father, thy Sustainer with all*
thy heart, and with all thy soul, and with all thy mind. Thou shalt love
thy neighbour as thyself."

The Aramic/Hebrew Word For Law Is: **"Towrah"** Or **"Torah"**
(טורה) These Letters Are Equivalent To The Ashuric Syriac
(Arabic) Word **Wariyya** (وريه) Which Means "A View." In
Greek, The Word For Law Is: **"Nomos"**.
The Ashuric Syriac (Arabic) Word For Law Is **Shari'ah** (شريعه)
Which Means: "A Rule Established By Authority; Society Or
Custom 2. A Code Of Ethics Or Behavior. This Word Takes Its
Root From: **Shara'a** (شرع) Meaning To Introduce, Enact,
Prescribe, Give, Make Laws.

What is the difference between <u>Law</u> and <u>Commandments</u> in the KJV bible book of Exodus chapter 24 verse 12?

According to the KJV bible Hebrew Strong's Concordance
"#8451, the word for "<u>Law</u>" is: תּוֹרָה **Towrah or Torah** and
means: "**Law, a precept or statute, especially the Decalogue
or <u>Pentateuch</u>: law, codes of law, custom, manner, the
Deuteronomic or <u>Mosaic Law</u>.**"

91

Yashu'a (Jesus) said: "A new commandment I give unto
you, that ye love one another; as I have loved you,
that ye also love one another."

ASSASSINS of DISOBEDIENCE!
Invoking the Power of the Most High Through Obedience, is the Key to Living Your Best Life
as the Supreme Ingredient!
Heaven or Hell?

CHILDREN OF THE MOST HIGH:
PRISTINE YOUTH AND FAMILY SOLUTIONS, LLC.
SONS AND DAUGHTERS OF THE MOST HIGH PUBLISHERS ®

Oh, Gracious Most High Heavenly father, Holy is your name,
Your Will Be Done Now and Forever!
Yashu'a (Jesus) said: *"Thou shalt love the Most High Heavenly Father, thy Sustainer with all*
thy heart, and with all thy soul, and with all thy mind. Thou shalt love
thy neighbour as thyself."

תּוֹרָה f. (from the root יָרָה Hiph. No. 4. to teach).
—(1) *instruction, doctrine,* Job 22:22.—(*a*) human, as that of parents, Prov. 1:8; 3:1; 4:2; 7:2.
—(*b*) divine through prophets, Isa. 1:10; 8:16, 20; 42:4, 21.

(2) *law.*—(*a*) human, the manner and principles which men follow, 2 Sa. 7:19.—(*b*) divine, whether one, followed by a genit. of the object, e. g. *the law of sacrifice,* Leviticus 6:7; 7:7; or collect. *laws*; סֵפֶר הַתּוֹרָה the book of the law, Josh. 1:8; 8:34; 2 Ki. 22:8, 11; Neh. 8:3; plur. תּוֹרוֹת laws, Exod. 18:20; Lev. 26:46.

According to the KJV bible Hebrew Strong's Concordance "#4687, the word for "**Commandments**" is: מִצְוָה **Mits-waw or Mitsvah**) and means: "**commandments, precept, commanded, ordinances.**"

92

Yashu'a (Jesus) said: *"A new commandment I give unto you, that ye love one another; as I have loved you, that ye also love one another."*

ASSASSINS of DISOBEDIENCE!
Invoking the Power of the Most High Through Obedience, is the Key to Living Your Best Life
as the Supreme Ingredient!
Heaven or Hell?

CHILDREN OF THE MOST HIGH:
PRISTINE YOUTH AND FAMILY SOLUTIONS, LLC.
SONS AND DAUGHTERS OF THE MOST HIGH PUBLISHERS ®

Oh, Gracious Most High Heavenly father, Holy is your name,
Your Will Be Done Now and Forever!
Yashu'a (Jesus) said: *"Thou shalt love the Most High Heavenly Father, thy Sustainer with all*
thy heart, and with all thy soul, and with all thy mind. Thou shalt love
thy neighbour as thyself."

מִצְוָה f. (from the root צָוָה) pl. מִצְוֹת *a command,*
a precept, 2 Ki. 18:36; especially used of the precepts of God, Deuteron. 6:1, 25; 7:11; of a human
teacher, Proverbs 7:1, 2. The idea of *prohibition* is
found Lev. 4:13, אַחַת מִכָּל־מִצְוֹת יְהֹוָה אֲשֶׁר לֹא־תֵעָשֶׂינָה
" any of the commandments of Jehovah which
ought not to be done," i. e. things prohibited by his
precepts. מִצְוַת הַלְוִיִּם what was due to the Levites,
Neh. 13:5; comp. מִשְׁפָּט.

93

Yashu'a (Jesus) said: *"A new commandment I give unto*
you, that ye love one another; as I have loved you,
that ye also love one another."

ASSASSINS of DISOBEDIENCE!
Invoking the Power of the Most High Through Obedience, is the Key to Living Your Best Life
as the Supreme Ingredient!
Heaven or Hell?

CHILDREN OF THE MOST HIGH:
PRISTINE YOUTH AND FAMILY SOLUTIONS, LLC.
SONS AND DAUGHTERS OF THE MOST HIGH PUBLISHERS ®

Oh, Gracious Most High Heavenly father, Holy is your name,
Your Will Be Done Now and Forever!
Yashu'a (Jesus) said: *"Thou shalt love the Most High Heavenly Father, thy Sustainer with all*
thy heart, and with all thy soul, and with all thy mind. Thou shalt love
thy neighbour as thyself."

In the KJV bible book of John chapter 14 verse 21; the Messiah Yashu'a (Jesus) said: "He [or she] that hath my commandments (ἐντολή Entolē, pronounced as: **En-to-la'**, is the KJV bible Greek Strong's Concordance#1785 word ἐντολή Entolē and means: **injunction, i.e. an authoritative prescription: commandment, precept, an order, command, charge**), and keepeth them, he [or she] it is that loveth me: and he [or she] that loveth me shall be loved of my Father, and I will love him [or her], and will manifest myself to him [or her]." According to the Lane Arabic/English Lexicon (2003), in Ashuric/Syraic (Arabic), the word for "Commandment" is Wasiah (وصيه) and means direction, instruction, injunction, order."

94

Yashu'a (Jesus) said: "A new commandment I give unto
you, that ye love one another; as I have loved you,
that ye also love one another."

ASSASSINS of DISOBEDIENCE!
Invoking the Power of the Most High Through Obedience, is the Key to Living Your Best Life
as the Supreme Ingredient!
Heaven or Hell?

CHILDREN OF THE MOST HIGH:
PRISTINE YOUTH AND FAMILY SOLUTIONS, LLC.
SONS AND DAUGHTERS OF THE MOST HIGH PUBLISHERS ®

Oh, Gracious Most High Heavenly father, Holy is your name,
Your Will Be Done Now and Forever!
Yashu'a (Jesus) said: "Thou shalt love the Most High Heavenly Father, thy Sustainer with all thy heart, and with all thy soul, and with all thy mind. Thou shalt love thy neighbour as thyself."

What is the Pentateuch or Pentateuchus? The "**Pentateuchus**" is **Latin** for the **Greek** word: "**Pentateuch**" for the **Aramic (Hebrew)** word: "**Law**" תּוֹרָה **Towrah or Torah**. The Greek word **Penta** means **five** and **Teuch** means **tool, book, rolls. Pentateuch** means "collection of **five rolls (scrolls) in reference to the first five books of the bible which are: Barashith** מראשית **(means "The Reconstruction" in Aramic (Hebrew)** for the first book of **Genesis. Shimut** שמות **(means "Names" in Aramic (Hebrew)** for the second book of **Exodus. Wayikra** ויקרא **(means "And He Called" in Aramic (Hebrew)** for the third book of **Leviticus. Bimidbar** במדבר **(means "In the Wilderness" in Aramic (Hebrew)** for the fourth book of **Numbers**, (Safrai, Stern, Flusser, & Van Unnik, 1976)."

95

Yashu'a (Jesus) said: "A new commandment I give unto you, that ye love one another; as I have loved you, that ye also love one another."

ASSASSINS of DISOBEDIENCE!
Invoking the Power of the Most High Through Obedience, is the Key to Living Your Best Life
as the Supreme Ingredient!
Heaven or Hell?

CHILDREN OF THE MOST HIGH:
PRISTINE YOUTH AND FAMILY SOLUTIONS, LLC.
SONS AND DAUGHTERS OF THE MOST HIGH PUBLISHERS ®

Oh, Gracious Most High Heavenly father, Holy is your name,
Your Will Be Done Now and Forever!
Yashu'a (Jesus) said: *"Thou shalt love the Most High Heavenly Father, thy Sustainer with all thy heart, and with all thy soul, and with all thy mind. Thou shalt love thy neighbour as thyself."*

Dibarim רבד **(means "Words" in Aramic (Hebrew)** for the fifth book of **Deuteronomy** that combined with the other four, are called "**The Book of Moses**".

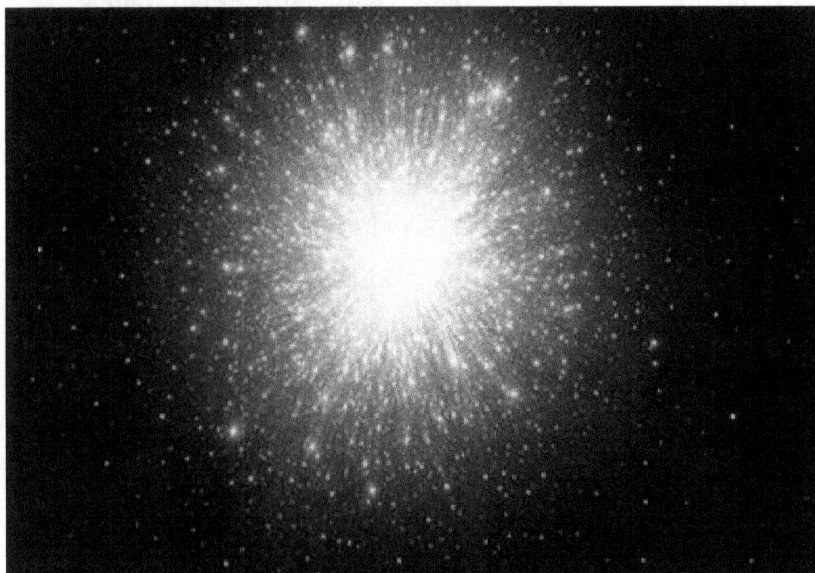

96

Yashu'a (Jesus) said: "A new commandment I give unto you, that ye love one another; as I have loved you, that ye also love one another."

ASSASSINS of DISOBEDIENCE!
Invoking the Power of the Most High Through Obedience, is the Key to Living Your Best Life
as the Supreme Ingredient!
Heaven or Hell?

CHILDREN OF THE MOST HIGH:
PRISTINE YOUTH AND FAMILY SOLUTIONS, LLC.
SONS AND DAUGHTERS OF THE MOST HIGH PUBLISHERS ®

Oh, Gracious Most High Heavenly father, Holy is your name,
Your Will Be Done Now and Forever!
Yashu'a (Jesus) said: "Thou shalt love the Most High Heavenly Father, thy Sustainer with all
thy heart, and with all thy soul, and with all thy mind. Thou shalt love
thy neighbour as thyself."

In the KJV bible book of Matthew chapter 10 verses 34-40; it states: "Think not that I am come to send peace on earth: I came not to send peace, but a sword. For I am come to set a man at variance against his father, and the daughter against her mother, and the daughter in law against her mother in law. And a man's foes *shall be* they of his own household."

"He that loveth father or mother more than me is not worthy of me: and he that loveth son or daughter more than me is not worthy of me. And he that taketh not his cross, and followeth after me, is not worthy of me. He that findeth his life shall lose it: and he that loseth his life for my sake shall find it. He that receiveth you receiveth me, and he that receiveth me receiveth him that sent me."

97

Yashu'a (Jesus) said: "A new commandment I give unto you, that ye love one another; as I have loved you, that ye also love one another."

ASSASSINS of DISOBEDIENCE!
Invoking the Power of the Most High Through Obedience, is the Key to Living Your Best Life
as the Supreme Ingredient!
Heaven or Hell?

CHILDREN OF THE MOST HIGH:
PRISTINE YOUTH AND FAMILY SOLUTIONS, LLC.
SONS AND DAUGHTERS OF THE MOST HIGH PUBLISHERS ®

Oh, Gracious Most High Heavenly father, Holy is your name,
Your Will Be Done Now and Forever!
Yashu'a (Jesus) said: "Thou shalt love the Most High Heavenly Father, thy Sustainer with all
thy heart, and with all thy soul, and with all thy mind. Thou shalt love
thy neighbour as thyself."

According to the above verses; the children of the Most High are to love the Messiah Yashu'a more than our loved ones on the planet earth. To embrace the doctrine of the Most High that the Messiah Yashu'a (Jesus) taught, and to be obedient to the Most High and Messiah Yashu'a (Jesus) **will create foes (enemies) on personal and professional levels**. The children of the Most High who work each moment, and each breath to master becoming **Assassins of Disobedience**; have an obligation according to the KJV bible book of Psalms, chapter 82, verses 3-8; to: "**Defend the poor and fatherless: do justice to the afflicted and needy. Deliver the poor and needy: rid them out of the hand of the wicked. They know not, neither will they understand; they walk on in darkness: all the foundations of the earth are out of course.**"

98

Yashu'a (Jesus) said: "A new commandment I give unto
you, that ye love one another; as I have loved you,
that ye also love one another."

ASSASSINS of DISOBEDIENCE!
Invoking the Power of the Most High Through Obedience, is the Key to Living Your Best Life
as the Supreme Ingredient!
Heaven or Hell?

CHILDREN OF THE MOST HIGH:
PRISTINE YOUTH AND FAMILY SOLUTIONS, LLC.
SONS AND DAUGHTERS OF THE MOST HIGH PUBLISHERS ®

Oh, Gracious Most High Heavenly father, Holy is your name,
Your Will Be Done Now and Forever!
Yashu'a (Jesus) said: *"Thou shalt love the Most High Heavenly Father, thy Sustainer with all thy heart, and with all thy soul, and with all thy mind. Thou shalt love thy neighbour as thyself."*

"I have said, Ye are gods; and all of you are children of the Most High. But ye shall die like men, and fall like one of the princes. Arise, O God, judge the earth: for thou shalt inherit all nations."

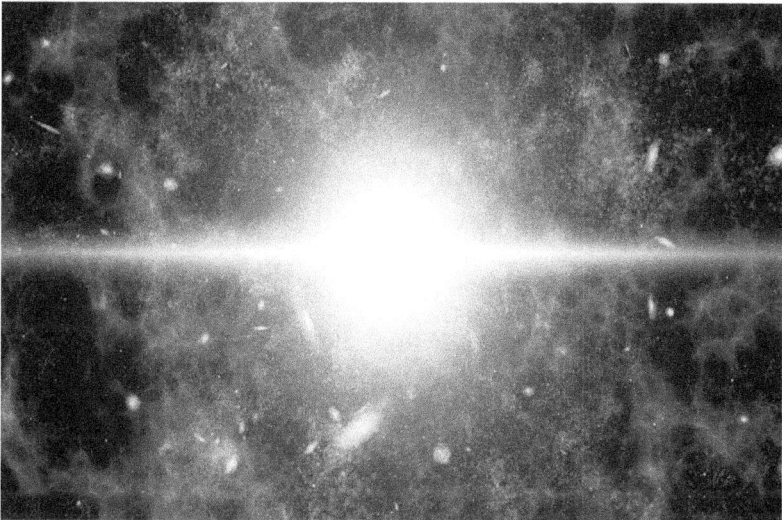

99

Yashu'a (Jesus) said: *"A new commandment I give unto you, that ye love one another; as I have loved you, that ye also love one another."*

ASSASSINS of DISOBEDIENCE!
Invoking the Power of the Most High Through Obedience, is the Key to Living Your Best Life
as the Supreme Ingredient!
Heaven or Hell?

CHILDREN OF THE MOST HIGH:
PRISTINE YOUTH AND FAMILY SOLUTIONS, LLC.
SONS AND DAUGHTERS OF THE MOST HIGH PUBLISHERS ®

Oh, Gracious Most High Heavenly father, Holy is your name,
Your Will Be Done Now and Forever!
Yashu'a (Jesus) said: "Thou shalt love the Most High Heavenly Father, thy Sustainer with all
thy heart, and with all thy soul, and with all thy mind. Thou shalt love
thy neighbour as thyself."

How do the children of the Most High put the KJV bible book of Psalms chapter 82 into action, mentally, physically, spiritually, and emotionally? By remembering and practicing **the KJV bible book of Deuteronomy chapter 6 verses 1-2; and 4-7.** These verses state: "Now these are the commandments, the statutes, and the judgments, which the LORD your God commanded to teach you, that ye might do them in the land whither ye go to possess it. That thou mightest fear the LORD thy God, to keep all his statutes and his commandments, which I command thee, thou, and thy son, and thy son's son, all the days of thy life; and that thy days may be prolonged. The LORD our God *is* one LORD. And thou shalt love the LORD thy God with all thine heart, and with all thy soul, and with all thy might."

Yashu'a (Jesus) said: "A new commandment I give unto you, that ye love one another; as I have loved you, that ye also love one another."

ASSASSINS of DISOBEDIENCE!
Invoking the Power of the Most High Through Obedience, is the Key to Living Your Best Life
as the Supreme Ingredient!
Heaven or Hell?

CHILDREN OF THE MOST HIGH:
PRISTINE YOUTH AND FAMILY SOLUTIONS, LLC.
SONS AND DAUGHTERS OF THE MOST HIGH PUBLISHERS ®

Oh, Gracious Most High Heavenly father, Holy is your name,
Your Will Be Done Now and Forever!
Yashu'a (Jesus) said: "Thou shalt love the Most High Heavenly Father, thy Sustainer with all
thy heart, and with all thy soul, and with all thy mind. Thou shalt love
thy neighbour as thyself."

"And these words, which I command thee this day, shall be in thine heart: And thou shalt teach them diligently unto thy children, and shalt talk of them when thou sittest in thine house, and when thou walkest by the way, and when thou liest down, and when thou risest up, KJV bible book of Deuteronomy chapter 6 verses 1-2, and 4-7." So, **a commandment is what is asked of the children of the Most High**. **For example:** In the KJV bible book of Genesis chapter 2 verse 17; it states: "But of the tree of the knowledge of good and evil, thou shalt not eat of it: for in the day that thou eatest thereof thou shalt surely die." This is the **first biblical commandment**.

101

Yashu'a (Jesus) said: "A new commandment I give unto
you, that ye love one another; as I have loved you,
that ye also love one another."

ASSASSINS of DISOBEDIENCE!
Invoking the Power of the Most High Through Obedience, is the Key to Living Your Best Life
as the Supreme Ingredient!
Heaven or Hell?

CHILDREN OF THE MOST HIGH:
PRISTINE YOUTH AND FAMILY SOLUTIONS, LLC.
SONS AND DAUGHTERS OF THE MOST HIGH PUBLISHERS ®

Oh, Gracious Most High Heavenly father, Holy is your name,
Your Will Be Done Now and Forever!
Yashu'a (Jesus) said: "Thou shalt love the Most High Heavenly Father, thy Sustainer with all
thy heart, and with all thy soul, and with all thy mind. Thou shalt love
thy neighbour as thyself."

Therefore; the difference between the word for "**Law**" is: תּוֹרָה **Towrah or Torah** and or ἐντολή **Entolē** or **Wasiah** وصيه; is "**Law**" תּוֹרָה **Towrah or Torah** means: "Law, a precept or statute, especially the Decalogue or **Pentateuch**: law, codes of law, custom, manner, the Deuteronomic or Mosaic Law." "**Commandments**" is: מִצְוָה **Mits-waw or Mitsvah**) or ἐντολή **Entolē** or **Wasiah** وصيه; which means: "commandments, precept, commanded, ordinances, directions, instruction and order."

102

Yashu'a (Jesus) said: "A new commandment I give unto
you, that ye love one another; as I have loved you,
that ye also love one another."

ASSASSINS of DISOBEDIENCE!
Invoking the Power of the Most High Through Obedience, is the Key to Living Your Best Life
as the Supreme Ingredient!
Heaven or Hell?

CHILDREN OF THE MOST HIGH:
PRISTINE YOUTH AND FAMILY SOLUTIONS, LLC.
SONS AND DAUGHTERS OF THE MOST HIGH PUBLISHERS ®

Oh, Gracious Most High Heavenly father, Holy is your name,
Your Will Be Done Now and Forever!
Yashu'a (Jesus) said: "Thou shalt love the Most High Heavenly Father, thy Sustainer with all
thy heart, and with all thy soul, and with all thy mind. Thou shalt love
thy neighbour as thyself."

Chapter 4: What are the Consequences of the Children of the Most High, for Disobeying God's (אֱלֹהִים 'Elohiym) Commandments?

The Messiah Yashu'a (Jesus) said: "Think not that I am come to destroy the law, or the prophets: I am not come to destroy, but to fulfil. For verily I say unto you, Till heaven and earth pass, one jot or one tittle shall in no wise pass from the law, till all be fulfilled. Matthew 5:17-18; KJV Bible."

The Most High Heavenly Father is "The Holy One."

In the KJV bible book of Isaiah chapter 45 verse 11; it states:
"Thus, saith the Lord, The Holy One of Israel, and his Maker, Ask me
of things to come concerning my sons, and concerning the work of my
hands command ye me."

103

Yashu'a (Jesus) said: "A new commandment I give unto
you, that ye love one another; as I have loved you,
that ye also love one another."

ASSASSINS of DISOBEDIENCE!
*Invoking the Power of the Most High Through Obedience, is the Key to Living Your Best Life
as the Supreme Ingredient!
Heaven or Hell?*

CHILDREN OF THE MOST HIGH:
PRISTINE YOUTH AND FAMILY SOLUTIONS, LLC.
SONS AND DAUGHTERS OF THE MOST HIGH PUBLISHERS ®

*Oh, Gracious Most High Heavenly father, Holy is your name,
Your Will Be Done Now and Forever!*
Yashu'a (Jesus) said: *"Thou shalt love the Most High Heavenly Father, thy Sustainer with all
thy heart, and with all thy soul, and with all thy mind. Thou shalt love
thy neighbour as thyself."*

In the KJV bible book of Mathews chapter 5 verses 17-18; the Messiah Yashu'a (Jesus) said: "Think not that I am come to destroy the law, or the prophets: I am not come to destroy, but to fulfil. For verily I say unto you, till heaven and earth pass, one jot or one tittle shall in no wise pass from the law, till all be fulfilled." In the above verse, the KJV bible Greek Strong's Concordance **#3928** word for "**pass**" is "παρέρχομαι **Parerchomain**, pronounced as: **Pä-re'r-kho-mi** and means **pass, come forth, to pass by**." According to this verse, the children of the Most High **shall in no way pass from the law until all be fulfilled**. When did the Messiah Yashu'a say that this would occur? The Messiah Yashu'a (Jesus) said: "For verily I say unto you, till heaven and earth pass, one jot or one tittle shall in no wise pass from the law, till all be fulfilled."

104

Yashu'a (Jesus) said: *"A new commandment I give unto
you, that ye love one another; as I have loved you,
that ye also love one another."*

ASSASSINS of DISOBEDIENCE!
Invoking the Power of the Most High Through Obedience, is the Key to Living Your Best Life
as the Supreme Ingredient!
Heaven or Hell?

CHILDREN OF THE MOST HIGH:
PRISTINE YOUTH AND FAMILY SOLUTIONS, LLC.
SONS AND DAUGHTERS OF THE MOST HIGH PUBLISHERS ®

Oh, Gracious Most High Heavenly father, Holy is your name,
Your Will Be Done Now and Forever!
Yashu'a (Jesus) said: *"Thou shalt love the Most High Heavenly Father, thy Sustainer with all*
thy heart, and with all thy soul, and with all thy mind. Thou shalt love
thy neighbour as thyself."

Did heaven and earth pass? No, heaven and earth did not pass. According to the KJV bible, when does **heaven and earth pass away?** In the book of **Revelation chapter 21 verses 1-3**; it states: "**And I saw a new heaven and a new earth**: **for the first heaven and the first earth were passed away**; and there was no more sea. And I John saw the holy city, new Jerusalem, coming down from God out of heaven, prepared as a bride adorned for her husband. And I heard a great voice out of heaven saying, Behold, the tabernacle of God is with men, and he will dwell with them, and **they shall be his people**, and God himself shall be with them, and be their God." In the KJV book of Matthew chapter 10 verse 22; the Messiah Yashu'a (Jesus) said: "**And ye shall be hated of all men for my name's sake: but he that endureth to the end shall be saved.**"

105

Yashu'a (Jesus) said: *"A new commandment I give unto you, that ye love one another; as I have loved you, that ye also love one another."*

ASSASSINS of DISOBEDIENCE!
Invoking the Power of the Most High Through Obedience, is the Key to Living Your Best Life
as the Supreme Ingredient!
Heaven or Hell?

CHILDREN OF THE MOST HIGH:
PRISTINE YOUTH AND FAMILY SOLUTIONS, LLC.
SONS AND DAUGHTERS OF THE MOST HIGH PUBLISHERS ®

Oh, Gracious Most High Heavenly father, Holy is your name,
Your Will Be Done Now and Forever!
Yashu'a (Jesus) said: "Thou shalt love the Most High Heavenly Father, thy Sustainer with all
thy heart, and with all thy soul, and with all thy mind. Thou shalt love
thy neighbour as thyself."

In the KJV book of Revelation chapter 1 verses 14-15; it physically describes the Messiah Yashu'a (Jesus) as: "**His head and his hairs were white like wool**, **as white as snow**; and his eyes were as a flame of fire; And **his feet like unto fine brass**, **as if they burned in a furnace**; and **his voice as the sound of many waters**." In the KJV book of Matthew chapter 10 verse 22; the Messiah Yashu'a (Jesus) said: "And ye shall be hated of all men for my name's sake: but he that endureth to the end shall be saved."

Mr. George Floyd being killed on local, national and international TV in front of the eyes of every human being that can see on May 25, 2020.

106

Yashu'a (Jesus) said: "A new commandment I give unto you, that ye love one another; as I have loved you, that ye also love one another."

ASSASSINS of DISOBEDIENCE!
Invoking the Power of the Most High Through Obedience, is the Key to Living Your Best Life
as the Supreme Ingredient!
Heaven or Hell?

CHILDREN OF THE MOST HIGH:
PRISTINE YOUTH AND FAMILY SOLUTIONS, LLC.
SONS AND DAUGHTERS OF THE MOST HIGH PUBLISHERS ®

Oh, Gracious Most High Heavenly father, Holy is your name,
Your Will Be Done Now and Forever!
Yashu'a (Jesus) said: "Thou shalt love the Most High Heavenly Father, thy Sustainer with all
thy heart, and with all thy soul, and with all thy mind. Thou shalt love
thy neighbour as thyself."

In the KJV book of Matthew chapter 24 verse 9; the Messiah Yashu'a (Jesus) also said: "Then shall they deliver you up to be afflicted, and shall kill you: and ye shall be hated of all nations for my name's sake."

The brutal abduction and murder of 14-years-old Emmett Till on August 28, 1955, galvanized the emerging Civil Rights Movement.

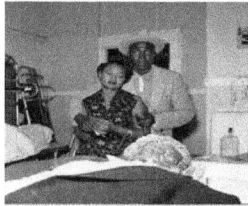

14-years-old Emmett Till's mother looking at her son's deceased body.

107

Yashu'a (Jesus) said: "A new commandment I give unto you, that ye love one another; as I have loved you, that ye also love one another."

ASSASSINS of DISOBEDIENCE!
Invoking the Power of the Most High Through Obedience, is the Key to Living Your Best Life
as the Supreme Ingredient!
Heaven or Hell?

CHILDREN OF THE MOST HIGH:
PRISTINE YOUTH AND FAMILY SOLUTIONS, LLC.
SONS AND DAUGHTERS OF THE MOST HIGH PUBLISHERS ®

Oh, Gracious Most High Heavenly father, Holy is your name,
Your Will Be Done Now and Forever!
Yashu'a (Jesus) said: "Thou shalt love the Most High Heavenly Father, thy Sustainer with all
thy heart, and with all thy soul, and with all thy mind. Thou shalt love
thy neighbour as thyself."

In the KJV bible book of Isaiah chapter 52 verses 1-6; it states: "**Awake, Awake (עוּר `Uwr, עוּר `Uwr, pronounced as ür - oor, עוּר `Uwr means: "the idea of opening the eyes); to wake (literally or figuratively): wake up), lift up (self), master, raise (up), stir up (self)."** (<u>Awake</u>, <u>Awake</u> [<u>mentally and spiritually</u>, <u>Your Life Matters!</u>] put on thy strength, O Zion; put on thy beautiful garments, O Jerusalem, the holy city: for **henceforth there shall no more come into thee the uncircumcised and the unclean**. Shake thyself from the dust; arise, and sit down, O Jerusalem: <u>**loose thyself from the bands of thy neck, O captive daughter of Zion**</u>.

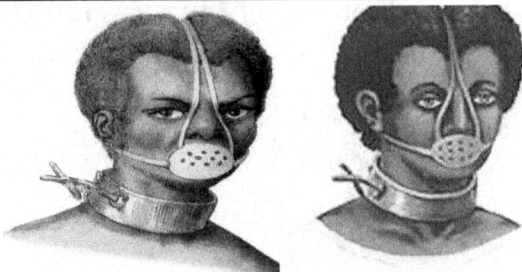

108

Yashu'a (Jesus) said: "A new commandment I give unto you, that ye love one another; as I have loved you, that ye also love one another."

ASSASSINS of DISOBEDIENCE!
Invoking the Power of the Most High Through Obedience, is the Key to Living Your Best Life
as the Supreme Ingredient!
Heaven or Hell?

CHILDREN OF THE MOST HIGH:
PRISTINE YOUTH AND FAMILY SOLUTIONS, LLC.
SONS AND DAUGHTERS OF THE MOST HIGH PUBLISHERS ®

Oh, Gracious Most High Heavenly father, Holy is your name,
Your Will Be Done Now and Forever!
Yashu'a (Jesus) said: "Thou shalt love the Most High Heavenly Father, thy Sustainer with all
thy heart, and with all thy soul, and with all thy mind. Thou shalt love
thy neighbour as thyself."

"For thus saith the LORD, **Ye have sold yourselves for nought**; and ye shall be redeemed without money."

109

Yashu'a (Jesus) said: "A new commandment I give unto
you, that ye love one another; as I have loved you,
that ye also love one another."

ASSASSINS of DISOBEDIENCE!
Invoking the Power of the Most High Through Obedience, is the Key to Living Your Best Life
as the Supreme Ingredient!
Heaven or Hell?

CHILDREN OF THE MOST HIGH:
PRISTINE YOUTH AND FAMILY SOLUTIONS, LLC.
SONS AND DAUGHTERS OF THE MOST HIGH PUBLISHERS ®

Oh, Gracious Most High Heavenly father, Holy is your name,
Your Will Be Done Now and Forever!
Yashu'a (Jesus) said: *"Thou shalt love the Most High Heavenly Father, thy Sustainer with all*
thy heart, and with all thy soul, and with all thy mind. Thou shalt love
thy neighbour as thyself."

"Whom the LORD of hosts shall bless, saying, **Blessed be Egypt my people**, and **Assyria** the work of my hands, and **Israel** mine inheritance (KJV Isaiah 19:25). "**For thus saith the Lord God**, **My people** went down aforetime into Egypt to sojourn there; and the Assyrian oppressed them without cause (KJV Isaiah 52:4). "**Now the sojourning of the children of Israel, who dwelt in Egypt, was four hundred and thirty years (430)** (KJV **Exodus 12:40**)." "Now therefore, what have I here, saith **the LORD**, that **my people are taken away for nought**? they that rule over them make them to **howl** (יְלֵל **Yawlal or Yalal, means to howl (with a wailing tone), yell, wail; cry excessively out of deep sorrow and pain; to make a long, loud, high-pitched cry, as in grief, sorrow, or fear.)** **saith the LORD**; **And my name continually every day is**

Yashu'a (Jesus) said: "A new commandment I give unto
you, that ye love one another; as I have loved you,
that ye also love one another."

ASSASSINS of DISOBEDIENCE!
Invoking the Power of the Most High Through Obedience, is the Key to Living Your Best Life
as the Supreme Ingredient!
Heaven or Hell?

CHILDREN OF THE MOST HIGH:
PRISTINE YOUTH AND FAMILY SOLUTIONS, LLC.
SONS AND DAUGHTERS OF THE MOST HIGH PUBLISHERS ®

Oh, Gracious Most High Heavenly father, Holy is your name,
Your Will Be Done Now and Forever!
Yashu'a (Jesus) said: "Thou shalt love the Most High Heavenly Father, thy Sustainer with all
thy heart, and with all thy soul, and with all thy mind. Thou shalt love
thy neighbour as thyself."

<u>blasphemed</u>, KJV Isaiah 52:5." Hosea 13:4 states: "<u>**Yet I am**</u>
<u>**the LORD thy God from the land of Egypt, and thou shalt**</u>
<u>**know no god but me: for there is no savior (יְשַׁע Yāsʷa,**</u>
<u>**Yâsha' or Yashu'a, means Savior) beside me**</u>. Therefore, my
people shall know *my name* <u>Yâsha' or Yashu'a</u> (<u>that is called</u>:
Ἰησοῦς Iēsous (**Jesus**) in the KJV John <u>**9:11**</u>. That's why <u>the</u>
<u>Lord   said: "my   name   continually   every   day   is</u>
<u>blasphemed</u>."): therefore, they shall know in that day that **I am**
he that doth speak: behold, it is I." In the KJV bible book of
Genesis chapter 15 verses 12-16; it states: "And when the sun
was going down, a deep sleep fell upon Abram; and, lo, a horror
of great darkness fell upon him."

111

Yashu'a (Jesus) said: "A new commandment I give unto
you, that ye love one another; as I have loved you,
that ye also love one another."

ASSASSINS of DISOBEDIENCE!
Invoking the Power of the Most High Through Obedience, is the Key to Living Your Best Life
as the Supreme Ingredient!
Heaven or Hell?

CHILDREN OF THE MOST HIGH:
PRISTINE YOUTH AND FAMILY SOLUTIONS, LLC.
SONS AND DAUGHTERS OF THE MOST HIGH PUBLISHERS ®

Oh, Gracious Most High Heavenly father, Holy is your name,
Your Will Be Done Now and Forever!
Yashu'a (Jesus) said: "Thou shalt love the Most High Heavenly Father, thy Sustainer with all
thy heart, and with all thy soul, and with all thy mind. Thou shalt love
thy neighbour as thyself."

And he (**the Lord GOD**, אֲדֹנָי **'Adonay** יְהֹוִה **Yahuwa or**
Yehovih or Yehovah) **said unto Abram**, **know of a surety**
that thy seed shall be a stranger in a land that is not theirs,
and shall serve them; and they **shall afflict** them **four**
hundred years (400);

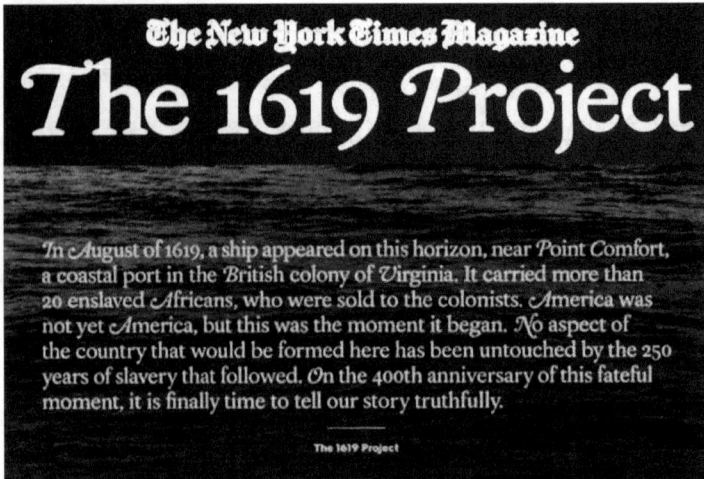

The New York Times Magazine

The 1619 Project

In August of 1619, a ship appeared on this horizon, near Point Comfort, a coastal port in the British colony of Virginia. It carried more than 20 enslaved Africans, who were sold to the colonists. America was not yet America, but this was the moment it began. No aspect of the country that would be formed here has been untouched by the 250 years of slavery that followed. On the 400th anniversary of this fateful moment, it is finally time to tell our story truthfully.

The 1619 Project

112

Yashu'a (Jesus) said: "A new commandment I give unto
you, that ye love one another; as I have loved you,
that ye also love one another."

ASSASSINS of DISOBEDIENCE!
Invoking the Power of the Most High Through Obedience, is the Key to Living Your Best Life
as the Supreme Ingredient!
Heaven or Hell?

CHILDREN OF THE MOST HIGH:
PRISTINE YOUTH AND FAMILY SOLUTIONS, LLC.
SONS AND DAUGHTERS OF THE MOST HIGH PUBLISHERS ®

Oh, Gracious Most High Heavenly father, Holy is your name,
Your Will Be Done Now and Forever!
Yashu'a (Jesus) said: *"Thou shalt love the Most High Heavenly Father, thy Sustainer with all*
thy heart, and with all thy soul, and with all thy mind. Thou shalt love
thy neighbour as thyself."

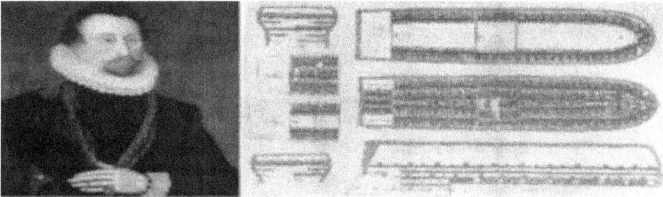

'Jesus' was the name of the Slave Ship captained by Sir John Hawkins in 1564 by appointment of the Queen of England

113

Yashu'a (Jesus) said: *"A new commandment I give unto*
you, that ye love one another; as I have loved you,
that ye also love one another."

ASSASSINS of DISOBEDIENCE!
Invoking the Power of the Most High Through Obedience, is the Key to Living Your Best Life
as the Supreme Ingredient!
Heaven or Hell?

CHILDREN OF THE MOST HIGH:
PRISTINE YOUTH AND FAMILY SOLUTIONS, LLC.
SONS AND DAUGHTERS OF THE MOST HIGH PUBLISHERS ®

Oh, Gracious Most High Heavenly father, Holy is your name,
Your Will Be Done Now and Forever!
Yashu'a (Jesus) said: "Thou shalt love the Most High Heavenly Father, thy Sustainer with all
thy heart, and with all thy soul, and with all thy mind. Thou shalt love
thy neighbour as thyself."

"**And also, that nation, whom they shall serve, will I judge**:

and afterward shall they come out with great substance.

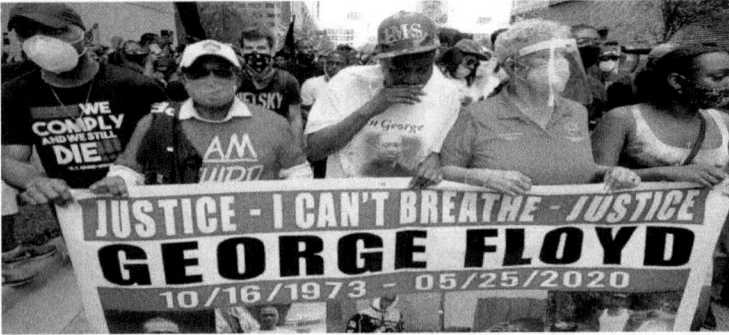

In the KJV bible book of Amos chapter 5 verse 16: it states:

"Therefore the Lord, the God of hosts, the Lord, saith thus;

Wailing shall be in all streets; and they shall say in all the

highways, Alas! alas! and they shall call the husbandman to

mourning, and such as are skillful of lamentation to **wailing**."

114

Yashu'a (Jesus) said: "A new commandment I give unto
you, that ye love one another; as I have loved you,
that ye also love one another."

ASSASSINS of DISOBEDIENCE!
Invoking the Power of the Most High Through Obedience, is the Key to Living Your Best Life
as the Supreme Ingredient!
Heaven or Hell?

CHILDREN OF THE MOST HIGH:
PRISTINE YOUTH AND FAMILY SOLUTIONS, LLC.
SONS AND DAUGHTERS OF THE MOST HIGH PUBLISHERS ®

Oh, Gracious Most High Heavenly father, Holy is your name,
Your Will Be Done Now and Forever!
Yashu'a (Jesus) said: *"Thou shalt love the Most High Heavenly Father, thy Sustainer with all thy heart, and with all thy soul, and with all thy mind. Thou shalt love thy neighbour as thyself."*

"And thou shalt go to thy fathers in **peace**; (KJV Matthew 5:9; **the Messiah Yashu'a (Jesus) said: "Blessed are the peacemakers**, for they **shall** (**future tense**) be called the children of God"), **thou shalt be buried in a good old age**."

U.S. Representative, Congressman John Lewis on the left, and Rev. C.T. Vivian on the right, were Civil Rights Leaders and members of Rev. Dr. Martin Luther King Jr.'s inner cabinet. They died on the same day, Friday, July 17, 2020. Rev. C.T. Vivian was 95 years old, and Congressman John Lewis was 80 years old.

Mr. James Charles Evers was the older brother of Civil Rights icon, Mr. Medgar Evers. Mr. James Charles Evers died on Wednesday, July 22, 2020. He was 97 years old.

Yashu'a (Jesus) said: *"A new commandment I give unto you, that ye love one another; as I have loved you, that ye also love one another."*

ASSASSINS of DISOBEDIENCE!
Invoking the Power of the Most High Through Obedience, is the Key to Living Your Best Life
as the Supreme Ingredient!
Heaven or Hell?

CHILDREN OF THE MOST HIGH:
PRISTINE YOUTH AND FAMILY SOLUTIONS, LLC.
SONS AND DAUGHTERS OF THE MOST HIGH PUBLISHERS ℗

Oh, Gracious Most High Heavenly father, Holy is your name,
Your Will Be Done Now and Forever!
Yashu'a (Jesus) said: "*Thou shalt love the Most High Heavenly Father, thy Sustainer with all*
thy heart, and with all thy soul, and with all thy mind. Thou shalt love
thy neighbour as thyself."

Mr. Jon Batiste organized a **"WE ARE" – A Peaceful Protest** March with Music, which took place in New York City on Saturday and saw thousands join him to confront police brutality and racial injustice. The New York City protest is just one of many happening around the world following the unlawful deaths of **George Floyd**, **Breonna Taylor**, and **Ahmaud Arbery**.

116

Yashu'a (Jesus) said: "*A new commandment I give unto*
you, that ye love one another; as I have loved you,
that ye also love one another."

CHILDREN OF THE MOST HIGH:
PRISTINE YOUTH AND FAMILY SOLUTIONS, LLC.
SONS AND DAUGHTERS OF THE MOST HIGH PUBLISHERS ®

Oh, Gracious Most High Heavenly father, Holy is your name,
Your Will Be Done Now and Forever!
Yashu'a (Jesus) said: *"Thou shalt love the Most High Heavenly Father, thy Sustainer with all thy heart, and with all thy soul, and with all thy mind. Thou shalt love thy neighbour as thyself."*

"This is our response to the **deep-rooted systemic injustice** we have yet to fix, a fact made abundantly clear by the public execution of another black person," **said Batiste** in an Instagram post announcing the event. He continued, **"This is a movement that exists because I believe the power of the arts and music is divine. Our ancestors used this power to create a better world for us and now we have the chance to do the same. We are the ones to change the world. We are the golden ones."** In 1967, Reverend Dr. Martin Luther King Jr. said: "We must face the hard fact that many Americans would like to have a nation which is a democracy for white Americans but simultaneously a dictatorship over black Americans."

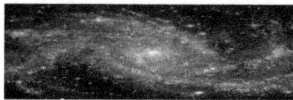

117

Yashu'a (Jesus) said: *"A new commandment I give unto you, that ye love one another; as I have loved you, that ye also love one another."*

ASSASSINS of DISOBEDIENCE!
Invoking the Power of the Most High Through Obedience, is the Key to Living Your Best Life
as the Supreme Ingredient!
Heaven or Hell?

CHILDREN OF THE MOST HIGH:
PRISTINE YOUTH AND FAMILY SOLUTIONS, LLC.
SONS AND DAUGHTERS OF THE MOST HIGH PUBLISHERS ®

Oh, Gracious Most High Heavenly father, Holy is your name,
Your Will Be Done Now and Forever!
Yashu'a (Jesus) said: "Thou shalt love the Most High Heavenly Father, thy Sustainer with all
thy heart, and with all thy soul, and with all thy mind. Thou shalt love
thy neighbour as thyself."

"**But in the fourth generation they shall come hither again**: **for the iniquity of the Amorites is not yet full**. KJV Genesis 15:16."

Donald Trump vs Hillary Clinton is ...
gq-magazine.co.uk

118

Yashu'a (Jesus) said: "A new commandment I give unto you, that ye love one another; as I have loved you, that ye also love one another."

ASSASSINS of DISOBEDIENCE!
Invoking the Power of the Most High Through Obedience, is the Key to Living Your Best Life
as the Supreme Ingredient!
Heaven or Hell?

CHILDREN OF THE MOST HIGH:
PRISTINE YOUTH AND FAMILY SOLUTIONS, LLC.
SONS AND DAUGHTERS OF THE MOST HIGH PUBLISHERS ®

Oh, Gracious Most High Heavenly father, Holy is your name,
Your Will Be Done Now and Forever!
Yashu'a (Jesus) said: "Thou shalt love the Most High Heavenly Father, thy Sustainer with all
thy heart, and with all thy soul, and with all thy mind. Thou shalt love
thy neighbour as thyself."

In 1921 a group of whites burnt the black community of Tulsa, Oklahoma to ground. It was the wealthiest black community in the United States, known as "black wall street." Firebombs were dropped from airplanes and hundreds were killed. This massacre was not acknowledged in state history records until 1996.

The 1921 Attack on Greenwood was one of the most significant events in Tulsa's history. Following World War, I, Tulsa was recognized nationally for its **affluent African American community** known as the **Greenwood District**. This thriving business district and surrounding residential area was referred to as **"Black Wall Street."** In June 1921, a series of events nearly destroyed the entire Greenwood area. <u>**A race massacre in which an estimated 300 people of mostly African American men, women and children, were killed by white people, and aircrafts were used to drop incendiary devices on a black neighborhood in Tulsa, Oklahoma**</u>.

119

Yashu'a (Jesus) said: "A new commandment I give unto
you, that ye love one another; as I have loved you,
that ye also love one another."

ASSASSINS of DISOBEDIENCE!
Invoking the Power of the Most High Through Obedience, is the Key to Living Your Best Life
as the Supreme Ingredient!
Heaven or Hell?

CHILDREN OF THE MOST HIGH:
PRISTINE YOUTH AND FAMILY SOLUTIONS, LLC.
SONS AND DAUGHTERS OF THE MOST HIGH PUBLISHERS ®

Oh, Gracious Most High Heavenly father, Holy is your name,
Your Will Be Done Now and Forever!
Yashu'a (Jesus) said: *"Thou shalt love the Most High Heavenly Father, thy Sustainer with all*
thy heart, and with all thy soul, and with all thy mind. Thou shalt love
thy neighbour as thyself."

Protests across the globe
after George Floyd's death

Updated 4:13 AM ET, Mon June 8, 2020

NO JUSTICE
NO PEACE

BLACK LIVES
MATTER

120

Yashu'a (Jesus) said: *"A new commandment I give unto*
you, that ye love one another; as I have loved you,
that ye also love one another."

ASSASSINS of DISOBEDIENCE!
Invoking the Power of the Most High Through Obedience, is the Key to Living Your Best Life
as the Supreme Ingredient!
Heaven or Hell?

CHILDREN OF THE MOST HIGH:
PRISTINE YOUTH AND FAMILY SOLUTIONS, LLC.
SONS AND DAUGHTERS OF THE MOST HIGH PUBLISHERS ®

Oh, Gracious Most High Heavenly father, Holy is your name,
Your Will Be Done Now and Forever!
Yashu'a (Jesus) said: *"Thou shalt love the Most High Heavenly Father, thy Sustainer with all*
thy heart, and with all thy soul, and with all thy mind. Thou shalt love
thy neighbour as thyself."

In the KJV bible book of Galatians chapter 6 verses 7-8; it states: **"Be not deceived; God is not mocked: for whatsoever a man soweth, that shall he also reap. For he that soweth to his flesh shall of the flesh reap corruption; but he that soweth to the Spirit shall of the Spirit reap life everlasting."**

121

Yashu'a (Jesus) said: *"A new commandment I give unto you, that ye love one another; as I have loved you, that ye also love one another."*

ASSASSINS of DISOBEDIENCE!
Invoking the Power of the Most High Through Obedience, is the Key to Living Your Best Life
as the Supreme Ingredient!
Heaven or Hell?

CHILDREN OF THE MOST HIGH:
PRISTINE YOUTH AND FAMILY SOLUTIONS, LLC.
SONS AND DAUGHTERS OF THE MOST HIGH PUBLISHERS ®

Oh, Gracious Most High Heavenly father, Holy is your name,
Your Will Be Done Now and Forever!
Yashu'a (Jesus) said: *"Thou shalt love the Most High Heavenly Father, thy Sustainer with all*
thy heart, and with all thy soul, and with all thy mind. Thou shalt love
thy neighbour as thyself."

What are the consequences of the children of the Most High for disobeying God's (אֱלֹהִים 'Elohiym) commandments due to a lack of knowledge and a rejection of knowledge?

The Messiah Yashu'a (Jesus) said: "If ye love me, keep my commandments, KJV John 14:15." According to the KJV bible book of Hosea chapter 4 verses 5-7; **the consequences of the children of the Most High disobeying God's (אֱלֹהִים 'Elohiym) commandments due to a lack of knowledge and a rejection of knowledge are: "<u>My people are destroyed for lack of knowledge</u>: <u>because thou hast rejected knowledge</u>, <u>I will also reject thee</u>, <u>that thou shalt be no priest to me</u>: <u>seeing thou hast forgotten the law of thy God</u>, <u>I will also forget thy children</u>."**

Yashu'a (Jesus) said: "A new commandment I give unto
you, that ye love one another; as I have loved you,
that ye also love one another."

ASSASSINS of DISOBEDIENCE!
Invoking the Power of the Most High Through Obedience, is the Key to Living Your Best Life
as the Supreme Ingredient!
Heaven or Hell?

CHILDREN OF THE MOST HIGH:
PRISTINE YOUTH AND FAMILY SOLUTIONS, LLC.
SONS AND DAUGHTERS OF THE MOST HIGH PUBLISHERS ®

Oh, Gracious Most High Heavenly father, Holy is your name,
Your Will Be Done Now and Forever!
Yashu'a (Jesus) said: "Thou shalt love the Most High Heavenly Father, thy Sustainer with all thy heart, and with all thy soul, and with all thy mind. Thou shalt love thy neighbour as thyself."

"As they were increased, so they sinned against me: **therefore, will I change their glory into shame**. They eat up the sin of my people, and they set their heart on their iniquity."

123

Yashu'a (Jesus) said: "A new commandment I give unto you, that ye love one another; as I have loved you, that ye also love one another."

ASSASSINS of DISOBEDIENCE!
Invoking the Power of the Most High Through Obedience, is the Key to Living Your Best Life
as the Supreme Ingredient!
Heaven or Hell?

CHILDREN OF THE MOST HIGH:
PRISTINE YOUTH AND FAMILY SOLUTIONS, LLC.
SONS AND DAUGHTERS OF THE MOST HIGH PUBLISHERS ®

Oh, Gracious Most High Heavenly father, Holy is your name,
Your Will Be Done Now and Forever!
Yashu'a (Jesus) said: "Thou shalt love the Most High Heavenly Father, thy Sustainer with all
thy heart, and with all thy soul, and with all thy mind. Thou shalt love
thy neighbour as thyself."

Therefore; **the consequences of the children of the Most High disobeying God's (אֱלֹהִים 'Elohiym) commandments due to a lack of knowledge and a rejection of knowledge** are **sorrow, preventable suffering,** and **death**. The KJV bible book of Romans chapter 6 verse 23; it states: **"For the wages of sin [is] death; but the gift of God [is] eternal life through Jesus Christ our Lord**." So, we; the children of the Most High must continue to obey the commandments that the Messiah Yashu'a (Jesus) followed and those that he commanded us to obey under the **New Covenant. "If my people, which are called by my name, shall humble themselves, and pray, and seek my face, and turn from their wicked ways; then will I hear from heaven, and will forgive their sin, and will heal their land, KJV 2nd Chronicles 7:14."**

Yashu'a (Jesus) said: "A new commandment I give unto you, that ye love one another; as I have loved you, that ye also love one another."

ASSASSINS of DISOBEDIENCE!
Invoking the Power of the Most High Through Obedience, is the Key to Living Your Best Life
as the Supreme Ingredient!
Heaven or Hell?

CHILDREN OF THE MOST HIGH:
PRISTINE YOUTH AND FAMILY SOLUTIONS, LLC.
SONS AND DAUGHTERS OF THE MOST HIGH PUBLISHERS ®

Oh, Gracious Most High Heavenly father, Holy is your name,
Your Will Be Done Now and Forever!
Yashu'a (Jesus) said: *"Thou shalt love the Most High Heavenly Father, thy Sustainer with all*
thy heart, and with all thy soul, and with all thy mind. Thou shalt love
thy neighbour as thyself."

Chapter 5: What is the New Covenant of the Lord?

The Most High Heavenly Father is
"The Peaceful."

In the KJV bible book of Matthew chapter 5 verse 9;
The Messiah Yashu'a (Jesus) said: *"Blessed are the peacemakers: for*
they shall be called the children of God."

125

Yashu'a (Jesus) said: "A new commandment I give unto
you, that ye love one another; as I have loved you,
that ye also love one another."

ASSASSINS of DISOBEDIENCE!
Invoking the Power of the Most High Through Obedience, is the Key to Living Your Best Life
as the Supreme Ingredient!
Heaven or Hell?

CHILDREN OF THE MOST HIGH:
PRISTINE YOUTH AND FAMILY SOLUTIONS, LLC.
SONS AND DAUGHTERS OF THE MOST HIGH PUBLISHERS ®

Oh, Gracious Most High Heavenly father, Holy is your name,
Your Will Be Done Now and Forever!
Yashu'a (Jesus) said: "Thou shalt love the Most High Heavenly Father, thy Sustainer with all
thy heart, and with all thy soul, and with all thy mind. Thou shalt love
thy neighbour as thyself."

In the KJV bible book of Hebrews chapter 8 verses 6-10; it states: "But now hath he obtained a more excellent ministry, by how much also he is the mediator of a better covenant, which was established upon better promises. For if that first covenant had been faultless, then should no place have been sought for the second. For finding fault with them, he saith, Behold, the days come, saith the Lord, when **I will make a new covenant with the house of Israel and with the house of Judah**."

126

Yashu'a (Jesus) said: "A new commandment I give unto you, that ye love one another; as I have loved you, that ye also love one another."

ASSASSINS of DISOBEDIENCE!
Invoking the Power of the Most High Through Obedience, is the Key to Living Your Best Life
as the Supreme Ingredient!
Heaven or Hell?

CHILDREN OF THE MOST HIGH:
PRISTINE YOUTH AND FAMILY SOLUTIONS, LLC.
SONS AND DAUGHTERS OF THE MOST HIGH PUBLISHERS ®

Oh, Gracious Most High Heavenly father, Holy is your name,
Your Will Be Done Now and Forever!
Yashu'a (Jesus) said: *"Thou shalt love the Most High Heavenly Father, thy Sustainer with all thy heart, and with all thy soul, and with all thy mind. Thou shalt love thy neighbour as thyself."*

"Not according to the covenant that I made with their fathers in the day when I took them by the hand to lead them out of the land of Egypt; because they continued not in my covenant, and I regarded them not, saith the Lord. **For this is the covenant that I will make with the house of Israel after those days, saith the Lord; I will put my laws into their mind, and write them in their hearts: and I will be to them a God, and they shall be to me a people**." In the KJV bible book of Hebrews chapter 10 verses 16-17; it states: **"This is the covenant that I will make with them after those days, saith the Lord, I will put my laws into their hearts, and in their minds will I write them; And their sins and iniquities will I remember no more."**

Yashu'a (Jesus) said: *"A new commandment I give unto you, that ye love one another; as I have loved you, that ye also love one another."*

ASSASSINS of DISOBEDIENCE!
Invoking the Power of the Most High Through Obedience, is the Key to Living Your Best Life
as the Supreme Ingredient!
Heaven or Hell?

CHILDREN OF THE MOST HIGH:
PRISTINE YOUTH AND FAMILY SOLUTIONS, LLC.
SONS AND DAUGHTERS OF THE MOST HIGH PUBLISHERS ®

Oh, Gracious Most High Heavenly father, Holy is your name,
Your Will Be Done Now and Forever!
Yashu'a (Jesus) said: *"Thou shalt love the Most High Heavenly Father, thy Sustainer with all*
thy heart, and with all thy soul, and with all thy mind. Thou shalt love
thy neighbour as thyself."

How does the KJV bible define the word "sin?" According to the KJV bible book of Psalms chapter 51 verses1-2; it states: "[To the chief Musician, A Psalm of David, when Nathan the prophet came unto him, after he had gone in to Bathsheba.] Have mercy upon me, O God, according to thy lovingkindness: according unto the multitude of thy tender mercies blot out my transgressions. Wash me thoroughly from mine **iniquity**, and cleanse me from my **sin**." In the KJV bible book of Psalms chapter 51 verse 2, the word for **iniquity** is the "KJV bible Hebrew Strong's Concordance**#5771** word: עָוֹן `Avon, which means: "**perversity**, **depravity**, **iniquity**, **guilt or punishment of iniquity**, **guilt of iniquity**, guilt (as great), guilt (of condition), **consequence of or punishment for iniquity, moral) evil**:—**fault, mischief, sin**."

128

Yashu'a (Jesus) said: "A new commandment I give unto
you, that ye love one another; as I have loved you,
that ye also love one another."

ASSASSINS of DISOBEDIENCE!
Invoking the Power of the Most High Through Obedience, is the Key to Living Your Best Life
as the Supreme Ingredient!
Heaven or Hell?

CHILDREN OF THE MOST HIGH:
PRISTINE YOUTH AND FAMILY SOLUTIONS, LLC.
SONS AND DAUGHTERS OF THE MOST HIGH PUBLISHERS ®

Oh, Gracious Most High Heavenly father, Holy is your name,
Your Will Be Done Now and Forever!
Yashu'a (Jesus) said: "Thou shalt love the Most High Heavenly Father, thy Sustainer with all
thy heart, and with all thy soul, and with all thy mind. Thou shalt love
thy neighbour as thyself."

עָוֹן Ex. 28:43; 34:7; more rarely עָוֹן 2 Ki. 7:9; Ps. 51:7; const. עָוֹן, עָוֹן 1 Chron. 21:8, pl. absol. and const. עֲוֹנוֹת with suff. עֲוֹנָיו, עֲוֹנֶיךָ, more often עֲוֹנֹתַי, עֲוֹנֹתָיו etc.; m. pr. *perversity, depravity* (from the root עָוָה); hence—(1) *a depraved action, a crime, a sin,* Genesis 4:13; 44:16. Job 31:11, עָוֹן פְּלִילִים "a crime to be punished by the judges," comp. Job 31:28; 19:29, עֲוֹנוֹת חָרֶב "crimes to be punished by the sword." Eze. 21:30, עֲוֹן קֵץ "crime of end," i. e. which brings an end or destruction. Eze. 21:34; 35:5. It is often *guilt contracted by sinning,* as עֲוֹן אָבוֹת "the guilt of the fathers," Ex. 20:5; 34:7; עֲוֹן הָאֱמֹרִי "the guilt of the Amorites," Gen. 15:16. עֲוֹן חַטָּאתִי "the guilt of my sin," Ps. 32:5; also *any thing unjustly acquired,* Hos. 12:9, "they shall not find in my possession עָוֹן אֲשֶׁר חֵטְא any thing unjustly acquired which (would be) sin," (fein Unrecht, das Sünde wäre). In speaking of pardon and expiation of sin, the words נָשָׂא, כָּפַּר, הֶעֱבִיר, סָלַח No. 2, c, are used; of punishing it, the verb פָּקַד is used; of bearing or suffering its penalty, the verb נָשָׂא No. 2, b.

(2) Sometimes it is *the penalty* of sin, Isaiah 5:18; *calamity, misery,* Ps. 31:11. [The common meaning does very well in this place.]

129

Yashu'a (Jesus) said: "A new commandment I give unto
you, that ye love one another; as I have loved you,
that ye also love one another."

ASSASSINS of DISOBEDIENCE!
Invoking the Power of the Most High Through Obedience, is the Key to Living Your Best Life
as the Supreme Ingredient!
Heaven or Hell?

CHILDREN OF THE MOST HIGH:
PRISTINE YOUTH AND FAMILY SOLUTIONS, LLC.
SONS AND DAUGHTERS OF THE MOST HIGH PUBLISHERS ®

Oh, Gracious Most High Heavenly father, Holy is your name,
Your Will Be Done Now and Forever!
Yashu'a (Jesus) said: "Thou shalt love the Most High Heavenly Father, thy Sustainer with all
thy heart, and with all thy soul, and with all thy mind. Thou shalt love
thy neighbour as thyself."

The word "<u>sin</u>" is the "KJV bible Hebrew Strong's Concordance "#2403 word: חַטָּאת **Chatta'ath**, which means: **an offence (sometimes habitual sinfulness), sin, sinful, sin offering, condition of sin, guilt of sin, punishment for sin, purification from sins of ceremonial uncleanness, and its penalty, occasion, sacrifice, or expiation. Also (concretely) an offender: punishment (of sin), purifying (-fication for sin), sin (-ner, offering).**"

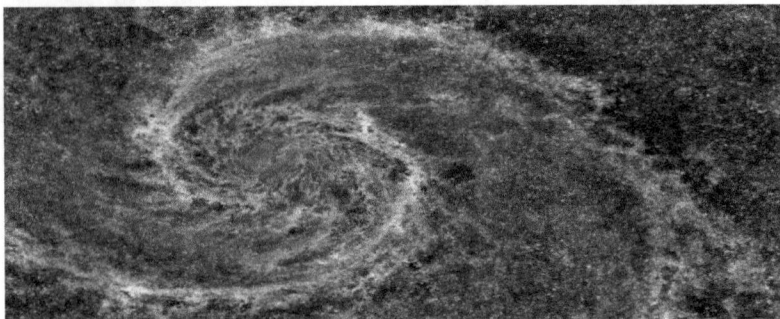

130

Yashu'a (Jesus) said: "A new commandment I give unto you, that ye love one another; as I have loved you, that ye also love one another."

CHILDREN OF THE MOST HIGH:
PRISTINE YOUTH AND FAMILY SOLUTIONS, LLC.
SONS AND DAUGHTERS OF THE MOST HIGH PUBLISHERS ®

Oh, Gracious Most High Heavenly father, Holy is your name,
Your Will Be Done Now and Forever!
Yashu'a (Jesus) said: "Thou shalt love the Most High Heavenly Father, thy Sustainer with all thy heart, and with all thy soul, and with all thy mind. Thou shalt love thy neighbour as thyself."

חֲטָאָה —(1) f. of the word חֹטֵא *a sinner* f., or *sinful*, Am. 9:8.

(2) i. q. חַטָּאת —(a) *sin*, Ex. 34:7. —(b) *penalty of sin* (like חַטָּאת No. 3), Isa. 5:18.

חַטָּאת constr. חַטַּאת plur. חַטָּאוֹת f. ["*a miss, misstep, slip with the foot*, Pro. 13:6"].

(1) *sin*, Ex. 28:9; Isa. 6:27, etc. ["Rarely for the habit of sinning, *sinfulness*, Prov. 14:34; Isa. 3:9."] Also applied to that by which any one sins, e.g. idols, Hos. 10:8; Deut. 9:21; comp. 2 Ki. 13:2, *water of sin*, i. e. of expiation or purifying, Num. 8:7.

(2) *a sin offering*, Levit. 6:18, 23; as to its difference from אָשָׁם see that word.

(3) *penalty*, Lam. 3:39; Zec. 14:19; hence *calamity, misfortune*, Isa. 40:2; Prov. 10:16 (opp. to חַיִּים). [Is not this last sense wholly needless? and would not its introduction utterly mar the sense of the passages referred to in support of it?]

131

Yashu'a (Jesus) said: "A new commandment I give unto you, that ye love one another; as I have loved you, that ye also love one another."

ASSASSINS of DISOBEDIENCE!
Invoking the Power of the Most High Through Obedience, is the Key to Living Your Best Life
as the Supreme Ingredient!
Heaven or Hell?

CHILDREN OF THE MOST HIGH:
PRISTINE YOUTH AND FAMILY SOLUTIONS, LLC.
SONS AND DAUGHTERS OF THE MOST HIGH PUBLISHERS ®

Oh, Gracious Most High Heavenly father, Holy is your name,
Your Will Be Done Now and Forever!
Yashu'a (Jesus) said: *"Thou shalt love the Most High Heavenly Father, thy Sustainer with all*
thy heart, and with all thy soul, and with all thy mind. Thou shalt love
thy neighbour as thyself."

According to the KJV bible book of 1st John chapter 1 verse 9; it states: "If we confess our **sins**, he is faithful and just to forgive us our **sins**, **and to cleanse us from all unrighteousness**." In the KJV bible book of 1st John chapter 1 verses 9, the word "**sins**" in the "KJV bible Greek Strong's Concordance "**#266** word: ἁμαρτία **Hamartia**, which means: **to be without a share in, to miss the mark, to err, be mistaken to miss or wander from the path of uprightness and honor, to do or go wrong, to wander from the law of God, violate God's law, sin that which is done wrong, sin, an offence, a violation of the divine law in thought or in act collectively, the complex or aggregate of sins committed either by a single person or by many**"

132

ASSASSINS of DISOBEDIENCE!
Invoking the Power of the Most High Through Obedience, is the Key to Living Your Best Life
as the Supreme Ingredient!
Heaven or Hell?

CHILDREN OF THE MOST HIGH:
PRISTINE YOUTH AND FAMILY SOLUTIONS, LLC.
SONS AND DAUGHTERS OF THE MOST HIGH PUBLISHERS ®

Oh, Gracious Most High Heavenly father, Holy is your name,
Your Will Be Done Now and Forever!
Yashu'a (Jesus) said: "Thou shalt love the Most High Heavenly Father, thy Sustainer with all
thy heart, and with all thy soul, and with all thy mind. Thou shalt love
thy neighbour as thyself."

According to the KJV bible book of Genesis chapter 4 verse 7; it states: "If (אִם 'Im) thou doest well (יָטַב Yatab) shalt thou not be accepted (שְׂאֵת Sĕ'eth) and if thou doest not well (יָטַב Yatab) <u>sin</u> (חַטָּאת Chatta'ath) lieth (רֹבֵץ Rabats) at the door (פֶּתַח Pethach) And unto thee shall be his desire (תְּשׁוּקָה Tĕshuwqah) and thou shalt rule (מְשַׁל Mashal) over him."

133

Yashu'a (Jesus) said: "A new commandment I give unto
you, that ye love one another; as I have loved you,
that ye also love one another."

ASSASSINS of DISOBEDIENCE!
Invoking the Power of the Most High Through Obedience, is the Key to Living Your Best Life
as the Supreme Ingredient!
Heaven or Hell?

CHILDREN OF THE MOST HIGH:
PRISTINE YOUTH AND FAMILY SOLUTIONS, LLC.
SONS AND DAUGHTERS OF THE MOST HIGH PUBLISHERS ®

Oh, Gracious Most High Heavenly father, Holy is your name,
Your Will Be Done Now and Forever!
Yashu'a (Jesus) said: *"Thou shalt love the Most High Heavenly Father, thy Sustainer with all*
thy heart, and with all thy soul, and with all thy mind. Thou shalt love
thy neighbour as thyself."

In the KJV bible book of Genesis chapter 4 verse 5 with Hebrew inserts; it states:

5: וְאֶל־קַיִן וְאֶל־מִנְחָתוֹ לֹא שָׁעָה וַיִּחַר לְקַיִן מְאֹד וַיִּפְּלוּ פָּנָיו

"But unto Cain and to his offering he had not respect. And Cain was very **wroth** (the word "**wroth**" is the KJV bible Hebrew Strong's Concordance#2734 חָרָה **Charah**, which means: **to be very angry**, to glow or grow warm; figuratively (usually) **to blaze up, of anger, zeal, jealousy: —be angry, burn**, be displeased, × earnestly, fret self, grieve, be (wax) hot, be incensed, kindle, × very, be wroth." his **countenance (Paniym** – Pronunciation **Pä·nēm'**) fell, and is defined as: "**when a person face frowns when they don't get their way**", and then he became wroth or very angry."

Yashu'a (Jesus) said: *"A new commandment I give unto you, that ye love one another; as I have loved you, that ye also love one another."*

ASSASSINS of DISOBEDIENCE!
Invoking the Power of the Most High Through Obedience, is the Key to Living Your Best Life
as the Supreme Ingredient!
Heaven or Hell?

CHILDREN OF THE MOST HIGH:
PRISTINE YOUTH AND FAMILY SOLUTIONS, LLC.
SONS AND DAUGHTERS OF THE MOST HIGH PUBLISHERS ®

Oh, Gracious Most High Heavenly father, Holy is your name,
Your Will Be Done Now and Forever!
Yashu'a (Jesus) said: *"Thou shalt love the Most High Heavenly Father, thy Sustainer with all*
thy heart, and with all thy soul, and with all thy mind. Thou shalt love
thy neighbour as thyself."

So, according to the previous verses, we learn that when Cain was disrespectful to the **Yahuwa** or **Yehovah (יְהֹוָה LORD)** and he did not get his way, **he became very <u>angry</u>,** and it led to him committing the <u>**sin**</u> of killing his brother Abel in the KJV bible book of Genesis chapter 4 verse 8. **<u>Anger and alcohol can impair the prefrontal lobe of the brain</u>** which is responsible for making sound decisions and can negatively affect the body (Hendricks, Bore, Aslinia, & Morriss, 2013). Therefore; the aforementioned KJV bible verses teach us that, **"Sin"** "lays and waits at the door" for the **essence (soul)** of people in hopes that the great dragon, that old serpent called the devil and **satan and his angels (Jinn - evil angels)** can seduce people to commit **"Sin".** Cain's encounter with **"Sin"** is a warning and sign for the children of the Most High who seek to obey the Most High.

135

Yashu'a (Jesus) said: *"A new commandment I give unto*
you, that ye love one another; as I have loved you,
that ye also love one another."

ASSASSINS of DISOBEDIENCE!
*Invoking the Power of the Most High Through Obedience, is the Key to Living Your Best Life
as the Supreme Ingredient!
Heaven or Hell?*

CHILDREN OF THE MOST HIGH:
PRISTINE YOUTH AND FAMILY SOLUTIONS, LLC.
SONS AND DAUGHTERS OF THE MOST HIGH PUBLISHERS ®

*Oh, Gracious Most High Heavenly father, Holy is your name,
Your Will Be Done Now and Forever!*
*Yashu'a (Jesus) said: "Thou shalt love the Most High Heavenly Father, thy Sustainer with all
thy heart, and with all thy soul, and with all thy mind. Thou shalt love
thy neighbour as thyself."*

How does the American Heritage Dictionary (2020) define the word "sin?"

The American Heritage Dictionary defines the word "**sin**" as:

"1. A transgression of a religious or moral law, especially when deliberate. 2. Theology, a. Deliberate disobedience to the known will of God. b. A condition of estrangement from God resulting from such disobedience. 3. Something regarded as being shameful, deplorable, or utterly wrong. intr.v. sinned, sin·ning, sins to violate a religious or moral law. Idioms: live in sin; To cohabit in a sexual relationship without being married. as sin; Completely or extremely: He is guilty as sin. [Middle English **sinne**, from Old English **synn**; see es- in the Appendix of Indo-European roots]."

*Yashu'a (Jesus) said: "A new commandment I give unto
you, that ye love one another; as I have loved you,
that ye also love one another."*

ASSASSINS of DISOBEDIENCE!
Invoking the Power of the Most High Through Obedience, is the Key to Living Your Best Life
as the Supreme Ingredient!
Heaven or Hell?

CHILDREN OF THE MOST HIGH:
PRISTINE YOUTH AND FAMILY SOLUTIONS, LLC.
SONS AND DAUGHTERS OF THE MOST HIGH PUBLISHERS ®

Oh, Gracious Most High Heavenly father, Holy is your name,
Your Will Be Done Now and Forever!
Yashu'a (Jesus) said: "Thou shalt love the Most High Heavenly Father, thy Sustainer with all thy heart, and with all thy soul, and with all thy mind. Thou shalt love thy neighbour as thyself."

Why is it important to take the time to research our English translations of the bible, word by word in the original languages (Tongues γλῶσσα Glōssa), KJV bible book of Acts chapter 2 verses 7-8) they were revealed in? That is an excellent question! The Messiah Yashu'a (Jesus) said in the KJV bible book of Matthews chapter 24 verses 4-5; states: **"Take heed (βλέπω Blepō, is the KJV bible Greek Strong's Concordance #991 word: βλέπω Blepō, which means to be aware of)** that no **man (τις Tis, is the KJV bible Greek Strong's Concordance #5100 word: τις Tis, which means any one, inclusive of all people regardless of gender) deceive you."**

137

Yashu'a (Jesus) said: "A new commandment I give unto you, that ye love one another; as I have loved you, that ye also love one another."

ASSASSINS of DISOBEDIENCE!
Invoking the Power of the Most High Through Obedience, is the Key to Living Your Best Life
as the Supreme Ingredient!
Heaven or Hell?

CHILDREN OF THE MOST HIGH:
PRISTINE YOUTH AND FAMILY SOLUTIONS, LLC.
SONS AND DAUGHTERS OF THE MOST HIGH PUBLISHERS ®

Oh, Gracious Most High Heavenly father, Holy is your name,
Your Will Be Done Now and Forever!
Yashu'a (Jesus) said: *"Thou shalt love the Most High Heavenly Father, thy Sustainer with all thy heart, and with all thy soul, and with all thy mind. Thou shalt love thy neighbour as thyself."*

The Messiah Yashu'a (Jesus) also said in the KJV bible book of John chapter 8 verse 32; "And ye shall know the truth, and the truth shall make you free." "**Ye shall know**" (γινώσκω **Ginōskō**, is the KJV bible Greek Strong's Concordance **#1097** word: γινώσκω **Ginōskō**, which means **to know, understand, perceive**). The word "**translation**" means **the act or process of translating, especially from one language into another**." So, in order to ensure that sincere-hearted people who have accepted the real Messiah Yashu'a (Jesus) as their Savior are not being deceived by modern day mistranslations of the bible, and to ensure that we know the truth; we must make the time to do intense, evidence-based, non-bias, rigorous research into the original languages that the bible and other scriptures were revealed in, to know the truth that can make us free.

138

Yashu'a (Jesus) said: *"A new commandment I give unto you, that ye love one another; as I have loved you, that ye also love one another."*

ASSASSINS of DISOBEDIENCE!
Invoking the Power of the Most High Through Obedience, is the Key to Living Your Best Life
as the Supreme Ingredient!
Heaven or Hell?

CHILDREN OF THE MOST HIGH:
PRISTINE YOUTH AND FAMILY SOLUTIONS, LLC.
SONS AND DAUGHTERS OF THE MOST HIGH PUBLISHERS ®

Oh, Gracious Most High Heavenly father, Holy is your name,
Your Will Be Done Now and Forever!
Yashu'a (Jesus) said: "Thou shalt love the Most High Heavenly Father, thy Sustainer with all
thy heart, and with all thy soul, and with all thy mind. Thou shalt love
thy neighbour as thyself."

This process can begin for a person by utilizing 21st century free online Hebrew and Greek Languages Strong's Concordances, or Lexicons, and online dictionaries. http://www.eliyah.com/lexicon.html, and **free cell phone Bible Hub KJV Strong's Exhaustive Concordance of the Bible app**. This on-going process of studying the bible and other scriptures, word by word in the original languages they were revealed in may help prevent the sincere-hearted truth seeker from being capable of being deceived by mistranslations, blind faith, and nonconfirmed beliefs with no substantiated facts. In the KJV bible book of 2nd Timothy chapter 2 verse 15; it states: "<u>**Study to shew thyself approved unto God, a workman that needeth not to be ashamed, rightly dividing the word of truth**</u>".

Yashu'a (Jesus) said: "A new commandment I give unto
you, that ye love one another; as I have loved you,
that ye also love one another."

ASSASSINS of DISOBEDIENCE!
Invoking the Power of the Most High Through Obedience, is the Key to Living Your Best Life
as the Supreme Ingredient!
Heaven or Hell?

CHILDREN OF THE MOST HIGH:
PRISTINE YOUTH AND FAMILY SOLUTIONS, LLC.
SONS AND DAUGHTERS OF THE MOST HIGH PUBLISHERS ®

Oh, Gracious Most High Heavenly father, Holy is your name,
Your Will Be Done Now and Forever!
Yashu'a (Jesus) said: *"Thou shalt love the Most High Heavenly Father, thy Sustainer with all thy heart, and with all thy soul, and with all thy mind. Thou shalt love thy neighbour as thyself."*

Therefore, the Children of the Most High: Pristine Youth and Family Solutions, LLC. utilize the Hebrew-Greek Key Word Study King James Version of the Bible and Strong's Concordance to start with the English translation in the process of researching the original words and meanings from the original languages that the bible was revealed in. This ensures that all readers receive the original message or messages and information that the **God (אֱלֹהִים 'Elohiym)** intended for members of humanity to receive, and this also helps to eliminate misinformation. Seek out the "**Spiritual Trillionaire**" book for more information on this topic.

Yashu'a (Jesus) said: *"A new commandment I give unto you, that ye love one another; as I have loved you, that ye also love one another."*

ASSASSINS of DISOBEDIENCE!
Invoking the Power of the Most High Through Obedience, is the Key to Living Your Best Life
as the Supreme Ingredient!
Heaven or Hell?

CHILDREN OF THE MOST HIGH:
PRISTINE YOUTH AND FAMILY SOLUTIONS, LLC.
SONS AND DAUGHTERS OF THE MOST HIGH PUBLISHERS ®

Oh, Gracious Most High Heavenly father, Holy is your name,
Your Will Be Done Now and Forever!
Yashu'a (Jesus) said: *"Thou shalt love the Most High Heavenly Father, thy Sustainer with all*
thy heart, and with all thy soul, and with all thy mind. Thou shalt love
thy neighbour as thyself."

141

Yashu'a (Jesus) said: *"A new commandment I give unto*
you, that ye love one another; as I have loved you,
that ye also love one another."

ASSASSINS of DISOBEDIENCE!
Invoking the Power of the Most High Through Obedience, is the Key to Living Your Best Life
as the Supreme Ingredient!
Heaven or Hell?

CHILDREN OF THE MOST HIGH:
PRISTINE YOUTH AND FAMILY SOLUTIONS, LLC.
SONS AND DAUGHTERS OF THE MOST HIGH PUBLISHERS ®

Oh, Gracious Most High Heavenly father, Holy is your name,
Your Will Be Done Now and Forever!
Yashu'a (Jesus) said: "Thou shalt love the Most High Heavenly Father, thy Sustainer with all
thy heart, and with all thy soul, and with all thy mind. Thou shalt love
thy neighbour as thyself."

What does the word "Covenant" mean in the KJV bible book in the Old Testament and in the New Testament?

In the KJV bible book of Genesis chapter 9 verses 9-10; it states: "And God spake unto Noah, and to his sons with him, saying, And I, behold, I establish my **covenant** with you, and with your seed after you." The KJV bible Hebrew Strong's Concordance "**#1285** word: בְּרִית **Ber-eeth or Beriyth**, is the word for **covenant** and it means: "**covenant, alliance, treaty pledge, agreement**." In the KJV bible book of Hebrews chapter 10 verse 16; it states: "This is the **covenant** that I will make with them after those days, saith the Lord, I will put my laws into their hearts, and in their minds will I write them."

Yashu'a (Jesus) said: "A new commandment I give unto you, that ye love one another; as I have loved you, that ye also love one another."

ASSASSINS of DISOBEDIENCE!
Invoking the Power of the Most High Through Obedience, is the Key to Living Your Best Life
as the Supreme Ingredient!
Heaven or Hell?

CHILDREN OF THE MOST HIGH:
PRISTINE YOUTH AND FAMILY SOLUTIONS, LLC.
SONS AND DAUGHTERS OF THE MOST HIGH PUBLISHERS ®

Oh, Gracious Most High Heavenly father, Holy is your name,
Your Will Be Done Now and Forever!
Yashu'a (Jesus) said: "Thou shalt love the Most High Heavenly Father, thy Sustainer with all
thy heart, and with all thy soul, and with all thy mind. Thou shalt love
thy neighbour as thyself."

The KJV bible Greek Strong's Concordance "**#1242** word: διαθήκη Diathēkē, is the word for **covenant** and it means: "**a compact, a covenant, a testament; God's covenant with Noah, etc., a disposition, arrangement, of any sort, which one wishes to be valid, the last disposition which one makes of his earthly possessions after his death, a testament or will.**"

So, what is the New Covenant of the Lord?

The <u>**New Covenant**</u> διαθήκη Diathēkē, **(God's covenant)**; is through obeying the Most High's laws and commandments, and through obeying the Messiah Yashu'a (Jesus) commandments. The Messiah Yashu'a said: "I am the way, the truth, and the life: no man cometh unto the Father, but by me, KJV John 14:6." This is why the KJV bible book of Hebrews chapter 10 verse 16; it states: "This is the **covenant** that I will make with them after those days, saith the Lord, I will put my laws into their hearts, and in their minds will I write them."

143

Yashu'a (Jesus) said: "A new commandment I give unto
you, that ye love one another; as I have loved you,
that ye also love one another."

ASSASSINS of DISOBEDIENCE!
Invoking the Power of the Most High Through Obedience, is the Key to Living Your Best Life
as the Supreme Ingredient!
Heaven or Hell?

CHILDREN OF THE MOST HIGH:
PRISTINE YOUTH AND FAMILY SOLUTIONS, LLC.
SONS AND DAUGHTERS OF THE MOST HIGH PUBLISHERS ®

Oh, Gracious Most High Heavenly father, Holy is your name,
Your Will Be Done Now and Forever!
Yashu'a (Jesus) said: *"Thou shalt love the Most High Heavenly Father, thy Sustainer with all*
thy heart, and with all thy soul, and with all thy mind. Thou shalt love
thy neighbour as thyself."

Chapter 6: Does the 48 Laws of Power Align with God's (אֱלֹהִים 'Elohiym) Commandments and Laws; and the Doctrine of the Most High that the Messiah Yashu'a (Jesus) Taught?

The Messiah Yashu'a (Jesus) said: "He [or she] that hath my commandments, and keepeth them, he [or she] it is that loveth me: and he [or she] that loveth me shall be loved of my Father, and I will love him [or her], and will manifest myself to him [or her]. He [or she] that hath an ear, let him hear what the Spirit saith unto the churches.

The Most High Heavenly Father is The Faithful."

In the KJV bible book of Deuteronomy chapter 7 verse 9; it states: "Know therefore that the LORD thy God, he is God, the faithful God, which keepeth covenant and mercy with them that love him and keep his commandments to a thousand generations."

144

Yashu'a (Jesus) said: "A new commandment I give unto you, that ye love one another; as I have loved you, that ye also love one another."

ASSASSINS of DISOBEDIENCE!
Invoking the Power of the Most High Through Obedience, is the Key to Living Your Best Life
as the Supreme Ingredient!
Heaven or Hell?

CHILDREN OF THE MOST HIGH:
PRISTINE YOUTH AND FAMILY SOLUTIONS, LLC.
SONS AND DAUGHTERS OF THE MOST HIGH PUBLISHERS ®

Oh, Gracious Most High Heavenly father, Holy is your name,
Your Will Be Done Now and Forever!
Yashu'a (Jesus) said: *"Thou shalt love the Most High Heavenly Father, thy Sustainer with all*
thy heart, and with all thy soul, and with all thy mind. Thou shalt love
thy neighbour as thyself."

What are the 48 Laws of Power?

The 48 Laws of Power (1998) is a **non-fiction book** written by an American author named **Mr. Robert Greene**. The book is a bestseller, and has sold over 1.2 million copies in the United States of America. **Define Power?** The Online American Heritage Dictionary (2020) defines power as: "1. a. **The ability or capacity to act or do something effectively**: Is it in your power to undo this injustice? b. often powers A specific **capacity**, **faculty**, or **aptitude**: her powers of concentration. 2. a. **Physical strength or force exerted or capable of being exerted**: the power of the waves. See Synonyms at strength."

Yashu'a (Jesus) said: *"A new commandment I give unto*
you, that ye love one another; as I have loved you,
that ye also love one another."

ASSASSINS of DISOBEDIENCE!
Invoking the Power of the Most High Through Obedience, is the Key to Living Your Best Life
as the Supreme Ingredient!
Heaven or Hell?

CHILDREN OF THE MOST HIGH:
PRISTINE YOUTH AND FAMILY SOLUTIONS, LLC.
SONS AND DAUGHTERS OF THE MOST HIGH PUBLISHERS ®

Oh, Gracious Most High Heavenly father, Holy is your name,
Your Will Be Done Now and Forever!
Yashu'a (Jesus) said: *"Thou shalt love the Most High Heavenly Father, thy Sustainer with all thy heart, and with all thy soul, and with all thy mind. Thou shalt love thy neighbour as thyself."*

"b. **Effectiveness at moving one's emotions or changing how one thinks**: a novel of great power. 3. a. **The ability or official capacity to exercise control**; **authority**: How long has that party been in power? b. **The military strength or economic or political influence of a nation or other group**: That country projects its power throughout the region. c. A country, nation, or other political unit having great influence or control over others: the western powers. 4. a. **A supernatural being**: **the powers of evil**. 5. a. **The energy or motive force by which a physical system or machine is operated**: turbines turned by steam power; a sailing ship driven by wind power. b. **The capacity of a system or machine to operate**: a vehicle that runs under its own power. c. **Electrical or mechanical energy, especially as used to assist or replace human energy**."

146

ASSASSINS of DISOBEDIENCE!
Invoking the Power of the Most High Through Obedience, is the Key to Living Your Best Life
as the Supreme Ingredient!
Heaven or Hell?

CHILDREN OF THE MOST HIGH:
PRISTINE YOUTH AND FAMILY SOLUTIONS, LLC.
SONS AND DAUGHTERS OF THE MOST HIGH PUBLISHERS ®

Oh, Gracious Most High Heavenly father, Holy is your name,
Your Will Be Done Now and Forever!
Yashu'a (Jesus) said: *"Thou shalt love the Most High Heavenly Father, thy Sustainer with all*
thy heart, and with all thy soul, and with all thy mind. Thou shalt love
thy neighbour as thyself."

"d. **Electricity supplied** to a home, building, or community: a storm that cut off power to the whole region. 6. **In Physics, the rate at which work is done, expressed as the amount of work per unit time and commonly measured in units such as the watt and horsepower**. 7. **Electricity**: a. **The product of applied potential difference and current in a direct-current circuit**. b. **The product of the effective values of the voltage and current with the cosine of the phase angle between current and voltage in an alternating-current circuit**. 8. Mathematics; a. See exponent. b. The number of elements in a finite set. 9. Statistics; In a statistical test, the probability of correctly rejecting the null hypothesis when it is false. 10. **A measure of the magnification of an optical instrument, such as a microscope or telescope**."

Yashu'a (Jesus) said: *"A new commandment I give unto you, that ye love one another; as I have loved you, that ye also love one another."*

ASSASSINS of DISOBEDIENCE!
Invoking the Power of the Most High Through Obedience, is the Key to Living Your Best Life
as the Supreme Ingredient!
Heaven or Hell?

CHILDREN OF THE MOST HIGH:
PRISTINE YOUTH AND FAMILY SOLUTIONS, LLC.
SONS AND DAUGHTERS OF THE MOST HIGH PUBLISHERS ®

Oh, Gracious Most High Heavenly father, Holy is your name,
Your Will Be Done Now and Forever!
Yashu'a (Jesus) said: *"Thou shalt love the Most High Heavenly Father, thy Sustainer with all thy heart, and with all thy soul, and with all thy mind. Thou shalt love thy neighbour as thyself."*

"11. Chiefly Upper Southern US A large number or amount. See Note at powerful. 12. Archaic An armed force. adj. 1. **Of or relating to political, social, or economic control**: a power struggle; a power base. 2. Operated with mechanical or electrical energy in place of bodily exertion: a power tool; power car windows. 3. Of or relating to the generation or transmission of electricity: power companies; power lines. 4. **Informal of or relating to influential business or professional practices**: a pinstriped suit with a power tie; met with high-level executives at a power breakfast. tr.v. pow·ered, pow·er·ing, pow·ers; To supply with power, especially mechanical or electrical power. Idiom: powers that be: **Those who hold effective power in a system or situation**: a plan vetoed by the powers that be."

148

Yashu'a (Jesus) said: "A new commandment I give unto you, that ye love one another; as I have loved you, that ye also love one another."

ASSASSINS of DISOBEDIENCE!
Invoking the Power of the Most High Through Obedience, is the Key to Living Your Best Life
as the Supreme Ingredient!
Heaven or Hell?

CHILDREN OF THE MOST HIGH:
PRISTINE YOUTH AND FAMILY SOLUTIONS, LLC.
SONS AND DAUGHTERS OF THE MOST HIGH PUBLISHERS ®

Oh, Gracious Most High Heavenly father, Holy is your name,
Your Will Be Done Now and Forever!
Yashu'a (Jesus) said: "Thou shalt love the Most High Heavenly Father, thy Sustainer with all
thy heart, and with all thy soul, and with all thy mind. Thou shalt love
thy neighbour as thyself."

"[Middle English, from Old **French pooir, to be able, power, from Vulgar Latin *potēre, to be able, from Latin potis, able, powerful; see poti- in the Appendix of Indo-European roots**]." Is there a correlation between the definitions of "**Power**" and "**Potential**?" **Define Potential**? The Online American Heritage Dictionary (2020) defines potential as: "1. **Capable of being but not yet in existence**; latent or **undeveloped**: a potential problem; a substance with many potential uses. 2. Grammar of, relating to, or being a verbal construction with auxiliaries such as may or can; for example, it may snow. n. 1. **The inherent ability or capacity for growth**, **development**, **or future success**: an investment with a lot of potential; a singer who has the potential to become a major star."

Yashu'a (Jesus) said: "A new commandment I give unto
you, that ye love one another; as I have loved you,
that ye also love one another."

ASSASSINS of DISOBEDIENCE!
Invoking the Power of the Most High Through Obedience, is the Key to Living Your Best Life
as the Supreme Ingredient!
Heaven or Hell?

CHILDREN OF THE MOST HIGH:
PRISTINE YOUTH AND FAMILY SOLUTIONS, LLC.
SONS AND DAUGHTERS OF THE MOST HIGH PUBLISHERS ®

Oh, Gracious Most High Heavenly father, Holy is your name,
Your Will Be Done Now and Forever!
Yashu'a (Jesus) said: "Thou shalt love the Most High Heavenly Father, thy Sustainer with all
thy heart, and with all thy soul, and with all thy mind. Thou shalt love
thy neighbour as thyself."

2. **The possibility that something might happen or result from given conditions**: a tense situation with the potential to turn into a riot; farming practices that increase the potential for the erosion of topsoil. 3. Physics; a. See electric potential. b. See gravitational potential. c. See magnetic potential. 4. Grammar A potential verb form. [Middle English potencial, from **Old French potenciel, from Late Latin potentiālis, powerful, from Latin potentia, power, from potēns, potent**, present participle of posse, **to be able**; see POTENT.] po·ten-tial·ly adv." So, the aforementioned, **Old French potenciel, from Late Latin potentiālis, powerful, from Latin potentia, power, from potēns, potent**; shows that the etymological root meaning of "**potential**" is "**power**."

Yashu'a (Jesus) said: "A new commandment I give unto you, that ye love one another; as I have loved you, that ye also love one another."

ASSASSINS of DISOBEDIENCE!
Invoking the Power of the Most High Through Obedience, is the Key to Living Your Best Life
as the Supreme Ingredient!
Heaven or Hell?

CHILDREN OF THE MOST HIGH:
PRISTINE YOUTH AND FAMILY SOLUTIONS, LLC.
SONS AND DAUGHTERS OF THE MOST HIGH PUBLISHERS &

Oh, Gracious Most High Heavenly father, Holy is your name,
Your Will Be Done Now and Forever!
Yashu'a (Jesus) said: *"Thou shalt love the Most High Heavenly Father, thy Sustainer with all thy heart, and with all thy soul, and with all thy mind. Thou shalt love thy neighbour as thyself."*

How does the 48 Laws of <u>Power</u> correlate with some of the youth and adults who are children of the Most High? Youth and adults who are children of the Most High do not want to be ruled by the children of the devil who utilize their power to control the most vulnerable and marginalized populations of the global members of humanity through **systemic racism, dominance, fear, inequalities, and inequities**. The **<u>48 Laws of Power</u>** correlates with some of the children of the Most High who also seek power over evil and receive their power from the Most High Heavenly Father. Therefore; the correlation is wanting power, and **the differences are the root foundations of power of the 48 Laws of Power** and the **power over evil that comes to the children of the Most High from the Most High Heavenly Father**.

151

Yashu'a (Jesus) said: *"A new commandment I give unto you, that ye love one another; as I have loved you, that ye also love one another."*

ASSASSINS of DISOBEDIENCE!
Invoking the Power of the Most High Through Obedience, is the Key to Living Your Best Life
as the Supreme Ingredient!
Heaven or Hell?

CHILDREN OF THE MOST HIGH:
PRISTINE YOUTH AND FAMILY SOLUTIONS, LLC.
SONS AND DAUGHTERS OF THE MOST HIGH PUBLISHERS ®

Oh, Gracious Most High Heavenly father, Holy is your name,
Your Will Be Done Now and Forever!
Yashu'a (Jesus) said: "Thou shalt love the Most High Heavenly Father, thy Sustainer with all
thy heart, and with all thy soul, and with all thy mind. Thou shalt love
thy neighbour as thyself."

Does the 48 Laws of Power Align with God's (אֱלֹהִים 'Elohiym) Commandments and Laws, and the Doctrine of the Most High that the Messiah Yashu'a (Jesus) taught?

That's a great question! Let's examine the 48 Laws of Power to inquire if the **48 Laws of Power** align with **the Commandments and Laws of the Doctrine of the Most High that the Messiah Yashu'a (Jesus) taught.**

Yashu'a (Jesus) said: "A new commandment I give unto you, that ye love one another; as I have loved you, that ye also love one another."

ASSASSINS of DISOBEDIENCE!
Invoking the Power of the Most High Through Obedience, is the Key to Living Your Best Life
as the Supreme Ingredient!
Heaven or Hell?

CHILDREN OF THE MOST HIGH:
PRISTINE YOUTH AND FAMILY SOLUTIONS, LLC.
SONS AND DAUGHTERS OF THE MOST HIGH PUBLISHERS ®

Oh, Gracious Most High Heavenly father, Holy is your name,
Your Will Be Done Now and Forever!
Yashu'a (Jesus) said: *"Thou shalt love the Most High Heavenly Father, thy Sustainer with all*
thy heart, and with all thy soul, and with all thy mind. Thou shalt love
thy neighbour as thyself."

Are there any other reasons why the children of the Most High may consider examining the 48 Laws of Power? The children of the Most High are also examining the 48 Laws of Power in accordance with the KJV bible book of 1st John chapter 4 verses 1; it states: "Beloved, believe not every spirit, but **try** (the word "**try**" is the KJV bible Greek Strong's Concordance "**#1381** word: δοκιμάζω **Dokimazō** and means: **to test, examine, prove, scrutinize; to recognize as genuine after examination, to approve, deem worthy**) **the spirits whether they are of God**: because many false prophets are gone out into the world. So, the children of the Most High are examining the **48 Laws of Power to test and examine whether they are of the Most High Heavenly Father or not.**

Yashu'a (Jesus) said: "A new commandment I give unto
you, that ye love one another; as I have loved you,
that ye also love one another."

CHILDREN OF THE MOST HIGH:
PRISTINE YOUTH AND FAMILY SOLUTIONS, LLC.
SONS AND DAUGHTERS OF THE MOST HIGH PUBLISHERS ®

Oh, Gracious Most High Heavenly father, Holy is your name,
Your Will Be Done Now and Forever!
Yashu'a (Jesus) said: *"Thou shalt love the Most High Heavenly Father, thy Sustainer with all thy heart, and with all thy soul, and with all thy mind. Thou shalt love thy neighbour as thyself."*

In the KJV bible book of 1st John chapter 4 verses 1-3; it states: "Beloved, believe not every spirit, but **try (δοκιμάζω Dokimazō-to test, examine, prove, scrutinize; to recognize as genuine after examination, to approve, deem worthy) the spirits whether they are of God**: because many false prophets are gone out into the world. Hereby know ye the Spirit of God: Every spirit that confesseth that Jesus Christ is come in the flesh is of God: **And every spirit that confesseth not that Jesus Christ is come in the flesh is not of God: and this is that spirit of antichrist, whereof ye have heard that it should come; and even now already is it in the world**."

154

Yashu'a (Jesus) said: *"A new commandment I give unto you, that ye love one another; as I have loved you, that ye also love one another."*

ASSASSINS of DISOBEDIENCE!
Invoking the Power of the Most High Through Obedience, is the Key to Living Your Best Life
as the Supreme Ingredient!
Heaven or Hell?

CHILDREN OF THE MOST HIGH:
PRISTINE YOUTH AND FAMILY SOLUTIONS, LLC.
SONS AND DAUGHTERS OF THE MOST HIGH PUBLISHERS ®

Oh, Gracious Most High Heavenly father, Holy is your name,
Your Will Be Done Now and Forever!
Yashu'a (Jesus) said: "Thou shalt love the Most High Heavenly Father, thy Sustainer with all
thy heart, and with all thy soul, and with all thy mind. Thou shalt love
thy neighbour as thyself."

Examining The 48 Laws of Power

"The **first (1) out of 48 Laws of Power** states: <u>**NEVER OUTSHINE THE MASTER**</u>. Always make those above you feel comfortably superior. In your desire to please and impress them, do not go too far in displaying your talents or you might accomplish the opposite—inspire fear and insecurity. Make your masters appear more brilliant than they are and you will attain the heights of power (Greene 1998, p.1)."

155

Yashu'a (Jesus) said: "A new commandment I give unto you, that ye love one another; as I have loved you, that ye also love one another."

ASSASSINS of DISOBEDIENCE!
Invoking the Power of the Most High Through Obedience, is the Key to Living Your Best Life
as the Supreme Ingredient!
Heaven or Hell?

CHILDREN OF THE MOST HIGH:
PRISTINE YOUTH AND FAMILY SOLUTIONS, LLC.
SONS AND DAUGHTERS OF THE MOST HIGH PUBLISHERS ®

Oh, Gracious Most High Heavenly father, Holy is your name,
Your Will Be Done Now and Forever!
Yashu'a (Jesus) said: "Thou shalt love the Most High Heavenly Father, thy Sustainer with all
thy heart, and with all thy soul, and with all thy mind. Thou shalt love
thy neighbour as thyself."

The Messiah Yashu'a (Jesus) said in the KJV bible book of Matthew chapter 6 verse 24 states: "No man can serve two masters: for either he will hate the one, and love the other; or else he will hold to the one, and despise the other. Ye cannot serve God and <u>mammon</u> (μαμωνᾶς **Mamōnas**, KJV bible Greek Strong's Concordance **#3126**; μαμωνᾶς **Mamōnas** **means: wealth, personified; avarice (deified), treasure; riches (where it is personified and opposed to God).**" So, if you are a child of the Most High, we seek to be like **Rabboni (Master) Yashu'a (Jesus)**, and must remember, that only Lucifer and the likes; aspire to **be like the Most High**. In the KJV bible book of John chapter 20 verse 6; it states: "Jesus saith unto her, Mary. She turned herself, and saith unto him, **Rabboni; which is to say, Master.**"

156

Yashu'a (Jesus) said: "A new commandment I give unto you, that ye love one another; as I have loved you, that ye also love one another."

ASSASSINS of DISOBEDIENCE!
Invoking the Power of the Most High Through Obedience, is the Key to Living Your Best Life
as the Supreme Ingredient!
Heaven or Hell?

CHILDREN OF THE MOST HIGH:
PRISTINE YOUTH AND FAMILY SOLUTIONS, LLC.
SONS AND DAUGHTERS OF THE MOST HIGH PUBLISHERS ®

Oh, Gracious Most High Heavenly father, Holy is your name,
Your Will Be Done Now and Forever!
Yashu'a (Jesus) said: *"Thou shalt love the Most High Heavenly Father, thy Sustainer with all thy heart, and with all thy soul, and with all thy mind. Thou shalt love thy neighbour as thyself."*

In the KJV bible book of John chapter 14 verse 6; the Messiah Yashu'a (Jesus) said: "I am the way, the truth, and the life: no man cometh unto the Father, but by me." In the KJV bible book of Isaiah chapter 14 verses 12-16; it states: "How art thou fallen from heaven, O Lucifer, son of the morning! how art thou cut down to the ground, which didst weaken the nations! For thou hast said in thine heart, I will ascend into heaven, I will exalt my throne above the stars of God: I will sit also upon the mount of the congregation, in the sides of the north: I will ascend above the heights of the clouds; I will **be like the Most High**. Yet thou shalt be brought down to hell, to the sides of the pit. They that see thee shall narrowly look upon thee, and consider thee, saying, <u>**is this the man that made the earth to tremble**</u>, that did shake kingdoms."

157

ASSASSINS of DISOBEDIENCE!
Invoking the Power of the Most High Through Obedience, is the Key to Living Your Best Life
as the Supreme Ingredient!
Heaven or Hell?

CHILDREN OF THE MOST HIGH:
PRISTINE YOUTH AND FAMILY SOLUTIONS, LLC.
SONS AND DAUGHTERS OF THE MOST HIGH PUBLISHERS ®

Oh, Gracious Most High Heavenly father, Holy is your name,
Your Will Be Done Now and Forever!
Yashu'a (Jesus) said: *"Thou shalt love the Most High Heavenly Father, thy Sustainer with all thy heart, and with all thy soul, and with all thy mind. Thou shalt love thy neighbour as thyself."*

"The **second (2) out of 48 Laws of Power** is: <u>**NEVER PUT TOO MUCH TRUST IN FRIENDS, LEARN HOW TO USE ENEMIES**</u>. Be wary of friends—they will betray you more quickly, for they are easily aroused to envy. They also become spoiled and tyrannical. But hire a former enemy and he will be more loyal than a friend, because he has more to prove. In fact, you have more to fear from friends than from enemies. If you have no enemies, find a way to make them (Greene 1998, p.8)." According the KJV bible book of Proverbs chapter 18 verse 24; it states: "A man [that hath] **friends** must shew himself **friendly**: and there is a **friend** [that] sticketh closer than a brother." "A **friend** loveth at all times, and a brother is born for adversity, Proverbs 17:17."

158

Yashu'a (Jesus) said: "A new commandment I give unto you, that ye love one another; as I have loved you, that ye also love one another."

ASSASSINS of DISOBEDIENCE!
Invoking the Power of the Most High Through Obedience, is the Key to Living Your Best Life
as the Supreme Ingredient!
Heaven or Hell?

CHILDREN OF THE MOST HIGH:
PRISTINE YOUTH AND FAMILY SOLUTIONS, LLC.
SONS AND DAUGHTERS OF THE MOST HIGH PUBLISHERS ®

Oh, Gracious Most High Heavenly father, Holy is your name,
Your Will Be Done Now and Forever!
Yashu'a (Jesus) said: *"Thou shalt love the Most High Heavenly Father, thy Sustainer with all*
thy heart, and with all thy soul, and with all thy mind. Thou shalt love
thy neighbour as thyself."

The KJV bible book of James chapter 2 verse 23; states: "And the scripture was fulfilled which saith, Abraham believed God, and it was imputed unto him for righteousness: and he was called the **Friend** of God." In the KJV bible book of John chapter 15 verses 5-21; the Messiah Yashu'a (Jesus) said: "I am the vine, ye are the branches: He that abideth in me, and I in him, the same bringeth forth much fruit: for without me ye can do nothing. If a man abides not in me, he is cast forth as a branch, and is withered; and men gather them, and cast them into the fire, and they are burned. If ye abide in me, and my words abide in you, ye shall ask what ye will, and it shall be done unto you. Herein is my Father glorified, that ye bear much fruit; so, shall ye be my disciples."

159

Yashu'a (Jesus) said: "A new commandment I give unto
you, that ye love one another; as I have loved you,
that ye also love one another."

ASSASSINS of DISOBEDIENCE!
Invoking the Power of the Most High Through Obedience, is the Key to Living Your Best Life
as the Supreme Ingredient!
Heaven or Hell?

CHILDREN OF THE MOST HIGH:
PRISTINE YOUTH AND FAMILY SOLUTIONS, LLC.
SONS AND DAUGHTERS OF THE MOST HIGH PUBLISHERS ®

Oh, Gracious Most High Heavenly father, Holy is your name,
Your Will Be Done Now and Forever!
Yashu'a (Jesus) said: *"Thou shalt love the Most High Heavenly Father, thy Sustainer with all*
thy heart, and with all thy soul, and with all thy mind. Thou shalt love
thy neighbour as thyself."

As the Father hath loved me, so have I loved you: continue ye in my love. If ye keep my commandments, ye shall abide in my love; even as I have kept my Father's commandments, and abide in his love. These things have I spoken unto you, that my joy might remain in you, and that your joy might be full. This is my commandment, that ye love one another, as I have loved you. Greater love hath no man than this, that a man lay down his life for his friends. Ye are my friends, if ye do whatsoever I command you. Henceforth I call you not servants; for the servant knoweth not what his lord doeth: but I have called you friends; for all things that I have heard of my Father I have made known unto you."

160

Yashu'a (Jesus) said: *"A new commandment I give unto you, that ye love one another; as I have loved you, that ye also love one another."*

ASSASSINS of DISOBEDIENCE!
Invoking the Power of the Most High Through Obedience, is the Key to Living Your Best Life
as the Supreme Ingredient!
Heaven or Hell?

CHILDREN OF THE MOST HIGH:
PRISTINE YOUTH AND FAMILY SOLUTIONS, LLC.
SONS AND DAUGHTERS OF THE MOST HIGH PUBLISHERS ®

Oh, Gracious Most High Heavenly father, Holy is your name,
Your Will Be Done Now and Forever!
Yashu'a (Jesus) said: *"Thou shalt love the Most High Heavenly Father, thy Sustainer with all*
thy heart, and with all thy soul, and with all thy mind. Thou shalt love
thy neighbour as thyself."

"Ye have not chosen me, but I have chosen you, and ordained you, that ye should go and bring forth fruit, and that your fruit should remain: that whatsoever ye shall ask of the Father in my name, he may give it you. These things I command you, that ye love one another. If the world hates you, ye know that it hated me before it hated you. If ye were of the world, the world would love his own: but because ye are not of the world, but I have chosen you out of the world, therefore the world hateth you. Remember the word that I said unto you, the servant is not greater than his lord. If they have persecuted me, they will also persecute you; if they have kept my saying, they will keep yours also. But all these things will they do unto you for my name's sake, because they know not him that sent me."

161

Yashu'a (Jesus) said: *"A new commandment I give unto you, that ye love one another; as I have loved you, that ye also love one another."*

ASSASSINS of DISOBEDIENCE!
Invoking the Power of the Most High Through Obedience, is the Key to Living Your Best Life
as the Supreme Ingredient!
Heaven or Hell?

CHILDREN OF THE MOST HIGH:
PRISTINE YOUTH AND FAMILY SOLUTIONS, LLC.
SONS AND DAUGHTERS OF THE MOST HIGH PUBLISHERS ®

Oh, Gracious Most High Heavenly father, Holy is your name,
Your Will Be Done Now and Forever!
Yashu'a (Jesus) said: "Thou shalt love the Most High Heavenly Father, thy Sustainer with all
thy heart, and with all thy soul, and with all thy mind. Thou shalt love
thy neighbour as thyself."

"The **third (3) out of 48 Laws of Power** is: <u>**CONCEAL**</u>

<u>**YOUR INTENTIONS**</u>. Keep people off-balance and in the

dark by never revealing the purpose behind your actions. If they

have no clue what you are up to, they cannot prepare a defense.

Guide them far enough down the wrong path, envelop them in

enough smoke, and by the time they realize your intentions, it

will be too late (Greene 1998, p.16)." The KJV bible Hebrew

Strong's Concordance **#3680** for the word "<u>**conceal**</u>" is

"**covereth** כָּסָה **Kacah**." According to the KJV bible book of

Proverbs chapter 28 verse 13; it states: "He that **covereth** (כָּסָה

Kacah, means to conceal, to cover, hide) his sins shall not

prosper: but whoso confesseth and forsaketh them shall have

mercy."

162

Yashu'a (Jesus) said: "A new commandment I give unto
you, that ye love one another; as I have loved you,
that ye also love one another."

ASSASSINS of DISOBEDIENCE!
Invoking the Power of the Most High Through Obedience, is the Key to Living Your Best Life
as the Supreme Ingredient!
Heaven or Hell?

CHILDREN OF THE MOST HIGH:
PRISTINE YOUTH AND FAMILY SOLUTIONS, LLC.
SONS AND DAUGHTERS OF THE MOST HIGH PUBLISHERS ®

Oh, Gracious Most High Heavenly father, Holy is your name,
Your Will Be Done Now and Forever!
Yashu'a (Jesus) said: *"Thou shalt love the Most High Heavenly Father, thy Sustainer with all*
thy heart, and with all thy soul, and with all thy mind. Thou shalt love
thy neighbour as thyself."

In the KJV bible book of Ezekiel chapter 28 verse 14; it states: "Ezekiel Thou [art] **the anointed cherub** (כְּרוּב Keruwb)." A **Keruwb כְּרוּב is a disagreeable angelic-being)** that **covereth** (כָּסָה **Kacah, means to conceal, to cover, hide)** and I have set thee [so]: thou wast upon the holy mountain of God; thou hast walked up and down in the midst of the stones of fire. Thou wast perfect in thy ways from the day that thou wast created, till **iniquity** (the KJV bible Hebrew Strong's Concordance **#5766** word for **iniquity** is עָוֶל **`Evel, and means: iniquity, perverseness, unjust(-ly), unrighteousness(-ly); wicked(-ness), injustice, unrighteousness, wrong, violent deeds of injustice, injustice (of speech), injustice (generally)** was found in thee."

163

Yashu'a (Jesus) said: "A new commandment I give unto
you, that ye love one another; as I have loved you,
that ye also love one another."

ASSASSINS of DISOBEDIENCE!
Invoking the Power of the Most High Through Obedience, is the Key to Living Your Best Life
as the Supreme Ingredient!
Heaven or Hell?

CHILDREN OF THE MOST HIGH:
PRISTINE YOUTH AND FAMILY SOLUTIONS, LLC.
SONS AND DAUGHTERS OF THE MOST HIGH PUBLISHERS ®

Oh, Gracious Most High Heavenly father, Holy is your name,
Your Will Be Done Now and Forever!
Yashu'a (Jesus) said: "Thou shalt love the Most High Heavenly Father, thy Sustainer with all
thy heart, and with all thy soul, and with all thy mind. Thou shalt love
thy neighbour as thyself."

The Messiah Yashu'a (Jesus) said: "And ye shall know the truth, and the truth shall make you free, KJV John 8:32." "The **fourth (4) out of 48 Laws of Power** is: **ALWAYS SAY LESS THAN NECESSARY**. When you are trying to impress people with words, the more you say, the more common you appear, and the less in control. Even if you are saying something banal, it will seem original if you make it vague, open-ended, and sphinxlike. Powerful people **impress** and **intimidate** by saying less. The more you say, the more likely you are to say something foolish (Greene 1998, p.31)." The Online American Heritage Dictionary (2020) defines **impress** as: "to affect especially forcibly or deeply: gain the **admiration** or interest of. **Intimidate** is defined as: "**To make timid**; **fill with fear**: to coerce or deter, as with threats."

164

Yashu'a (Jesus) said: "A new commandment I give unto you, that ye love one another; as I have loved you, that ye also love one another."

ASSASSINS of DISOBEDIENCE!
Invoking the Power of the Most High Through Obedience, is the Key to Living Your Best Life
as the Supreme Ingredient!
Heaven or Hell?

CHILDREN OF THE MOST HIGH:
PRISTINE YOUTH AND FAMILY SOLUTIONS, LLC.
SONS AND DAUGHTERS OF THE MOST HIGH PUBLISHERS ®

Oh, Gracious Most High Heavenly father, Holy is your name,
Your Will Be Done Now and Forever!
Yashu'a (Jesus) said: "Thou shalt love the Most High Heavenly Father, thy Sustainer with all thy heart, and with all thy soul, and with all thy mind. Thou shalt love thy neighbour as thyself."

According to the KJV bible book of 2 Timothy chapter 1 verse 7; it states: "For God **hath not given us the spirit of fear**; but of power, and of love, and of a sound mind. The KJV bible book of Deuteronomy chapter 31 verse 6; states: "Be strong and of a good courage, **fear not**, **nor be afraid of them**: for the LORD thy God, he [it is] that doth go with thee; he will not fail thee, nor forsake thee."

165

Yashu'a (Jesus) said: "A new commandment I give unto you, that ye love one another; as I have loved you, that ye also love one another."

ASSASSINS of DISOBEDIENCE!
Invoking the Power of the Most High Through Obedience, is the Key to Living Your Best Life
as the Supreme Ingredient!
Heaven or Hell?

CHILDREN OF THE MOST HIGH:
PRISTINE YOUTH AND FAMILY SOLUTIONS, LLC.
SONS AND DAUGHTERS OF THE MOST HIGH PUBLISHERS ®

Oh, Gracious Most High Heavenly father, Holy is your name,
Your Will Be Done Now and Forever!
Yashu'a (Jesus) said: "Thou shalt love the Most High Heavenly Father, thy Sustainer with all
thy heart, and with all thy soul, and with all thy mind. Thou shalt love
thy neighbour as thyself."

In the KJV bible book of 1st Samuel chapter 16 verse 7; it states: "But the LORD said unto Samuel, **look not on his countenance** (the KJV bible Hebrew Strong's Concordance for this phrase is #777 for the word: מַרְאֶה **Mar'eh**, and means: **admiration of appearance, sight, phenomenon, spectacle, appearance, vision, what is seen or on the height of his stature**); because I have refused him: for the LORD seeth not as man seeth; for man looketh on the outward appearance, but the LORD looketh on the heart."

166

Yashu'a (Jesus) said: "A new commandment I give unto you, that ye love one another; as I have loved you, that ye also love one another."

ASSASSINS of DISOBEDIENCE!
Invoking the Power of the Most High Through Obedience, is the Key to Living Your Best Life
as the Supreme Ingredient!
Heaven or Hell?

CHILDREN OF THE MOST HIGH:
PRISTINE YOUTH AND FAMILY SOLUTIONS, LLC.
SONS AND DAUGHTERS OF THE MOST HIGH PUBLISHERS ®

Oh, Gracious Most High Heavenly father, Holy is your name,
Your Will Be Done Now and Forever!
Yashu'a (Jesus) said: "Thou shalt love the Most High Heavenly Father, thy Sustainer with all
thy heart, and with all thy soul, and with all thy mind. Thou shalt love
thy neighbour as thyself."

"The **fifth (5) out of 48 Laws of Power** is: <u>**SO MUCH DEPENDS ON REPUTATION—GUARD IT WITH YOUR LIFE**</u>. Reputation is the cornerstone of power. Through reputation alone you can intimidate and win; once it slips, however, you are vulnerable, and will be attacked on all sides. Make your reputation unassailable. Always be alert to potential attacks and thwart them before they happen. Meanwhile, learn to destroy your enemies by opening holes in their own reputations. Then stand aside and let public opinion hang them (Greene 1998, p.37)." The KJV bible book of Proverbs chapter 22 verse 1; states: "Proverbs 22:1 - A [good] name [is] rather to be chosen than great riches, [and] loving favor rather than silver and gold."

Yashu'a (Jesus) said: "A new commandment I give unto
you, that ye love one another; as I have loved you,
that ye also love one another."

ASSASSINS of DISOBEDIENCE!
Invoking the Power of the Most High Through Obedience, is the Key to Living Your Best Life
as the Supreme Ingredient!
Heaven or Hell?

CHILDREN OF THE MOST HIGH:
PRISTINE YOUTH AND FAMILY SOLUTIONS, LLC.
SONS AND DAUGHTERS OF THE MOST HIGH PUBLISHERS ®

Oh, Gracious Most High Heavenly father, Holy is your name,
Your Will Be Done Now and Forever!
Yashu'a (Jesus) said: "Thou shalt love the Most High Heavenly Father, thy Sustainer with all
thy heart, and with all thy soul, and with all thy mind. Thou shalt love
thy neighbour as thyself."

"The **sixth (6) out of 48 Laws of Power** is: <u>**COURT ATTENTION AT ALL COST**</u>. Everything is judged by its appearance; what is unseen counts for nothing. Never let yourself get lost in the crowd, then, or buried in oblivion. Stand out. Be conspicuous, at all cost. Make yourself a magnet of attention by appearing larger, more colorful, more mysterious than the bland and timid masses (Greene 1998, p.44)." In the KJV bible book of John chapter 7 verse 18; the Messiah Yashu'a (Jesus) said: **"He that speaketh of himself seeketh his own glory: but he that seeketh his glory that sent him, the same is true, and no unrighteousness is in him."**

168

Yashu'a (Jesus) said: "A new commandment I give unto you, that ye love one another; as I have loved you, that ye also love one another."

ASSASSINS of DISOBEDIENCE!
Invoking the Power of the Most High Through Obedience, is the Key to Living Your Best Life
as the Supreme Ingredient!
Heaven or Hell?

CHILDREN OF THE MOST HIGH:
PRISTINE YOUTH AND FAMILY SOLUTIONS, LLC.
SONS AND DAUGHTERS OF THE MOST HIGH PUBLISHERS ®

Oh, Gracious Most High Heavenly father, Holy is your name,
Your Will Be Done Now and Forever!
Yashu'a (Jesus) said: *"Thou shalt love the Most High Heavenly Father, thy Sustainer with all thy heart, and with all thy soul, and with all thy mind. Thou shalt love thy neighbour as thyself."*

In the KJV bible book of John chapter 8 verses 44-50; the Messiah Yashu'a (Jesus) also said: "**Ye are of your father the devil, and the lusts of your father ye will do. He was a murderer from the beginning, and abode not in the truth, because there is no truth in him. When he speaketh a lie, he speaketh of his own: for he is a liar, and the father of it. And because I tell you the truth, ye believe me not. Which of you convinceth me of sin? And if I say the truth, why do ye not believe me? He that is of God heareth God's words: ye therefore hear them not, because ye are not of God.**"

169

Yashu'a (Jesus) said: *"A new commandment I give unto you, that ye love one another; as I have loved you, that ye also love one another."*

ASSASSINS of DISOBEDIENCE!
*Invoking the Power of the Most High Through Obedience, is the Key to Living Your Best Life
as the Supreme Ingredient!
Heaven or Hell?*

CHILDREN OF THE MOST HIGH:
PRISTINE YOUTH AND FAMILY SOLUTIONS, LLC.
SONS AND DAUGHTERS OF THE MOST HIGH PUBLISHERS ®

*Oh, Gracious Most High Heavenly father, Holy is your name,
Your Will Be Done Now and Forever!*
*Yashu'a (Jesus) said: "Thou shalt love the Most High Heavenly Father, thy Sustainer with all
thy heart, and with all thy soul, and with all thy mind. Thou shalt love
thy neighbour as thyself."*

"Then answered the Jews, and said unto him, Say we not well that thou art a Samaritan, and hast a devil? Jesus answered, I have not a devil; but I honour my Father, and ye do dishonor me. And I seek not mine own glory: there is one that seeketh and judgeth."

"The **seventh (7) out of 48 Laws of Power** is: <u>**GET OTHERS TO DO THE WORK FOR YOU, BUT ALWAYS TAKE THE CREDIT**</u>. Use the wisdom, knowledge, and legwork of other people to further your own cause. Not only will such assistance save you valuable time and energy, it will give you a godlike aura of efficiency and speed. In the end your helpers will be forgotten and you will be remembered. Never do yourself what others can do for you (Greene 1998, p.56)."

170

*Yashu'a (Jesus) said: "A new commandment I give unto
you, that ye love one another; as I have loved you,
that ye also love one another."*

ASSASSINS of DISOBEDIENCE!
Invoking the Power of the Most High Through Obedience, is the Key to Living Your Best Life
as the Supreme Ingredient!
Heaven or Hell?

CHILDREN OF THE MOST HIGH:
PRISTINE YOUTH AND FAMILY SOLUTIONS, LLC.
SONS AND DAUGHTERS OF THE MOST HIGH PUBLISHERS ®

Oh, Gracious Most High Heavenly father, Holy is your name,
Your Will Be Done Now and Forever!
Yashu'a (Jesus) said: *"Thou shalt love the Most High Heavenly Father, thy Sustainer with all*
thy heart, and with all thy soul, and with all thy mind. Thou shalt love
thy neighbour as thyself."

In the KJV bible book of Matthew chapter 6 verse 5; and Matthew 5 verse 44; the Messiah Yashu'a (Jesus) said: "And when thou prayest, thou shalt not be as the hypocrites are: for they love to pray standing in the synagogues and in the corners of the streets, that they may be seen of men. Verily I say unto you, they have their reward. But I say unto you, love your enemies, bless them that curse you, do good to them that hate you, and pray for them which despitefully use you, and persecute you."

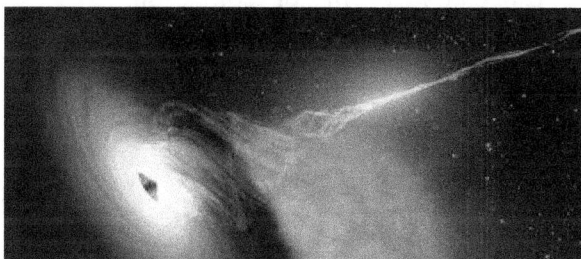

171

Yashu'a (Jesus) said: "A new commandment I give unto
you, that ye love one another; as I have loved you,
that ye also love one another."

ASSASSINS of DISOBEDIENCE!
Invoking the Power of the Most High Through Obedience, is the Key to Living Your Best Life
as the Supreme Ingredient!
Heaven or Hell?

CHILDREN OF THE MOST HIGH:
PRISTINE YOUTH AND FAMILY SOLUTIONS, LLC.
SONS AND DAUGHTERS OF THE MOST HIGH PUBLISHERS ®

Oh, Gracious Most High Heavenly father, Holy is your name,
Your Will Be Done Now and Forever!
Yashu'a (Jesus) said: *"Thou shalt love the Most High Heavenly Father, thy Sustainer with all*
thy heart, and with all thy soul, and with all thy mind. Thou shalt love
thy neighbour as thyself."

"The **eighth (8) out of 48 Laws of Power** is: <u>**MAKE OTHER PEOPLE COME TO YOU—USE BAIT IF NECESSARY**</u>. When you force the other person to act, <u>**you are the one in control**</u>. It is always better to make your opponent come to you, abandoning his own plans in the process. **Lure** him with fabulous gains—then attack. You hold the cards (Greene 1998, p.62)." The Online American Heritage Dictionary (2020) defines **control** as: "To **exercise authoritative** or dominating influence over; direct. **Lure** is defined as: Something that **tempts or attracts** with the promise of pleasure or reward; to attract or entice, especially by wiles or temptation."

172

Yashu'a (Jesus) said: "A new commandment I give unto
you, that ye love one another; as I have loved you,
that ye also love one another."

ASSASSINS of DISOBEDIENCE!
Invoking the Power of the Most High Through Obedience, is the Key to Living Your Best Life
as the Supreme Ingredient!
Heaven or Hell?

CHILDREN OF THE MOST HIGH:
PRISTINE YOUTH AND FAMILY SOLUTIONS, LLC.
SONS AND DAUGHTERS OF THE MOST HIGH PUBLISHERS ®

Oh, Gracious Most High Heavenly father, Holy is your name,
Your Will Be Done Now and Forever!
Yashu'a (Jesus) said: "Thou shalt love the Most High Heavenly Father, thy Sustainer with all
thy heart, and with all thy soul, and with all thy mind. Thou shalt love
thy neighbour as thyself."

In the KJV bible book of Matthew chapter 28 verse 18; the Messiah Yashu'a (Jesus) said: "All power is given unto me in heaven and in earth. When the righteous are in authority, the people rejoice: but when the wicked beareth rule, the people mourn, Proverbs 29:2." The Messiah Yashu'a (Jesus) also said: "After this manner therefore pray ye: Our Father which art in heaven, Hallowed be thy name. Thy kingdom come. Thy will be done in earth, as it is in heaven. Give us this day our daily bread. And forgive us our debts, as we forgive our debtors. And lead us not into temptation, but deliver us from evil: For thine is the kingdom, and the power, and the glory, forever. Amen.

173

Yashu'a (Jesus) said: "A new commandment I give unto you, that ye love one another; as I have loved you, that ye also love one another."

ASSASSINS of DISOBEDIENCE!
Invoking the Power of the Most High Through Obedience, is the Key to Living Your Best Life
as the Supreme Ingredient!
Heaven or Hell?

CHILDREN OF THE MOST HIGH:
PRISTINE YOUTH AND FAMILY SOLUTIONS, LLC.
SONS AND DAUGHTERS OF THE MOST HIGH PUBLISHERS ®

Oh, Gracious Most High Heavenly father, Holy is your name,
Your Will Be Done Now and Forever!
Yashu'a (Jesus) said: "Thou shalt love the Most High Heavenly Father, thy Sustainer with all
thy heart, and with all thy soul, and with all thy mind. Thou shalt love
thy neighbour as thyself."

"The **nineth (9) out of 48 Laws of Power** is: <u>**WIN THROUGH YOUR ACTIONS, NEVER THROUGH ARGUMENT**</u>. Any momentary triumph you think you have gained through argument is really a Pyrrhic victory: The resentment and ill will you stir up is stronger and lasts longer than any momentary change of opinion. It is much more powerful to get others to agree with you through your actions, without saying a word. Demonstrate, do not explicate (Greene 1998, p.69)."

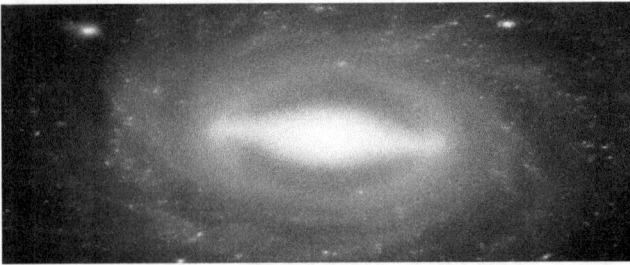

174

Yashu'a (Jesus) said: "A new commandment I give unto you, that ye love one another; as I have loved you, that ye also love one another."

ASSASSINS of DISOBEDIENCE!
Invoking the Power of the Most High Through Obedience, is the Key to Living Your Best Life
as the Supreme Ingredient!
Heaven or Hell?

CHILDREN OF THE MOST HIGH:
PRISTINE YOUTH AND FAMILY SOLUTIONS, LLC.
SONS AND DAUGHTERS OF THE MOST HIGH PUBLISHERS ®

Oh, Gracious Most High Heavenly father, Holy is your name,
Your Will Be Done Now and Forever!
Yashu'a (Jesus) said: *"Thou shalt love the Most High Heavenly Father, thy Sustainer with all thy heart, and with all thy soul, and with all thy mind. Thou shalt love thy neighbour as thyself."*

In the KJV bible book of Matthew chapter 7 verses 16-20; the Messiah Yashu'a (Jesus) said: "Beware of false prophets, which come to you in sheep's clothing, but inwardly they are ravening wolves."

"Ye shall know them by their fruits (καρπός **Karpos** is the KJV bible Greek Strong's Concordance#**2590** word for "**fruits**" in this verse, and it means: **work**, **act**, **actions**, **deeds**). Do men gather grapes of thorns, or figs of thistles? Even so every good tree bringeth forth good fruit; but a corrupt tree bringeth forth evil fruit."

175

Yashu'a (Jesus) said: *"A new commandment I give unto you, that ye love one another; as I have loved you, that ye also love one another."*

ASSASSINS of DISOBEDIENCE!
Invoking the Power of the Most High Through Obedience, is the Key to Living Your Best Life
as the Supreme Ingredient!
Heaven or Hell?

CHILDREN OF THE MOST HIGH:
PRISTINE YOUTH AND FAMILY SOLUTIONS, LLC.
SONS AND DAUGHTERS OF THE MOST HIGH PUBLISHERS

Oh, Gracious Most High Heavenly father, Holy is your name,
Your Will Be Done Now and Forever!
Yashu'a (Jesus) said: *"Thou shalt love the Most High Heavenly Father, thy Sustainer with all thy heart, and with all thy soul, and with all thy mind. Thou shalt love thy neighbour as thyself."*

"A good tree cannot bring forth evil fruit, neither can a corrupt tree bring forth good fruit. Every tree that bringeth not forth good fruit is hewn down, and cast into the fire. Wherefore by their <u>fruits</u> (καρπός **Karpos** means: **work**, **act**, **action**s, **deeds**) ye shall know them.

176

Yashu'a (Jesus) said: *"A new commandment I give unto you, that ye love one another; as I have loved you, that ye also love one another."*

ASSASSINS of DISOBEDIENCE!
Invoking the Power of the Most High Through Obedience, is the Key to Living Your Best Life
as the Supreme Ingredient!
Heaven or Hell?

CHILDREN OF THE MOST HIGH:
PRISTINE YOUTH AND FAMILY SOLUTIONS, LLC.
SONS AND DAUGHTERS OF THE MOST HIGH PUBLISHERS ®

Oh, Gracious Most High Heavenly father, Holy is your name,
Your Will Be Done Now and Forever!
Yashu'a (Jesus) said: "Thou shalt love the Most High Heavenly Father, thy Sustainer with all
thy heart, and with all thy soul, and with all thy mind. Thou shalt love
thy neighbour as thyself."

"The **tenth (10) out of 48 Laws of Power** is: **INFECTION: AVOID THE UNHAPPY AND UNLUCKY**. You can die from someone else's misery—emotional states are as infectious as diseases. You may feel you are helping the drowning man but you are only precipitating your own disaster. The unfortunate sometimes draw misfortune on themselves; they will also draw it on you. Associate with the happy and fortunate instead, (Greene 1998, p.76)." The Messiah Yashu'a (Jesus) said: "Peace I leave with you, my peace I give unto you: not as the world giveth, give I unto you. Let not your heart be troubled, neither let it be afraid, KJV John 14:27."

177

Yashu'a (Jesus) said: "A new commandment I give unto
you, that ye love one another; as I have loved you,
that ye also love one another."

ASSASSINS of DISOBEDIENCE!
Invoking the Power of the Most High Through Obedience, is the Key to Living Your Best Life
as the Supreme Ingredient!
Heaven or Hell?

CHILDREN OF THE MOST HIGH:
PRISTINE YOUTH AND FAMILY SOLUTIONS, LLC.
SONS AND DAUGHTERS OF THE MOST HIGH PUBLISHERS ®

Oh, Gracious Most High Heavenly father, Holy is your name,
Your Will Be Done Now and Forever!
Yashu'a (Jesus) said: *"Thou shalt love the Most High Heavenly Father, thy Sustainer with all*
thy heart, and with all thy soul, and with all thy mind. Thou shalt love
thy neighbour as thyself."

"Finally, brethren, whatsoever things are true, whatsoever things [are] honest, whatsoever things [are] just, whatsoever things [are] pure, whatsoever things [are] lovely, whatsoever things [are] of good report; if [there be] any virtue, and if [there be] any praise, think on these things, KJV Philippians 4:8." "A merry heart doeth good [like] a medicine: but a broken spirit drieth the bones, KJV Proverbs 17:22." The Messiah Yashu'a (Jesus) said: "**Either make the tree good, and his fruit good; or else make the tree corrupt, and his fruit corrupt: for the tree is known by [his] fruit. O generation of vipers, how can ye, being evil, speak good things? for out of the abundance of the heart the mouth speaketh. A good man out of the good treasure of the heart bringeth forth good things: and an evil man out of the evil treasure bringeth forth evil things.**"

178

Yashu'a (Jesus) said: *"A new commandment I give unto you, that ye love one another; as I have loved you, that ye also love one another."*

ASSASSINS of DISOBEDIENCE!
Invoking the Power of the Most High Through Obedience, is the Key to Living Your Best Life
as the Supreme Ingredient!
Heaven or Hell?

CHILDREN OF THE MOST HIGH:
PRISTINE YOUTH AND FAMILY SOLUTIONS, LLC.
SONS AND DAUGHTERS OF THE MOST HIGH PUBLISHERS ®

Oh, Gracious Most High Heavenly father, Holy is your name,
Your Will Be Done Now and Forever!
Yashu'a (Jesus) said: "Thou shalt love the Most High Heavenly Father, thy Sustainer with all
thy heart, and with all thy soul, and with all thy mind. Thou shalt love
thy neighbour as thyself."

"But I say unto you, that every idle word that men shall speak, they shall give account thereof in the day of judgment. For by thy words thou shalt be justified, and by thy words thou shalt be condemned, KJV Matthew 12:33-37." "The **eleventh (11) out of 48 Laws of Power** is: **LEARN TO KEEP PEOPLE DEPENDENT ON YOU**. To maintain your independence, you must always be needed and wanted. The more you are relied on, the more freedom you have. Make people depend on you for their happiness and prosperity and you have nothing to fear. Never teach them enough so that they can do without you, (Greene 1998, p.82)." In the KJV bible book of Matthew chapter 24 verse 4; the Messiah Yashu'a (Jesus) said: "Take heed that no man deceives you."

179

Yashu'a (Jesus) said: "A new commandment I give unto you, that ye love one another; as I have loved you, that ye also love one another."

ASSASSINS of DISOBEDIENCE!
Invoking the Power of the Most High Through Obedience, is the Key to Living Your Best Life
as the Supreme Ingredient!
Heaven or Hell?

CHILDREN OF THE MOST HIGH:
PRISTINE YOUTH AND FAMILY SOLUTIONS, LLC.
SONS AND DAUGHTERS OF THE MOST HIGH PUBLISHERS ®

Oh, Gracious Most High Heavenly father, Holy is your name,
Your Will Be Done Now and Forever!
Yashu'a (Jesus) said: "Thou shalt love the Most High Heavenly Father, thy Sustainer with all
thy heart, and with all thy soul, and with all thy mind. Thou shalt love
thy neighbour as thyself."

"But we had the sentence of death in ourselves, that we should not trust in ourselves, but in God which raiseth the dead, 2 Corinthians 1:9." "The LORD [is] my rock, and my fortress, and my deliverer; my God, my strength, in whom I will trust; my buckler, and the horn of my salvation, [and] my high tower, Psalms 18:2." "Trust in the LORD with all thine heart; and lean not unto thine own understanding. In all thy ways acknowledge him, and he shall direct thy paths, Proverbs 3:5-6."

180

Yashu'a (Jesus) said: "A new commandment I give unto you, that ye love one another; as I have loved you, that ye also love one another."

ASSASSINS of DISOBEDIENCE!
Invoking the Power of the Most High Through Obedience, is the Key to Living Your Best Life
as the Supreme Ingredient!
Heaven or Hell?

CHILDREN OF THE MOST HIGH:
PRISTINE YOUTH AND FAMILY SOLUTIONS, LLC.
SONS AND DAUGHTERS OF THE MOST HIGH PUBLISHERS ®

Oh, Gracious Most High Heavenly father, Holy is your name,
Your Will Be Done Now and Forever!
Yashu'a (Jesus) said: "Thou shalt love the Most High Heavenly Father, thy Sustainer with all
thy heart, and with all thy soul, and with all thy mind. Thou shalt love
thy neighbour as thyself."

"The **twelfth (12) out of 48 Laws of Power** is: <u>USE SELECTIVE HONESTY AND GENEROSITY TO DISARM YOUR VICTIM</u>. One sincere and honest move will cover over dozens of dishonest ones. Open-hearted gestures of honesty and generosity bring down the guard of even the most suspicious people. Once your selective honesty opens a hole in their armor, you can deceive and manipulate them at will. A timely gift—a Trojan horse—will serve the same purpose, (Greene 1998, p.89)." In the KJV bible book of Matthew chapter 24 verse 4; the Messiah Yashu'a (Jesus) said: "Take heed that no man deceives you."

181

Yashu'a (Jesus) said: "A new commandment I give unto you, that ye love one another; as I have loved you, that ye also love one another."

ASSASSINS of DISOBEDIENCE!
Invoking the Power of the Most High Through Obedience, is the Key to Living Your Best Life
as the Supreme Ingredient!
Heaven or Hell?

CHILDREN OF THE MOST HIGH:
PRISTINE YOUTH AND FAMILY SOLUTIONS, LLC.
SONS AND DAUGHTERS OF THE MOST HIGH PUBLISHERS ®

Oh, Gracious Most High Heavenly father, Holy is your name,
Your Will Be Done Now and Forever!
Yashu'a (Jesus) said: "Thou shalt love the Most High Heavenly Father, thy Sustainer with all
thy heart, and with all thy soul, and with all thy mind. Thou shalt love
thy neighbour as thyself."

In the KJV bible book of Proverbs chapter 6 verses 12-19; it states: "**A naughty person**, **a wicked man**, walketh with a **froward** (the word: "**froward**" is the KJV bible Hebrew Strong's Concordance#**6143** word: עִקְּשׁוּת `Iqqeshuwth and means: **distortion, crookedness, and perversity**) **mouth**. He winketh with his eyes, he speaketh with his feet, he teacheth with his fingers." "**Frowardness** (תַּהְפֻּכוֹת **Tahpukah, means: perversity, perverse thing**) **is in his heart**, **he deviseth mischief continually**; **he soweth discord**."

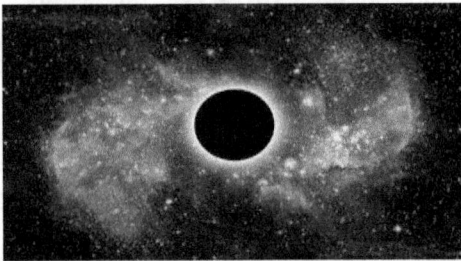

182

Yashu'a (Jesus) said: "A new commandment I give unto you, that ye love one another; as I have loved you, that ye also love one another."

ASSASSINS of DISOBEDIENCE!
Invoking the Power of the Most High Through Obedience, is the Key to Living Your Best Life
as the Supreme Ingredient!
Heaven or Hell?

CHILDREN OF THE MOST HIGH:
PRISTINE YOUTH AND FAMILY SOLUTIONS, LLC.
SONS AND DAUGHTERS OF THE MOST HIGH PUBLISHERS

Oh, Gracious Most High Heavenly father, Holy is your name,
Your Will Be Done Now and Forever!
Yashu'a (Jesus) said: "Thou shalt love the Most High Heavenly Father, thy Sustainer with all
thy heart, and with all thy soul, and with all thy mind. Thou shalt love
thy neighbour as thyself."

Therefore, shall his calamity come suddenly; suddenly shall he be broken without remedy, KJV Proverbs 6:15." "These six things doth the Lord hate: yea, seven are an abomination unto him: A proud look, **a lying tongue**, and hands that shed innocent blood, **An heart that deviseth wicked imaginations**, feet that be swift in running to mischief, **A false witness that speaketh lies**, and he that soweth discord among brethren, KJV Proverbs 6:16-19."

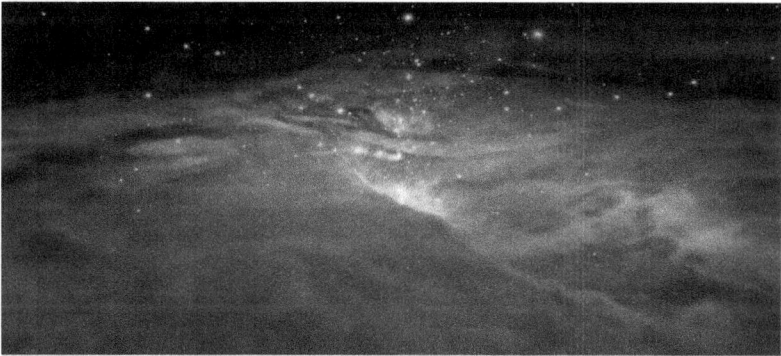

183

Yashu'a (Jesus) said: "A new commandment I give unto you, that ye love one another; as I have loved you, that ye also love one another."

ASSASSINS of DISOBEDIENCE!
Invoking the Power of the Most High Through Obedience, is the Key to Living Your Best Life
as the Supreme Ingredient!
Heaven or Hell?

CHILDREN OF THE MOST HIGH:
PRISTINE YOUTH AND FAMILY SOLUTIONS, LLC.
SONS AND DAUGHTERS OF THE MOST HIGH PUBLISHERS ®

Oh, Gracious Most High Heavenly father, Holy is your name,
Your Will Be Done Now and Forever!
Yashu'a (Jesus) said: *"Thou shalt love the Most High Heavenly Father, thy Sustainer with all*
thy heart, and with all thy soul, and with all thy mind. Thou shalt love
thy neighbour as thyself."

"The **thirteenth (13) out of 48 Laws of Power** is: <u>**WHEN ASKING FOR HELP, APPEAL TO PEOPLE'S SELF-INTEREST, NEVER TO THEIR MERCY OR GRATITUDE**</u>. If you need to turn to an ally for help, do not bother to remind him of your past assistance and good deeds. He will find a way to ignore you. Instead, uncover something in your request, or in your alliance with him, that will benefit him, and emphasize it out of all proportion. He will respond enthusiastically when he sees something to be gained for himself, (Greene 1998, p.95)." In the KJV bible book of Matthew chapter 24 verse 4; the Messiah Yashu'a (Jesus) said: "Take heed that no man deceives you."

184

Yashu'a (Jesus) said: "A new commandment I give unto you, that ye love one another; as I have loved you, that ye also love one another."

ASSASSINS of DISOBEDIENCE!
Invoking the Power of the Most High Through Obedience, is the Key to Living Your Best Life
as the Supreme Ingredient!
Heaven or Hell?

CHILDREN OF THE MOST HIGH:
PRISTINE YOUTH AND FAMILY SOLUTIONS, LLC.
SONS AND DAUGHTERS OF THE MOST HIGH PUBLISHERS ®

Oh, Gracious Most High Heavenly father, Holy is your name,
Your Will Be Done Now and Forever!
Yashu'a (Jesus) said: "Thou shalt love the Most High Heavenly Father, thy Sustainer with all
thy heart, and with all thy soul, and with all thy mind. Thou shalt love
thy neighbour as thyself."

The Messiah Yashu'a (Jesus) said: But I say unto you, Love your enemies, bless them that curse you, do good to them that hate you, and <u>pray for them which despitefully use you</u>, and persecute you; That ye may be the children of your Father which is in heaven: for he maketh his sun to rise on the evil and on the good, and sendeth rain on the just and on the unjust, KJV Matthew 5:44-45."

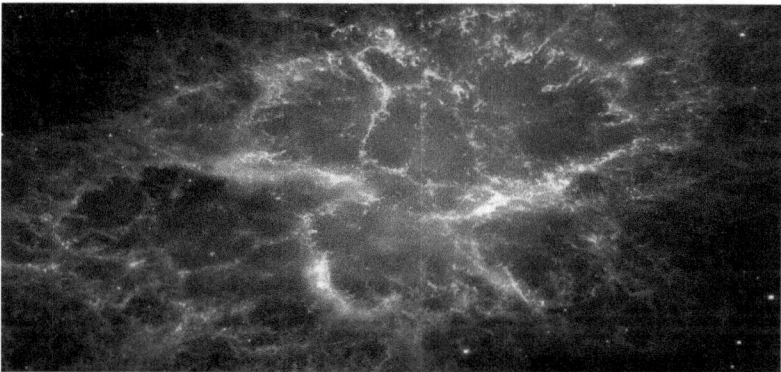

185

Yashu'a (Jesus) said: "A new commandment I give unto
you, that ye love one another; as I have loved you,
that ye also love one another."

ASSASSINS of DISOBEDIENCE!
Invoking the Power of the Most High Through Obedience, is the Key to Living Your Best Life
as the Supreme Ingredient!
Heaven or Hell?

CHILDREN OF THE MOST HIGH:
PRISTINE YOUTH AND FAMILY SOLUTIONS, LLC.
SONS AND DAUGHTERS OF THE MOST HIGH PUBLISHERS ®

Oh, Gracious Most High Heavenly father, Holy is your name,
Your Will Be Done Now and Forever!
Yashu'a (Jesus) said: *"Thou shalt love the Most High Heavenly Father, thy Sustainer with all*
thy heart, and with all thy soul, and with all thy mind. Thou shalt love
thy neighbour as thyself."

"The **fourteenth (14) out of 48 Laws of Power** is: <u>**POSE AS A FRIEND, WORK AS A SPY**</u>. Knowing about your rival is critical. Use spies to gather valuable information that will keep you a step ahead. Better still: Play the spy yourself. In polite social encounters, learn to probe. Ask indirect questions to get people to reveal their weaknesses and intentions. There is no occasion that is not an opportunity for artful spying, (Greene 1998, p. 101)." In the KJV bible book of Psalms 37 verse 32; it states: "The wicked <u>**watcheth**</u> (צָפָה **Tsaphah, means to spy on**) the righteous, and seeketh to slay him." The KJV bible Hebrew Strong's Concordance **#6822** for the word "**watcheth**" is: צָפָה **Tsaphah,** and means: **to spy on, to look out or about, spy, keep watch, observe, watch, to keep watch on, to watch, watch closely.**"

186

Yashu'a (Jesus) said: "A new commandment I give unto
you, that ye love one another; as I have loved you,
that ye also love one another."

ASSASSINS of DISOBEDIENCE!
Invoking the Power of the Most High Through Obedience, is the Key to Living Your Best Life
as the Supreme Ingredient!
Heaven or Hell?

CHILDREN OF THE MOST HIGH:
PRISTINE YOUTH AND FAMILY SOLUTIONS, LLC.
SONS AND DAUGHTERS OF THE MOST HIGH PUBLISHERS ®

Oh, Gracious Most High Heavenly father, Holy is your name,
Your Will Be Done Now and Forever!
Yashu'a (Jesus) said: *"Thou shalt love the Most High Heavenly Father, thy Sustainer with all thy heart, and with all thy soul, and with all thy mind. Thou shalt love thy neighbour as thyself."*

"The **fifteenth (15) out of 48 Laws of Power** is: <u>**CRUSH YOUR ENEMY TOTALLY**</u>. All great leaders since Moses have known that a feared enemy must be crushed completely. (Sometimes they have learned this the hard way.) If one ember is left alight, no matter how dimly it smolders, a fire will eventually break out. More is lost through stopping halfway than through total annihilation: The enemy will recover, and will seek revenge. Crush him, not only in body but in spirit, (Greene 1998, p.107)."

187

Yashu'a (Jesus) said: *"A new commandment I give unto you, that ye love one another; as I have loved you, that ye also love one another."*

CHILDREN OF THE MOST HIGH:
PRISTINE YOUTH AND FAMILY SOLUTIONS, LLC.
SONS AND DAUGHTERS OF THE MOST HIGH PUBLISHERS ®

Oh, Gracious Most High Heavenly father, Holy is your name,
Your Will Be Done Now and Forever!
Yashu'a (Jesus) said: *"Thou shalt love the Most High Heavenly Father, thy Sustainer with all thy heart, and with all thy soul, and with all thy mind. Thou shalt love thy neighbour as thyself."*

In the KJV bible book of Matthew chapter 5 verses 43-45; the Messiah Yashu'a (Jesus) said: "Ye have heard that it hath been said, thou shalt love thy neighbour, and hate thine enemy. But I say unto you, love your enemies, bless them that curse you, do good to them that hate you, and <u>pray for them which despitefully use you</u>, and persecute you. That ye may be the children of your Father which is in heaven: for he maketh his sun to rise on the evil and on the good, and sendeth rain on the just and on the unjust."

188

Yashu'a (Jesus) said: "A new commandment I give unto you, that ye love one another; as I have loved you, that ye also love one another."

ASSASSINS of DISOBEDIENCE!
Invoking the Power of the Most High Through Obedience, is the Key to Living Your Best Life
as the Supreme Ingredient!
Heaven or Hell?

CHILDREN OF THE MOST HIGH:
PRISTINE YOUTH AND FAMILY SOLUTIONS, LLC.
SONS AND DAUGHTERS OF THE MOST HIGH PUBLISHERS ®

Oh, Gracious Most High Heavenly father, Holy is your name,
Your Will Be Done Now and Forever!
Yashu'a (Jesus) said: "Thou shalt love the Most High Heavenly Father, thy Sustainer with all
thy heart, and with all thy soul, and with all thy mind. Thou shalt love
thy neighbour as thyself."

"The **sixteenth (16) out of 48 Laws of Power** is: <u>USE ABSENCE TO INCREASE RESPECT AND HONOR</u>. Too much circulation makes the price go down: The more you are seen and heard from, the more common you appear. If you are already established in a group, temporary withdrawal from it will make you more talked about, even more admired. You must learn when to leave. **Create value through scarcity**, (Greene 1998, p. 115)." The Online American Heritage Dictionary (2020) defines **scarcity** as: "Insufficiency of amount or supply; shortage: a scarcity of food that was caused by drought. Rarity of appearance or occurrence: antiques that are valued for their scarcity."

Yashu'a (Jesus) said: "A new commandment I give unto
you, that ye love one another; as I have loved you,
that ye also love one another."

ASSASSINS of DISOBEDIENCE!
Invoking the Power of the Most High Through Obedience, is the Key to Living Your Best Life
as the Supreme Ingredient!
Heaven or Hell?

CHILDREN OF THE MOST HIGH:
PRISTINE YOUTH AND FAMILY SOLUTIONS, LLC.
SONS AND DAUGHTERS OF THE MOST HIGH PUBLISHERS ®

Oh, Gracious Most High Heavenly father, Holy is your name,
Your Will Be Done Now and Forever!
Yashu'a (Jesus) said: "Thou shalt love the Most High Heavenly Father, thy Sustainer with all
thy heart, and with all thy soul, and with all thy mind. Thou shalt love
thy neighbour as thyself."

In the KJV bible book of Matthew chapter 6 verse 1; the Messiah Yashu'a (Jesus) said: "Take heed that ye do not your alms before men, to be seen of them: otherwise ye have no reward of your Father which is in heaven." "**[Let] nothing [be done] through strife or vainglory**; but in lowliness of mind let each esteem other better than themselves. Look not every man on his own things, but every man also on the things of others. Let this mind be in you, which was also in Christ Jesus, Philippians 2:3-5." In the aforementioned verses, the KJV bible Greek Strong's Concordance#2754 "κενοδοξία **Kenodoxia**" is the word for "**vainglory**" κενοδοξία **Kenodoxia** means: **self-conceit, groundless self-esteem, empty pride, vain-glory, a vain opinion; error**."

Yashu'a (Jesus) said: "A new commandment I give unto you, that ye love one another; as I have loved you, that ye also love one another."

ASSASSINS of DISOBEDIENCE!
Invoking the Power of the Most High Through Obedience, is the Key to Living Your Best Life
as the Supreme Ingredient!
Heaven or Hell?

CHILDREN OF THE MOST HIGH:
PRISTINE YOUTH AND FAMILY SOLUTIONS, LLC.
SONS AND DAUGHTERS OF THE MOST HIGH PUBLISHERS ®

Oh, Gracious Most High Heavenly father, Holy is your name,
Your Will Be Done Now and Forever!
Yashu'a (Jesus) said: "Thou shalt love the Most High Heavenly Father, thy Sustainer with all
thy heart, and with all thy soul, and with all thy mind. Thou shalt love
thy neighbour as thyself."

"The **seventeenth (17) out of 48 Laws of Power** is: <u>**KEEP OTHERS IN SUSPENDED TERROR: CULTIVATE AN AIR OF UNPREDICTABILITY**</u>. Humans are creatures of habit with an insatiable need to see familiarity in other people's actions. Your predictability gives them a sense of control. Turn the tables: Be deliberately unpredictable. **Behavior that seems to have no consistency or purpose will keep them off-balance, and they will wear themselves out trying to explain your moves**. Taken to an extreme, **this strategy can intimidate and terrorize**, (Greene 1998, p. 123)." In the KJV bible book of 2nd Timothy chapter 1 verse 7; it states: "For God hath not given us the spirit of fear; but of power, and of love, and of a sound mind."

191

Yashu'a (Jesus) said: "A new commandment I give unto
you, that ye love one another; as I have loved you,
that ye also love one another."

ASSASSINS of DISOBEDIENCE!
Invoking the Power of the Most High Through Obedience, is the Key to Living Your Best Life
as the Supreme Ingredient!
Heaven or Hell?

CHILDREN OF THE MOST HIGH:
PRISTINE YOUTH AND FAMILY SOLUTIONS, LLC.
SONS AND DAUGHTERS OF THE MOST HIGH PUBLISHERS ®

Oh, Gracious Most High Heavenly father, Holy is your name,
Your Will Be Done Now and Forever!
Yashu'a (Jesus) said: *"Thou shalt love the Most High Heavenly Father, thy Sustainer with all*
thy heart, and with all thy soul, and with all thy mind. Thou shalt love
thy neighbour as thyself."

In the KJV bible book of Job chapter 15 verse 35; it states: "They conceive mischief, and bring forth vanity, and their belly prepareth deceit." "His mouth is full of cursing and deceit and fraud: under his tongue [is] mischief and vanity, KJV Psalms 10:7." "He that worketh deceit shall not dwell within my house: he that telleth lies shall not tarry in my sight, KJV Psalms 101:7." "Deceit [is] in the heart of them that imagine evil: but to the counsellors of peace [is] joy, KJV Proverbs 12:20." "[Whose] hatred is covered by deceit, his wickedness shall be showed before the [whole] congregation, KJV Proverbs 26:26." "Thou lovest all devouring words, O [thou] deceitful tongue, Psalms 52:4." "For the mouth of the wicked and the mouth of the deceitful are opened against me: they have spoken against me with a lying tongue, KJV Psalms 109:2."

192

Yashu'a (Jesus) said: *"A new commandment I give unto you, that ye love one another; as I have loved you, that ye also love one another."*

ASSASSINS of DISOBEDIENCE!
*Invoking the Power of the Most High Through Obedience, is the Key to Living Your Best Life
as the Supreme Ingredient!*
Heaven or Hell?

CHILDREN OF THE MOST HIGH:
PRISTINE YOUTH AND FAMILY SOLUTIONS, LLC.
SONS AND DAUGHTERS OF THE MOST HIGH PUBLISHERS ®

*Oh, Gracious Most High Heavenly father, Holy is your name,
Your Will Be Done Now and Forever!*
Yashu'a (Jesus) said: *"Thou shalt love the Most High Heavenly Father, thy Sustainer with all
thy heart, and with all thy soul, and with all thy mind. Thou shalt love
thy neighbour as thyself."*

"The **eighteenth (18) out of 48 Laws of Power** is: <u>**DO NOT BUILD FORTRESSES TO PROTECT YOURSELF— ISOLATION IS DANGEROUS**</u>. The world is dangerous and enemies are everywhere—everyone has to protect themselves. A fortress seems the safest. But isolation exposes you to more dangers than it Protects you from—it cuts you off from valuable information, it makes you conspicuous and an easy target. Better to circulate among people, find allies, mingle. You are shielded from your enemies by the crowd, (Greene 1998, p. 130)." In the KJV bible book of Jeremiah chapter 16 verse 19; it states: "O LORD, my strength, and my fortress, and my refuge in the day of affliction, the Gentiles shall come unto thee from the ends of the earth, and shall say, Surely our fathers have inherited lies, vanity, and [things] wherein [there is] no profit."

193

*Yashu'a (Jesus) said: "A new commandment I give unto
you, that ye love one another; as I have loved you,
that ye also love one another."*

ASSASSINS of DISOBEDIENCE!
Invoking the Power of the Most High Through Obedience, is the Key to Living Your Best Life
as the Supreme Ingredient!
Heaven or Hell?

CHILDREN OF THE MOST HIGH:
PRISTINE YOUTH AND FAMILY SOLUTIONS, LLC.
SONS AND DAUGHTERS OF THE MOST HIGH PUBLISHERS

Oh, Gracious Most High Heavenly father, Holy is your name,
Your Will Be Done Now and Forever!
Yashu'a (Jesus) said: *"Thou shalt love the Most High Heavenly Father, thy Sustainer with all thy heart, and with all thy soul, and with all thy mind. Thou shalt love thy neighbour as thyself."*

"And he said, The LORD [is] my rock, and my fortress, and my deliverer, KJV 2nd Samuel 22:2." "The LORD [is] my rock, and my fortress, and my deliverer; my God, my strength, in whom I will trust; my buckler, and the horn of my salvation, [and] my high tower, KJV Psalms 18:2. "For thou [art] my rock and my fortress; therefore for thy name's sake lead me, and guide me, KJV Psalms 31:3." "Be thou my strong habitation, whereunto I may continually resort: thou hast given commandment to save me; for thou [art] my rock and my fortress, KJV Psalms 71:3." "I will say of the LORD, [He is] my refuge and my fortress: my God; in him will I trust, KJV Psalms 91:2."

194

Yashu'a (Jesus) said: "A new commandment I give unto you, that ye love one another; as I have loved you, that ye also love one another."

ASSASSINS of DISOBEDIENCE!
Invoking the Power of the Most High Through Obedience, is the Key to Living Your Best Life
as the Supreme Ingredient!
Heaven or Hell?

CHILDREN OF THE MOST HIGH:
PRISTINE YOUTH AND FAMILY SOLUTIONS, LLC.
SONS AND DAUGHTERS OF THE MOST HIGH PUBLISHERS ®

Oh, Gracious Most High Heavenly father, Holy is your name,
Your Will Be Done Now and Forever!
Yashu'a (Jesus) said: "Thou shalt love the Most High Heavenly Father, thy Sustainer with all
thy heart, and with all thy soul, and with all thy mind. Thou shalt love
thy neighbour as thyself."

"The **nineteenth (19) out of 48 Laws of Power** is: **KNOW WHO YOU'RE DEALING WITH—DO NOT OFFEND THE WRONG PERSON**. There are many different kinds of people in the world, and you can never assume that everyone will react to your strategies in the same way. **Deceive or outmaneuver some people** and they will spend the rest of their lives seeking revenge. They are wolves in lambs' clothing. Choose your victims and opponents carefully, then—never of fend or deceive the wrong person, (Greene 1998, p. 137)." In the KJV bible book of Job chapter 15 verse 35; it states: "They [the wicked] conceive mischief, and bring forth vanity, and their belly prepareth deceit." "His mouth is full of cursing and deceit and fraud: under his tongue [is] mischief and vanity, KJV Psalms 10:7."

195

Yashu'a (Jesus) said: "A new commandment I give unto you, that ye love one another; as I have loved you, that ye also love one another."

ASSASSINS of DISOBEDIENCE!
Invoking the Power of the Most High Through Obedience, is the Key to Living Your Best Life
as the Supreme Ingredient!
Heaven or Hell?

CHILDREN OF THE MOST HIGH:
PRISTINE YOUTH AND FAMILY SOLUTIONS, LLC.
SONS AND DAUGHTERS OF THE MOST HIGH PUBLISHERS ®

Oh, Gracious Most High Heavenly father, Holy is your name,
Your Will Be Done Now and Forever!
Yashu'a (Jesus) said: *"Thou shalt love the Most High Heavenly Father, thy Sustainer with all*
thy heart, and with all thy soul, and with all thy mind. Thou shalt love
thy neighbour as thyself."

"The **twentieth (20) out of 48 Laws of Power** is: <u>**DO NOT**</u> <u>**COMMIT TO ANYONE**</u>. If you allow people to feel they possess you to any degree, you lose all power over them. By not committing your affections, they will only try harder to win you over. Stay aloof and you gain the power that comes from their attention and frustrated desire. Play the Virgin Queen: **Give them hope but never satisfaction**, (Greene 1998, p. 145)." In the KJV bible book of Proverbs chapter 16 verse 3; it states: "<u>**Commit thy works unto the LORD**</u>, and thy thoughts shall be established." In the KJV bible book of Job chapter 15 verse 35; it states: "They [the wicked] conceive mischief, and bring forth vanity, and their belly prepareth deceit."

Yashu'a (Jesus) said: *"A new commandment I give unto*
you, that ye love one another; as I have loved you,
that ye also love one another."

ASSASSINS of DISOBEDIENCE!
Invoking the Power of the Most High Through Obedience, is the Key to Living Your Best Life
as the Supreme Ingredient!
Heaven or Hell?

CHILDREN OF THE MOST HIGH:
PRISTINE YOUTH AND FAMILY SOLUTIONS, LLC.
SONS AND DAUGHTERS OF THE MOST HIGH PUBLISHERS ®

Oh, Gracious Most High Heavenly father, Holy is your name,
Your Will Be Done Now and Forever!
Yashu'a (Jesus) said: "Thou shalt love the Most High Heavenly Father, thy Sustainer with all
thy heart, and with all thy soul, and with all thy mind. Thou shalt love
thy neighbour as thyself."

"The **twenty-first (21) out of 48 Laws of Power** is: <u>**PLAY A SUCKER TO CATCH A SUCKER—SEEM DUMBER THAN YOUR MARK**</u>. No one likes feeling stupider than the next person. The trick, then, is to make your victims feel smart—and not just smart, but smarter than you are. Once convinced of this, they will never suspect that you may have ulterior motives, (Greene 1998, p. 156)."

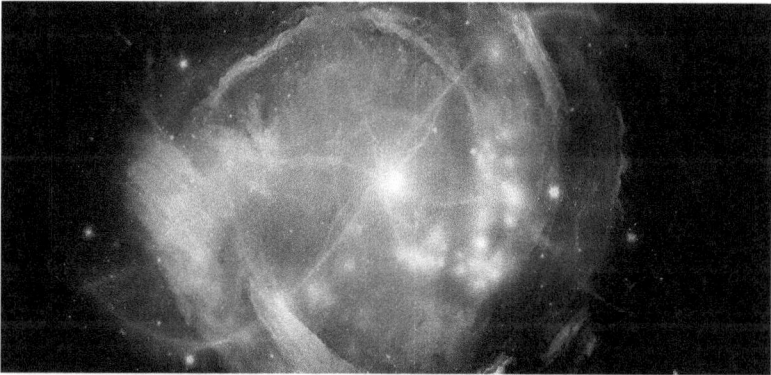

197

Yashu'a (Jesus) said: "A new commandment I give unto
you, that ye love one another; as I have loved you,
that ye also love one another."

ASSASSINS of DISOBEDIENCE!
Invoking the Power of the Most High Through Obedience, is the Key to Living Your Best Life
as the Supreme Ingredient!
Heaven or Hell?

CHILDREN OF THE MOST HIGH:
PRISTINE YOUTH AND FAMILY SOLUTIONS, LLC.
SONS AND DAUGHTERS OF THE MOST HIGH PUBLISHERS ®

Oh, Gracious Most High Heavenly father, Holy is your name,
Your Will Be Done Now and Forever!
Yashu'a (Jesus) said: "Thou shalt love the Most High Heavenly Father, thy Sustainer with all
thy heart, and with all thy soul, and with all thy mind. Thou shalt love
thy neighbour as thyself."

In the KJV bible book of Job chapter 15 verse 35; it states: "They [the wicked] conceive mischief, and bring forth vanity, and their belly prepareth deceit." In the KJV bible book of Matthew chapter 5 verses 43-45; the Messiah Yashu'a (Jesus) said: "Ye have heard that it hath been said, thou shalt love thy neighbour, and hate thine enemy. But I say unto you, love your enemies, bless them that curse you, do good to them that hate you, and <u>pray for them which despitefully use you</u>, and persecute you. That ye may be the children of your Father which is in heaven: for he maketh his sun to rise on the evil and on the good, and sendeth rain on the just and on the unjust."

198

Yashu'a (Jesus) said: "A new commandment I give unto
you, that ye love one another; as I have loved you,
that ye also love one another."

ASSASSINS of DISOBEDIENCE!
Invoking the Power of the Most High Through Obedience, is the Key to Living Your Best Life
as the Supreme Ingredient!
Heaven or Hell?

CHILDREN OF THE MOST HIGH:
PRISTINE YOUTH AND FAMILY SOLUTIONS, LLC.
SONS AND DAUGHTERS OF THE MOST HIGH PUBLISHERS ®

Oh, Gracious Most High Heavenly father, Holy is your name,
Your Will Be Done Now and Forever!
Yashu'a (Jesus) said: "Thou shalt love the Most High Heavenly Father, thy Sustainer with all
thy heart, and with all thy soul, and with all thy mind. Thou shalt love
thy neighbour as thyself."

"The **twenty-second (22) out of 48 Laws of Power** is: <u>USE</u> <u>THE SURRENDER TACTIC: TRANSFORM</u> <u>WEAKNESS INTO POWERLAY</u>. When you are weaker, never fight for honor's sake; choose surrender instead. Surrender gives you time to recover, time to torment and irritate your conqueror, time to wait for his power to wane. Do not give him the satisfaction of fighting and defeating you—surrender first. By turning the other cheek, you infuriate and unsettle him. Make surrender a tool of power, (Greene 1998, p. 163)." In the KJV bible book of James chapter 4 verse 8; it states: "Draw nigh to God, and he will draw nigh to you. Cleanse [your] hands, [ye] sinners; and purify [your] hearts, [ye] double minded." "Submit yourselves therefore to God. Resist the devil, and he will flee from you, KJV James 4:7."

Yashu'a (Jesus) said: "A new commandment I give unto
you, that ye love one another; as I have loved you,
that ye also love one another."

ASSASSINS of DISOBEDIENCE!
Invoking the Power of the Most High Through Obedience, is the Key to Living Your Best Life
as the Supreme Ingredient!
Heaven or Hell?

CHILDREN OF THE MOST HIGH:
PRISTINE YOUTH AND FAMILY SOLUTIONS, LLC.
SONS AND DAUGHTERS OF THE MOST HIGH PUBLISHERS ®

Oh, Gracious Most High Heavenly father, Holy is your name,
Your Will Be Done Now and Forever!
Yashu'a (Jesus) said: "Thou shalt love the Most High Heavenly Father, thy Sustainer with all
thy heart, and with all thy soul, and with all thy mind. Thou shalt love
thy neighbour as thyself."

"The **twenty-third (23) out of 48 Laws of Power** is: <u>**CONCENTRATE YOUR FORCES**</u>. Conserve your forces and energies by keeping them concentrated at their strongest point. You gain more by finding a rich mine and mining it deeper, than by flitting from one shallow mine to another—intensity defeats extensity every time. When looking for sources of power to elevate you, find the one key patron, the fat cow who will give you milk for a long time to come, (Greene 1998, p. 171)." In the KJV bible book of Romans chapter 12 verse 2; it states: "And be not conformed to this world: but be ye transformed by the renewing of your mind, that ye may prove what [is] that good, and acceptable, and perfect, will of God."

Yashu'a (Jesus) said: "A new commandment I give unto
you, that ye love one another; as I have loved you,
that ye also love one another."

ASSASSINS of DISOBEDIENCE!
Invoking the Power of the Most High Through Obedience, is the Key to Living Your Best Life
as the Supreme Ingredient!
Heaven or Hell?

CHILDREN OF THE MOST HIGH:
PRISTINE YOUTH AND FAMILY SOLUTIONS, LLC.
SONS AND DAUGHTERS OF THE MOST HIGH PUBLISHERS ®

Oh, Gracious Most High Heavenly father, Holy is your name,
Your Will Be Done Now and Forever!
Yashu'a (Jesus) said: *"Thou shalt love the Most High Heavenly Father, thy Sustainer with all*
thy heart, and with all thy soul, and with all thy mind. Thou shalt love
thy neighbour as thyself."

"Thine, O LORD, [is] the greatness, and the power, and the glory, and the victory, and the majesty: for all [that is] in the heaven and in the earth [is thine]; thine [is] the kingdom, O LORD, and thou art exalted as head above all, KJV 1 Chronicles 29:11." "The **twenty-fourth (24) out of 48 Laws of Power** is: <u>**PLAY THE PERFECT COURTIER**</u>. The perfect **courtier** thrives in a world where everything revolves around power and political dexterity. He has mastered the art of indirection; he flatters, yields to superiors, and asserts power over others in the most oblique and graceful manner. Learn and apply the laws of **courtiership** and there will be no limit to how far you can rise in the court, (Greene 1998, p. 178)."

Yashu'a (Jesus) said: "A new commandment I give unto
you, that ye love one another; as I have loved you,
that ye also love one another."

ASSASSINS of DISOBEDIENCE!
Invoking the Power of the Most High Through Obedience, is the Key to Living Your Best Life
as the Supreme Ingredient!
Heaven or Hell?

CHILDREN OF THE MOST HIGH:
PRISTINE YOUTH AND FAMILY SOLUTIONS, LLC.
SONS AND DAUGHTERS OF THE MOST HIGH PUBLISHERS ®

Oh, Gracious Most High Heavenly father, Holy is your name,
Your Will Be Done Now and Forever!
Yashu'a (Jesus) said: "Thou shalt love the Most High Heavenly Father, thy Sustainer with all
thy heart, and with all thy soul, and with all thy mind. Thou shalt love
thy neighbour as thyself."

The Online American Heritage Dictionary defines the word: "courtier" as: **"One who seeks favor, especially by insincere flattery or obsequious behavior**." In the KJV bible book of Psalms chapter 12 verse 3; states: "The LORD **shall cut off all flattering lips**, [and] the tongue that speaketh proud things." In the KJV bible book of Psalms chapter 5 verse 9; it states: **"For [there is] no faithfulness in their mouth; their inward part [is] very wickedness; their throat [is] an open sepulchre; they flatter with their tongue**." "A man that **flattereth** his neighbour spreadeth a net for his feet, KJV Proverbs 29:5." "He that hateth dissembleth with his lips, and layeth up deceit within him."

202

Yashu'a (Jesus) said: "A new commandment I give unto you, that ye love one another; as I have loved you, that ye also love one another."

ASSASSINS of DISOBEDIENCE!
Invoking the Power of the Most High Through Obedience, is the Key to Living Your Best Life
as the Supreme Ingredient!
Heaven or Hell?

CHILDREN OF THE MOST HIGH:
PRISTINE YOUTH AND FAMILY SOLUTIONS, LLC.
SONS AND DAUGHTERS OF THE MOST HIGH PUBLISHERS ®

Oh, Gracious Most High Heavenly father, Holy is your name,
Your Will Be Done Now and Forever!
Yashu'a (Jesus) said: "Thou shalt love the Most High Heavenly Father, thy Sustainer with all
thy heart, and with all thy soul, and with all thy mind. Thou shalt love
thy neighbour as thyself."

"When he speaketh fair, believe him not: for [there are] seven abominations in his heart. [Whose] hatred is covered by deceit; his wickedness shall be shewed before the [whole] congregation. Whoso diggeth a pit shall fall therein: and he that rolleth a stone, it will return upon him. A lying tongue hateth [those that are] afflicted by it; and a flattering mouth worketh ruin. KJV Proverbs 26:24-28."

203

Yashu'a (Jesus) said: "A new commandment I give unto you, that ye love one another; as I have loved you, that ye also love one another."

ASSASSINS of DISOBEDIENCE!
Invoking the Power of the Most High Through Obedience, is the Key to Living Your Best Life
as the Supreme Ingredient!
Heaven or Hell?

CHILDREN OF THE MOST HIGH:
PRISTINE YOUTH AND FAMILY SOLUTIONS, LLC.
SONS AND DAUGHTERS OF THE MOST HIGH PUBLISHERS ®

Oh, Gracious Most High Heavenly father, Holy is your name,
Your Will Be Done Now and Forever!
Yashu'a (Jesus) said: *"Thou shalt love the Most High Heavenly Father, thy Sustainer with all*
thy heart, and with all thy soul, and with all thy mind. Thou shalt love
thy neighbour as thyself."

Chapter 7: Does the 25th to 48th Laws of Power Align with God's (אֱלֹהִים 'Elohiym) Commandments and Laws; and the Doctrine of the Most High that the Messiah Yashu'a (Jesus) Taught?

CHILDREN OF THE MOST HIGH:
PRISTINE YOUTH AND FAMILY SOLUTIONS, LLC.
SONS AND DAUGHTERS OF THE MOST HIGH PUBLISHERS ®

The Most High Heavenly Father is "The Protector."

"Because thou hast made the LORD, [which is] my refuge, [even] the Most High, thy habitation; There shall no evil befall thee, neither shall any plague come nigh thy dwelling. For he shall give his angels charge over thee, to keep thee in all thy ways, KJV Psalms 91:9-11."

204

Yashu'a (Jesus) said: "A new commandment I give unto you, that ye love one another; as I have loved you, that ye also love one another."

ASSASSINS of DISOBEDIENCE!
Invoking the Power of the Most High Through Obedience, is the Key to Living Your Best Life
as the Supreme Ingredient!
Heaven or Hell?

CHILDREN OF THE MOST HIGH:
PRISTINE YOUTH AND FAMILY SOLUTIONS, LLC.
SONS AND DAUGHTERS OF THE MOST HIGH PUBLISHERS ®

Oh, Gracious Most High Heavenly father, Holy is your name,
Your Will Be Done Now and Forever!
Yashu'a (Jesus) said: *"Thou shalt love the Most High Heavenly Father, thy Sustainer with all*
thy heart, and with all thy soul, and with all thy mind. Thou shalt love
thy neighbour as thyself."

"The **twenty-fifth (25) out of 48 Laws of Power** is: **RE-CREATE YOURSELF**. Do not accept the roles that society foists on you. Re-create yourself by forging a new identity, one that commands attention and never bores the audience. Be the master of your own image rather than letting others define it for you. Incorporate dramatic devices into your public gestures and actions—your power will be enhanced and your character will seem larger than life, (Greene 1998, p. 191)." According to Hughes (2019), "When a person is in position of power in society, it does not change a person, it publicly reveals who the person who sits in the seat of power really is."

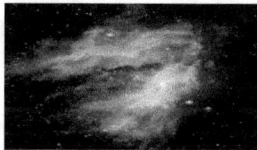

205

Yashu'a (Jesus) said: *"A new commandment I give unto you, that ye love one another; as I have loved you, that ye also love one another."*

ASSASSINS of DISOBEDIENCE!
Invoking the Power of the Most High Through Obedience, is the Key to Living Your Best Life
as the Supreme Ingredient!
Heaven or Hell?

CHILDREN OF THE MOST HIGH:
PRISTINE YOUTH AND FAMILY SOLUTIONS, LLC.
SONS AND DAUGHTERS OF THE MOST HIGH PUBLISHERS ®

Oh, Gracious Most High Heavenly father, Holy is your name,
Your Will Be Done Now and Forever!
Yashu'a (Jesus) said: *"Thou shalt love the Most High Heavenly Father, thy Sustainer with all*
thy heart, and with all thy soul, and with all thy mind. Thou shalt love
thy neighbour as thyself."

"Universal Love is against **I**ndividuality, which is why the word "Universe" consists of the two syllables of "**Uni**" (**One**) **Verse** (**Against**) or "**ALL**" or "**The ALL**" is against "**I**ndividuality" "**Pride**", and the **Me, Myself** and **I Trinity** are the children of the "**EGO**, the KJV bible Greek Strong's Concordance#**1473** word: ἐγώ **egō** which means: **I, me, my**; a primary pronoun of the first person **I**" and are the greatest barriers to experiencing the Most High Heavenly Father through obedience to the "**Will**" and "Commandments" of Most High, (Hughes 2019)."

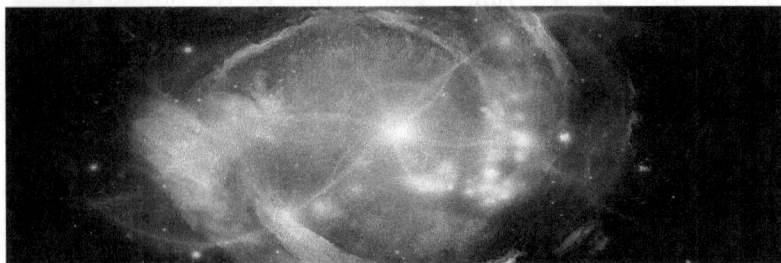

206

Yashu'a (Jesus) said: *"A new commandment I give unto you, that ye love one another; as I have loved you, that ye also love one another."*

ASSASSINS of DISOBEDIENCE!
Invoking the Power of the Most High Through Obedience, is the Key to Living Your Best Life
as the Supreme Ingredient!
Heaven or Hell?

CHILDREN OF THE MOST HIGH:
PRISTINE YOUTH AND FAMILY SOLUTIONS, LLC.
SONS AND DAUGHTERS OF THE MOST HIGH PUBLISHERS ®

Oh, Gracious Most High Heavenly father, Holy is your name,
Your Will Be Done Now and Forever!
Yashu'a (Jesus) said: "Thou shalt love the Most High Heavenly Father, thy Sustainer with all
thy heart, and with all thy soul, and with all thy mind. Thou shalt love
thy neighbour as thyself."

"Remember: it was the "**EGO**" of the great dragon, that old serpent called the devil and satan that filled his chest with "**Pride**", and he got **very hot with great wrath (when a person gets very angry, their body temperature rises and their personality can change from positive to negative)** before him and his **angels (ἄγγελος Angelos** means **messengers)** got into a war with the **Arch Angelic-Being Miykaa'el (Michael)** and his **Malaaikat (Angels/Messengers)** in the KJV bible book of Revelation chapter 12 verses 7-12. That's why the KJV bible book of Proverbs chapter 16 verse 18; states: "<u>**Pride goeth before destruction**</u>, **and a haughty** spirit before a fall."

207

Yashu'a (Jesus) said: "A new commandment I give unto you, that ye love one another; as I have loved you, that ye also love one another."

ASSASSINS of DISOBEDIENCE!
Invoking the Power of the Most High Through Obedience, is the Key to Living Your Best Life
as the Supreme Ingredient!
Heaven or Hell?

CHILDREN OF THE MOST HIGH:
PRISTINE YOUTH AND FAMILY SOLUTIONS, LLC.
SONS AND DAUGHTERS OF THE MOST HIGH PUBLISHERS ®

Oh, Gracious Most High Heavenly father, Holy is your name,
Your Will Be Done Now and Forever!
Yashu'a (Jesus) said: "Thou shalt love the Most High Heavenly Father, thy Sustainer with all
thy heart, and with all thy soul, and with all thy mind. Thou shalt love
thy neighbour as thyself."

The KJV bible Hebrew Strong's Concordance#1363 for the word phrase **"and a haughty"** is גֹּבַהּ **Gobahh and means arrogance, boastful, pouting out of anger, and full of pride**, (Hughes 2019)." "The KJV bible book of Revelation chapter 12 verses 7-12; states: "And there was war in heaven: Michael and his angels fought against the dragon; and the dragon fought and his angels, and prevailed not; neither was their place found any more in heaven. And the great dragon was cast out, that old serpent, called the Devil, and Satan, which deceiveth the whole world: he was cast out into the earth, and his angels were cast out with him. And I heard a loud voice saying in heaven, Now is come salvation, and strength, and the kingdom of our God, and the power of his Christ: for the accuser of our brethren is cast down, which accused them before our God day and night."

208

Yashu'a (Jesus) said: "A new commandment I give unto you, that ye love one another; as I have loved you, that ye also love one another."

ASSASSINS of DISOBEDIENCE!
Invoking the Power of the Most High Through Obedience, is the Key to Living Your Best Life
as the Supreme Ingredient!
Heaven or Hell?

CHILDREN OF THE MOST HIGH:
PRISTINE YOUTH AND FAMILY SOLUTIONS, LLC.
SONS AND DAUGHTERS OF THE MOST HIGH PUBLISHERS ®

Oh, Gracious Most High Heavenly father, Holy is your name,
Your Will Be Done Now and Forever!
Yashu'a (Jesus) said: *"Thou shalt love the Most High Heavenly Father, thy Sustainer with all*
thy heart, and with all thy soul, and with all thy mind. Thou shalt love
thy neighbour as thyself."

"And they overcame him by the blood of the Lamb, and by the word of their testimony; and they loved not their lives unto the death. Therefore rejoice, ye heavens, and ye that dwell in them. **Woe to the inhabitants of the earth and of the sea! for the devil is come down unto you, having great wrath, because he knoweth that he hath but a short time**." So, as it relates to a person who aspires to become an **Assassin of Disobedience**, **P**ride (**P**), **P**orne or Pornography (**P**) and the "**I**" principle that grows the "**I want to be seen or in-the-visual (individual)**" feeling of **P**ower (**P**) are all from the 9 Deadly Venoms of the great dragon which is revealed in the **3 PPPs'** being turned upside down as the numbers **666**. In the KJV bible book of **Revelation chapter 13 verse 18**; it states: "**Here is wisdom**, (Hughes 2019)."

Yashu'a (Jesus) said: *"A new commandment I give unto*
you, that ye love one another; as I have loved you,
that ye also love one another."

ASSASSINS of DISOBEDIENCE!
Invoking the Power of the Most High Through Obedience, is the Key to Living Your Best Life
as the Supreme Ingredient!
Heaven or Hell?

CHILDREN OF THE MOST HIGH:
PRISTINE YOUTH AND FAMILY SOLUTIONS, LLC.
SONS AND DAUGHTERS OF THE MOST HIGH PUBLISHERS ®

Oh, Gracious Most High Heavenly father, Holy is your name,
Your Will Be Done Now and Forever!
Yashu'a (Jesus) said: "Thou shalt love the Most High Heavenly Father, thy Sustainer with all
thy heart, and with all thy soul, and with all thy mind. Thou shalt love
thy neighbour as thyself."

"Let him that hath understanding count the number of the beast: **for it is the number of a man** (the KJV bible Greek Strong's Concordance#444 for the word "man" is ἄνθρωπος **Anthrōpos** and means a person or human being, whether male or female); and his (or her or their) number is Six hundred threescore and six (**666**). It is not possible to be an **Assassin of Disobedience** without surrendering the "**I**" principle and converting the "**EGO**" into the eternal obedient service to the "**Will**" of the Most High Heavenly Father. By surrendering the "**I**" principle, over time with a lot of personal hard work on yourself, a person may become free from all of the 9 Deadly Venoms of the Desires of the great dragon, that old serpent called the devil and satan, (Hughes 2019)."

210

Yashu'a (Jesus) said: "A new commandment I give unto you, that ye love one another; as I have loved you, that ye also love one another."

CHILDREN OF THE MOST HIGH:
PRISTINE YOUTH AND FAMILY SOLUTIONS, LLC.
SONS AND DAUGHTERS OF THE MOST HIGH PUBLISHERS

Oh, Gracious Most High Heavenly father, Holy is your name,
Your Will Be Done Now and Forever!
Yashu'a (Jesus) said: *"Thou shalt love the Most High Heavenly Father, thy Sustainer with all thy heart, and with all thy soul, and with all thy mind. Thou shalt love thy neighbour as thyself."*

"The **twenty-sixth (26) out of 48 Laws of Power** is: <u>**KEEP YOUR HANDS CLEAN**</u>. You must seem a paragon of civility and efficiency: Your hands are never soiled by mistakes and nasty deeds. <u>**Maintain such a spotless appearance by using others as scapegoats and cat's-paws to disguise your involvement**</u>, (Greene 1998, p. 200)." In the KJV bible book of Romans chapter 12 verses 17-21; it states: "Recompense to no man evil for evil. Provide things honest in the sight of all men. If it be possible, as much as lieth in you, live peaceably with all men. Dearly beloved, avenge not yourselves, but [rather] give place unto wrath: for it is written, Vengeance [is] mine; I will repay, saith the Lord."

Yashu'a (Jesus) said: *"A new commandment I give unto you, that ye love one another; as I have loved you, that ye also love one another."*

CHILDREN OF THE MOST HIGH:
PRISTINE YOUTH AND FAMILY SOLUTIONS, LLC.
SONS AND DAUGHTERS OF THE MOST HIGH PUBLISHERS &

*Oh, Gracious Most High Heavenly father, Holy is your name,
Your Will Be Done Now and Forever!*
Yashu'a (Jesus) said: *"Thou shalt love the Most High Heavenly Father, thy Sustainer with all thy heart, and with all thy soul, and with all thy mind. Thou shalt love thy neighbour as thyself."*

"Therefore, if thine enemy hunger, feed him; if he thirsts, give him drink: for in so doing thou shalt heap coals of fire on his head. Be not overcome of evil, but overcome evil with good."

"The **twenty-seventh (27) out of 48 Laws of Power** is: <u>**PLAY ON PEOPLE'S NEED TO BELIEVE TO CREATE A CULTLIKE FOLLOWING**</u>. People have an overwhelming desire to believe in something. **Become the focal point of such desire by offering them a cause, a new faith to follow.** Keep your words vague but full of promise; emphasize enthusiasm over rationality and clear thinking. Give your new disciples rituals to perform, ask them to make sacrifices on your behalf. In the absence of organized religion and grand causes, your new belief system will bring you untold power, (Greene 1998, p. 215)."

212

Yashu'a (Jesus) said: *"A new commandment I give unto you, that ye love one another; as I have loved you, that ye also love one another."*

ASSASSINS of DISOBEDIENCE!
Invoking the Power of the Most High Through Obedience, is the Key to Living Your Best Life
as the Supreme Ingredient!
Heaven or Hell?

CHILDREN OF THE MOST HIGH:
PRISTINE YOUTH AND FAMILY SOLUTIONS, LLC.
SONS AND DAUGHTERS OF THE MOST HIGH PUBLISHERS ®

Oh, Gracious Most High Heavenly father, Holy is your name,
Your Will Be Done Now and Forever!
Yashu'a (Jesus) said: *"Thou shalt love the Most High Heavenly Father, thy Sustainer with all*
thy heart, and with all thy soul, and with all thy mind. Thou shalt love
thy neighbour as thyself."

In the KJV bible book of John chapter 14 verse 6; the Messiah Yashu'a (Jesus) said: "I am the way, the truth, and the life: no man cometh unto the Father, but by me. In the KJV bible book of Matthew chapter 16 verse 24; the Messiah Yashu'a (Jesus) said: If any man will come after me, let him deny himself, and take up his cross, and follow me."

"The **twenty-eighth (28) out of 48 Laws of Power** is: **ENTER ACTION WITH BOLDNESS**. If you are unsure of a course of action, do not attempt it. Your doubts and hesitations will infect your execution. Timidity is dangerous: Better to enter with boldness. Any mistakes you commit through audacity are easily corrected with more audacity. Everyone admires the bold; no one honors the timid, (Greene 1998, p. 227)."

Yashu'a (Jesus) said: "A new commandment I give unto
you, that ye love one another; as I have loved you,
that ye also love one another."

ASSASSINS of DISOBEDIENCE!
Invoking the Power of the Most High Through Obedience, is the Key to Living Your Best Life
as the Supreme Ingredient!
Heaven or Hell?

CHILDREN OF THE MOST HIGH:
PRISTINE YOUTH AND FAMILY SOLUTIONS, LLC.
SONS AND DAUGHTERS OF THE MOST HIGH PUBLISHERS ®

Oh, Gracious Most High Heavenly father, Holy is your name,
Your Will Be Done Now and Forever!
Yashu'a (Jesus) said: "Thou shalt love the Most High Heavenly Father, thy Sustainer with all
thy heart, and with all thy soul, and with all thy mind. Thou shalt love
thy neighbour as thyself."

In the KJV bible book of John chapter 7 verse 26; it states: "But, lo, he speaketh boldly, and they say nothing unto him. Do the rulers know indeed that this is the very Christ?" "The wicked flee when no man pursueth: but the righteous are bold as a lion, Proverbs 28:1."

214

Yashu'a (Jesus) said: "A new commandment I give unto you, that ye love one another; as I have loved you, that ye also love one another."

ASSASSINS of DISOBEDIENCE!
Invoking the Power of the Most High Through Obedience, is the Key to Living Your Best Life
as the Supreme Ingredient!
Heaven or Hell?

CHILDREN OF THE MOST HIGH:
PRISTINE YOUTH AND FAMILY SOLUTIONS, LLC.
SONS AND DAUGHTERS OF THE MOST HIGH PUBLISHERS ®

Oh, Gracious Most High Heavenly father, Holy is your name,
Your Will Be Done Now and Forever!
Yashu'a (Jesus) said: "Thou shalt love the Most High Heavenly Father, thy Sustainer with all
thy heart, and with all thy soul, and with all thy mind. Thou shalt love
thy neighbour as thyself."

"The **twenty-nineth (29) out of 48 Laws of Power** is: <u>**PLAN**</u> <u>**ALL THE WAY TO THE END**</u>. The ending is everything. Plan all the way to it, taking into account all the possible consequences, obstacles, and twists of fortune that might reverse your hard work and give the glory to others. By planning to the end, you will not be overwhelmed by circumstances and you will know when to stop. Gently guide fortune and help determine the future by thinking far ahead, (Greene 1998, p. 236)." In the KJV bible book of Jeremiah chapter 29 verses 11-14; it states: "For I know the thoughts that I think toward you, saith the LORD, thoughts of peace, and not of evil, to give you an expected end. Then shall ye call upon me, and ye shall go and pray unto me, and I will hearken unto you."

Yashu'a (Jesus) said: "A new commandment I give unto
you, that ye love one another; as I have loved you,
that ye also love one another."

ASSASSINS of DISOBEDIENCE!
Invoking the Power of the Most High Through Obedience, is the Key to Living Your Best Life
as the Supreme Ingredient!
Heaven or Hell?

CHILDREN OF THE MOST HIGH:
PRISTINE YOUTH AND FAMILY SOLUTIONS, LLC.
SONS AND DAUGHTERS OF THE MOST HIGH PUBLISHERS ®

Oh, Gracious Most High Heavenly father, Holy is your name,
Your Will Be Done Now and Forever!
Yashu'a (Jesus) said: "Thou shalt love the Most High Heavenly Father, thy Sustainer with all
thy heart, and with all thy soul, and with all thy mind. Thou shalt love
thy neighbour as thyself."

"And ye shall seek me, and find [me], when ye shall search for me with all your heart. And I will be found of you, saith the LORD: and I will turn away your captivity, and I will gather you from all the nations, and from all the places whither I have driven you, saith the LORD; and I will bring you again into the place whence I caused you to be carried away captive." "A man's heart deviseth his way: but the LORD directeth his steps, KJV Proverbs 16:9."

216

Yashu'a (Jesus) said: "A new commandment I give unto
you, that ye love one another; as I have loved you,
that ye also love one another."

ASSASSINS of DISOBEDIENCE!
Invoking the Power of the Most High Through Obedience, is the Key to Living Your Best Life
as the Supreme Ingredient!
Heaven or Hell?

CHILDREN OF THE MOST HIGH:
PRISTINE YOUTH AND FAMILY SOLUTIONS, LLC.
SONS AND DAUGHTERS OF THE MOST HIGH PUBLISHERS ®

Oh, Gracious Most High Heavenly father, Holy is your name,
Your Will Be Done Now and Forever!
Yashu'a (Jesus) said: *"Thou shalt love the Most High Heavenly Father, thy Sustainer with all*
thy heart, and with all thy soul, and with all thy mind. Thou shalt love
thy neighbour as thyself."

"The **thirtieth (30) out of 48 Laws of Power** is: <u>MAKE YOUR ACCOMPLISHMENTS SEEM EFFORTLESS.</u> Your actions must seem natural and executed with ease. All the toil and practice that go into them, and also all the clever tricks, must be concealed. When you act, act effortlessly, as if you could do much more. Avoid the temptation of revealing how hard you work—it only raises questions. Teach no one your tricks or they will be used against you, (Greene 1998, p. 245)."

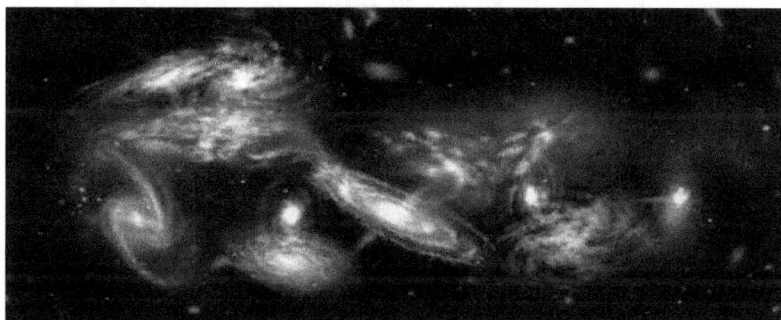

217

Yashu'a (Jesus) said: *"A new commandment I give unto you, that ye love one another; as I have loved you, that ye also love one another."*

ASSASSINS of DISOBEDIENCE!
Invoking the Power of the Most High Through Obedience, is the Key to Living Your Best Life
as the Supreme Ingredient!
Heaven or Hell?

CHILDREN OF THE MOST HIGH:
PRISTINE YOUTH AND FAMILY SOLUTIONS, LLC.
SONS AND DAUGHTERS OF THE MOST HIGH PUBLISHERS ®

Oh, Gracious Most High Heavenly father, Holy is your name,
Your Will Be Done Now and Forever!
Yashu'a (Jesus) said: "Thou shalt love the Most High Heavenly Father, thy Sustainer with all
thy heart, and with all thy soul, and with all thy mind. Thou shalt love
thy neighbour as thyself."

In the KJV bible book of Matthew chapter 15 verses 3-9; the Messiah Yashu'a (Jesus) said: "Why do ye also transgress the commandment of God by your tradition? For God commanded, saying, Honour thy father and mother: and, He that curseth father or mother, let him die the death. But ye say, whosoever shall say to his father or his mother, it is a gift, by whatsoever thou mightest be profited by me. And honour not his father or his mother, he shall be free. Thus, have ye made the commandment of God of none effect by your tradition. Ye hypocrites, well did Esaias prophesy of you, saying, this people draweth nigh unto me with their mouth, and honoureth me with their lips; but their heart is far from me. But in vain they do worship me, teaching for doctrines the commandments of men."

218

Yashu'a (Jesus) said: "A new commandment I give unto
you, that ye love one another; as I have loved you,
that ye also love one another."

ASSASSINS of DISOBEDIENCE!
Invoking the Power of the Most High Through Obedience, is the Key to Living Your Best Life
as the Supreme Ingredient!
Heaven or Hell?

CHILDREN OF THE MOST HIGH:
PRISTINE YOUTH AND FAMILY SOLUTIONS, LLC.
SONS AND DAUGHTERS OF THE MOST HIGH PUBLISHERS ®

Oh, Gracious Most High Heavenly father, Holy is your name,
Your Will Be Done Now and Forever!
Yashu'a (Jesus) said: *"Thou shalt love the Most High Heavenly Father, thy Sustainer with all thy heart, and with all thy soul, and with all thy mind. Thou shalt love thy neighbour as thyself."*

"The **thirty-first (31) out of 48 Laws of Power** is: <u>**CONTROL THE OPTIONS: GET OTHERS TO PLAY WITH THE CARDS YOU DEAL.**</u> The best deceptions are the ones that seem to give the other person a choice: Your victims feel they are in control, but are actually your puppets. Give people options that come out in your favor whichever one they choose. Force them to make choices between the lesser of two evils, both of which serve your purpose. Put them on the horns of a dilemma: They are gored wherever they turn, (Greene 1998, p. 254)."

219

Yashu'a (Jesus) said: *"A new commandment I give unto you, that ye love one another; as I have loved you, that ye also love one another."*

ASSASSINS of DISOBEDIENCE!
Invoking the Power of the Most High Through Obedience, is the Key to Living Your Best Life
as the Supreme Ingredient!
Heaven or Hell?

CHILDREN OF THE MOST HIGH:
PRISTINE YOUTH AND FAMILY SOLUTIONS, LLC.
SONS AND DAUGHTERS OF THE MOST HIGH PUBLISHERS ®

Oh, Gracious Most High Heavenly father, Holy is your name,
Your Will Be Done Now and Forever!
Yashu'a (Jesus) said: *"Thou shalt love the Most High Heavenly Father, thy Sustainer with all*
thy heart, and with all thy soul, and with all thy mind. Thou shalt love
thy neighbour as thyself."

In the KJV bible book of Matthew chapter 6 verse 24; the Messiah Yashu'a (Jesus) said: "No man can serve two masters: for either he will hate the one, and love the other; or else he will hold to the one, and despise the other. Ye cannot serve God and mammon (μαμωνᾶς **Mamōnas**-**wealth personified, avarice (deified); riches (where it is personified and opposed to God**)."

220

Yashu'a (Jesus) said: *"A new commandment I give unto you, that ye love one another; as I have loved you, that ye also love one another."*

ASSASSINS of DISOBEDIENCE!
Invoking the Power of the Most High Through Obedience, is the Key to Living Your Best Life
as the Supreme Ingredient!
Heaven or Hell?

CHILDREN OF THE MOST HIGH:
PRISTINE YOUTH AND FAMILY SOLUTIONS, LLC.
SONS AND DAUGHTERS OF THE MOST HIGH PUBLISHERS ®

Oh, Gracious Most High Heavenly father, Holy is your name,
Your Will Be Done Now and Forever!
Yashu'a (Jesus) said: "Thou shalt love the Most High Heavenly Father, thy Sustainer with all
thy heart, and with all thy soul, and with all thy mind. Thou shalt love
thy neighbour as thyself."

"The **thirty-second (32) out of 48 Laws of Power** is: **PLAY TO PEOPLE'S FANTASIES.** The truth is often avoided because it is ugly and unpleasant. Never appeal to truth and reality unless you are prepared for the anger that comes from disenchantment. Life is so harsh and distressing that people who can manufacture romance or conjure up fantasy are like oases in the desert: Everyone flocks to them. There is great power in tapping into the fantasies of the masses, (Greene 1998, p. 263)." In the KJV bible book of John chapter 8 verse 44; the Messiah Yashu'a (Jesus) said: "Ye are of [your] father the devil, and the lusts of your father ye will do. He was a murderer from the beginning, and abode not in the truth, because there is no truth in him. When he speaketh a lie, he speaketh of his own: for he is a liar, and the father of it."

221

Yashu'a (Jesus) said: "A new commandment I give unto you, that ye love one another; as I have loved you, that ye also love one another."

ASSASSINS of DISOBEDIENCE!
Invoking the Power of the Most High Through Obedience, is the Key to Living Your Best Life
as the Supreme Ingredient!
Heaven or Hell?

CHILDREN OF THE MOST HIGH:
PRISTINE YOUTH AND FAMILY SOLUTIONS, LLC.
SONS AND DAUGHTERS OF THE MOST HIGH PUBLISHERS ®

Oh, Gracious Most High Heavenly father, Holy is your name,
Your Will Be Done Now and Forever!
Yashu'a (Jesus) said: "Thou shalt love the Most High Heavenly Father, thy Sustainer with all
thy heart, and with all thy soul, and with all thy mind. Thou shalt love
thy neighbour as thyself."

"A false witness shall not be unpunished, and [he that] speaketh lies shall perish, KJV Proverbs 19:9." In the KJV bible book of Revelation chapter 21 verse 8; it states: "But the fearful, and unbelieving, and the abominable, and murderers, and whoremongers, and sorcerers, and idolaters, and all liars, shall have their part in the lake which burneth with fire and brimstone: which is the second death."

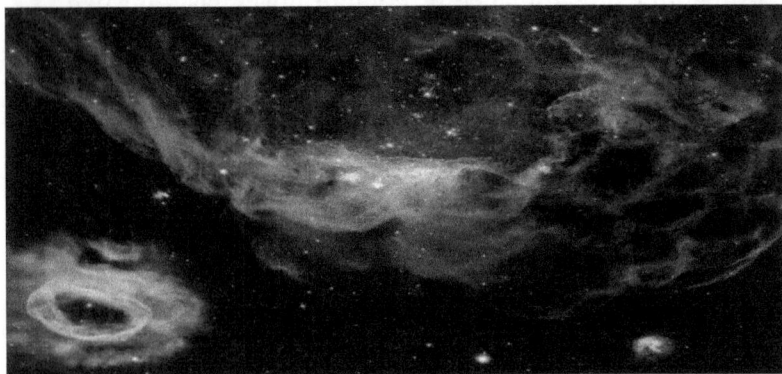

222

Yashu'a (Jesus) said: "A new commandment I give unto you, that ye love one another; as I have loved you, that ye also love one another."

ASSASSINS of DISOBEDIENCE!
Invoking the Power of the Most High Through Obedience, is the Key to Living Your Best Life
as the Supreme Ingredient!
Heaven or Hell?

CHILDREN OF THE MOST HIGH:
PRISTINE YOUTH AND FAMILY SOLUTIONS, LLC.
SONS AND DAUGHTERS OF THE MOST HIGH PUBLISHERS ®

Oh, Gracious Most High Heavenly father, Holy is your name,
Your Will Be Done Now and Forever!
Yashu'a (Jesus) said: "Thou shalt love the Most High Heavenly Father, thy Sustainer with all
thy heart, and with all thy soul, and with all thy mind. Thou shalt love
thy neighbour as thyself."

"The **thirty-third (33) out of 48 Laws of Power** is: **DISCOVER EACH MAN'S THUMBSCREW.** Everyone has a weakness, a gap in the castle wall. That weakness is usually an insecurity, an uncontrollable emotion or need; it can also be a small secret pleasure. Either way, once found, it is a thumbscrew you can turn to your advantage, (Greene 1998, p. 271)." In the KJV bible book of Matthew chapter 7 verse 12; the Messiah Yashu'a said: "Therefore all things whatsoever ye would that men should do to you, do ye even so to them: for this is the law and the prophets." The Messiah Yashu'a also said: "And as ye would that men should do to you, do ye also to them likewise, KJV Luke 6:31."

223

Yashu'a (Jesus) said: "A new commandment I give unto
you, that ye love one another; as I have loved you,
that ye also love one another."

ASSASSINS of DISOBEDIENCE!
Invoking the Power of the Most High Through Obedience, is the Key to Living Your Best Life
as the Supreme Ingredient!
Heaven or Hell?

CHILDREN OF THE MOST HIGH:
PRISTINE YOUTH AND FAMILY SOLUTIONS, LLC.
SONS AND DAUGHTERS OF THE MOST HIGH PUBLISHERS ®

Oh, Gracious Most High Heavenly father, Holy is your name,
Your Will Be Done Now and Forever!
Yashu'a (Jesus) said: "Thou shalt love the Most High Heavenly Father, thy Sustainer with all
thy heart, and with all thy soul, and with all thy mind. Thou shalt love
thy neighbour as thyself."

"Be not forgetful to entertain strangers: for thereby some have entertained angels unawares, KJV Hebrews 13:2." "The **thirty-fourth (34) out of 48 Laws of Power** is: "**BE ROYAL IN YOUR OWN FASHION: ACT LIKE A KING TO BE TREATED LIKE ONE.** The way you carry yourself will often determine how you are treated: In the long run, appearing vulgar or common will make people disrespect you. For a king respects himself and inspires the same sentiment in others. By acting regally and confident of your powers, you make yourself seem destined to wear a crown, (Greene 1998, p. 282)." In the KJV bible book of Proverbs chapter 8 verse 13; it states: "**The fear of the LORD is to hate evil: pride, and arrogancy, and the evil way, and the froward mouth, do I hate**."

224

Yashu'a (Jesus) said: "A new commandment I give unto
you, that ye love one another; as I have loved you,
that ye also love one another."

ASSASSINS of DISOBEDIENCE!
Invoking the Power of the Most High Through Obedience, is the Key to Living Your Best Life
as the Supreme Ingredient!
Heaven or Hell?

CHILDREN OF THE MOST HIGH:
PRISTINE YOUTH AND FAMILY SOLUTIONS, LLC.
SONS AND DAUGHTERS OF THE MOST HIGH PUBLISHERS ®

Oh, Gracious Most High Heavenly father, Holy is your name,
Your Will Be Done Now and Forever!
Yashu'a (Jesus) said: "Thou shalt love the Most High Heavenly Father, thy Sustainer with all
thy heart, and with all thy soul, and with all thy mind. Thou shalt love
thy neighbour as thyself."

"Pride goeth before destruction, and a haughty spirit before a fall. **Better it is to be of a humble spirit** with the lowly, than to divide the spoil with the proud, KJV Proverbs 16:18-19." In the KJV bible book of Luke chapter 14 verses 8-11; the Messiah Yashu'a (Jesus) said: "When thou art bidden of any man to a wedding, sit not down in the highest room; lest a more honorable man than thou be bidden of him. And he that bade thee and him come and say to thee, give this man place; and thou begin with shame to take the lowest room. But when thou art bidden, go and sit down in the lowest room; that when he that bade thee cometh, he may say unto thee, Friend, go up higher: then shalt thou have worship in the presence of them that sit at meat with thee."

225

Yashu'a (Jesus) said: "A new commandment I give unto you, that ye love one another; as I have loved you, that ye also love one another."

ASSASSINS of DISOBEDIENCE!
Invoking the Power of the Most High Through Obedience, is the Key to Living Your Best Life
as the Supreme Ingredient!
Heaven or Hell?

CHILDREN OF THE MOST HIGH:
PRISTINE YOUTH AND FAMILY SOLUTIONS, LLC.
SONS AND DAUGHTERS OF THE MOST HIGH PUBLISHERS ®

Oh, Gracious Most High Heavenly father, Holy is your name,
Your Will Be Done Now and Forever!
Yashu'a (Jesus) said: *"Thou shalt love the Most High Heavenly Father, thy Sustainer with all*
thy heart, and with all thy soul, and with all thy mind. Thou shalt love
thy neighbour as thyself."

"For whosoever exalted himself shall be abased; and he that humbled himself shall be exalted." In the KJV bible book of Revelation chapter 2 verse 10; the Messiah Yashu'a (Jesus) said: "Fear none of those things which thou shalt suffer: behold, the devil shall cast some of you into prison, that ye may be tried; and ye shall have tribulation ten days: be thou faithful unto death, and I will give thee a crown of life."

226

Yashu'a (Jesus) said: *"A new commandment I give unto you, that ye love one another; as I have loved you, that ye also love one another."*

ASSASSINS of DISOBEDIENCE!
Invoking the Power of the Most High Through Obedience, is the Key to Living Your Best Life
as the Supreme Ingredient!
Heaven or Hell?

CHILDREN OF THE MOST HIGH:
PRISTINE YOUTH AND FAMILY SOLUTIONS, LLC.
SONS AND DAUGHTERS OF THE MOST HIGH PUBLISHERS ®

Oh, Gracious Most High Heavenly father, Holy is your name,
Your Will Be Done Now and Forever!
Yashu'a (Jesus) said: "Thou shalt love the Most High Heavenly Father, thy Sustainer with all
thy heart, and with all thy soul, and with all thy mind. Thou shalt love
thy neighbour as thyself."

"The **thirty-fifth (35) out of 48 Laws of Power** is: <u>**MASTER THE ART OF TIMING.**</u> Never seem to be in a hurry-hurrying betrays a lack of control over yourself, and over time. Always seem patient, as if you know that everything will come to you eventually. Become a detective of the right moment; sniff out the spirit of the times, the trends that will carry you to power. Learn to stand back when the time is not yet ripe, and to strike fiercely when it has reached fruition, (Greene 1998, p. 291)." In the KJV bible book of Ecclesiastics chapter 3 verses 1-11, 14, 17; it states: "To everything there is a season, and a time to every purpose under the heaven. A time to be born, and a time to die; a time to plant, and a time to pluck up that which is planted. A time to kill, and a time to heal; a time to break down, and a time to build up."

Yashu'a (Jesus) said: "A new commandment I give unto
you, that ye love one another; as I have loved you,
that ye also love one another."

ASSASSINS of DISOBEDIENCE!
Invoking the Power of the Most High Through Obedience, is the Key to Living Your Best Life
as the Supreme Ingredient!
Heaven or Hell?

CHILDREN OF THE MOST HIGH:
PRISTINE YOUTH AND FAMILY SOLUTIONS, LLC.
SONS AND DAUGHTERS OF THE MOST HIGH PUBLISHERS ®

Oh, Gracious Most High Heavenly father, Holy is your name,
Your Will Be Done Now and Forever!
Yashu'a (Jesus) said: "Thou shalt love the Most High Heavenly Father, thy Sustainer with all
thy heart, and with all thy soul, and with all thy mind. Thou shalt love
thy neighbour as thyself."

"A time to weep, and a time to laugh; a time to mourn, and a time to dance. A time to cast away stones, and a time to gather stones together; a time to embrace, and a time to refrain from embracing. A time to get, and a time to lose; a time to keep, and a time to cast away. A time to rend, and a time to sew; a time to keep silence, and a time to speak. A time to love, and a time to hate; a time of war, and a time of peace. What profit hath he that worketh in that wherein he labored? I have seen the travail, which God hath given to the sons of men to be exercised in it. He hath made everything beautiful in his time: also, he hath set the world in their heart, so that no man can find out the work that God maketh from the beginning to the end."

228

Yashu'a (Jesus) said: "A new commandment I give unto
you, that ye love one another; as I have loved you,
that ye also love one another."

ASSASSINS of DISOBEDIENCE!
Invoking the Power of the Most High Through Obedience, is the Key to Living Your Best Life
as the Supreme Ingredient!
Heaven or Hell?

CHILDREN OF THE MOST HIGH:
PRISTINE YOUTH AND FAMILY SOLUTIONS, LLC.
SONS AND DAUGHTERS OF THE MOST HIGH PUBLISHERS ®

Oh, Gracious Most High Heavenly father, Holy is your name,
Your Will Be Done Now and Forever!
Yashu'a (Jesus) said: *"Thou shalt love the Most High Heavenly Father, thy Sustainer with all*
thy heart, and with all thy soul, and with all thy mind. Thou shalt love
thy neighbour as thyself."

"I know that, whatsoever God doeth, it shall be forever: nothing can be put to it, nor anything taken from it: and God doeth it, that men should fear before him. I said in mine heart, God shall judge the righteous and the wicked: for there is a time there for every purpose and for every work." "The **thirty-sixth (36) out of 48 Laws of Power** is: <u>**DISDAIN THINGS YOU CANNOT HAVE: IGNORING THEM IS THE BEST REVENGE.**</u> By acknowledging a petty problem, you give it existence and credibility. The more attention you pay an enemy, the stronger you make him; and a small mistake is often made worse and more visible when you try to fix it. It is sometimes best to leave things alone. If there is something you want but cannot have, show contempt for it. The less interest you reveal, the more superior you seem, (Greene 1998, p. 300)."

Yashu'a (Jesus) said: *"A new commandment I give unto you, that ye love one another; as I have loved you, that ye also love one another."*

CHILDREN OF THE MOST HIGH:
PRISTINE YOUTH AND FAMILY SOLUTIONS, LLC.
SONS AND DAUGHTERS OF THE MOST HIGH PUBLISHERS ®

Oh, Gracious Most High Heavenly father, Holy is your name,
Your Will Be Done Now and Forever!
Yashu'a (Jesus) said: "Thou shalt love the Most High Heavenly Father, thy Sustainer with all thy heart, and with all thy soul, and with all thy mind. Thou shalt love thy neighbour as thyself."

In the KJV bible book of 1 John chapter 2 verses 15-17; it states: "Love not the world, neither the things that are in the world. If any man loves the world, the love of the Father is not in him. For all that is in the world, the lust of the flesh, and the lust of the eyes, and the pride of life, is not of the Father, but is of the world. And the world passeth away, and the lust thereof: but he that doeth the will of God abideth forever." "The **thirty-seventh (37) out of 48 Laws of Power** is: **CREATE COMPELLING SPECTACLES.** Striking imagery and grand symbolic gestures create the aura of power—everyone responds to them. Stage spectacles for those around you, then, full of arresting visuals and radiant symbols that heighten your presence. Dazzled by appearances, no one will notice what you are really doing, (Greene 1998, p. 309)." In the KJV bible book of Matthew chapter 24 verse 4; the Messiah Yashu'a (Jesus) said: "Take heed that no man deceives you." In the KJV bible book of Matthew chapter 7 verses 15-20; the Messiah Yashu'a (Jesus) said: "Beware of false prophets, which come to you in sheep's clothing, but inwardly they are ravening wolves. Ye shall know them by their fruits. Do men gather grapes of thorns, or figs of thistles?

230

Yashu'a (Jesus) said: "A new commandment I give unto you, that ye love one another; as I have loved you, that ye also love one another."

ASSASSINS of DISOBEDIENCE!
Invoking the Power of the Most High Through Obedience, is the Key to Living Your Best Life
as the Supreme Ingredient!
Heaven or Hell?

CHILDREN OF THE MOST HIGH:
PRISTINE YOUTH AND FAMILY SOLUTIONS, LLC.
SONS AND DAUGHTERS OF THE MOST HIGH PUBLISHERS ®

Oh, Gracious Most High Heavenly father, Holy is your name,
Your Will Be Done Now and Forever!

Yashu'a (Jesus) said: "Thou shalt love the Most High Heavenly Father, thy Sustainer with all
thy heart, and with all thy soul, and with all thy mind. Thou shalt love
thy neighbour as thyself."

Even so every good tree bringeth forth good fruit; but a corrupt tree bringeth forth evil fruit. A good tree cannot bring forth evil fruit, neither can a corrupt tree bring forth good fruit. Every tree that bringeth not forth good fruit is hewn down, and cast into the fire. Wherefore by their fruits ye shall know them." In the KJV bible 2nd Timothy chapter 2 verse 11; it states: "And for this cause **God shall send them strong delusion, that they should believe a lie.**" For more information on "**delusion**", seek out the book below:

231

Yashu'a (Jesus) said: "A new commandment I give unto
you, that ye love one another; as I have loved you,
that ye also love one another."

ASSASSINS of DISOBEDIENCE!
Invoking the Power of the Most High Through Obedience, is the Key to Living Your Best Life
as the Supreme Ingredient!
Heaven or Hell?

CHILDREN OF THE MOST HIGH:
PRISTINE YOUTH AND FAMILY SOLUTIONS, LLC.
SONS AND DAUGHTERS OF THE MOST HIGH PUBLISHERS ®

Oh, Gracious Most High Heavenly father, Holy is your name,
Your Will Be Done Now and Forever!
Yashu'a (Jesus) said: "Thou shalt love the Most High Heavenly Father, thy Sustainer with all
thy heart, and with all thy soul, and with all thy mind. Thou shalt love
thy neighbour as thyself."

"The **thirty-eighth (38) out of 48 Laws of Power** is: **THINK AS YOU LIKE BUT BEHAVE LIKE OTHERS.** If you make a show of going against the times, flaunting your unconventional ideas and unorthodox ways, people will think that you only want attention and that you look down upon them. They will find a way to punish you for making them feel inferior. It is far safer to blend in and nurture the common touch. Share your originality only with tolerant friends and those who are sure to appreciate your uniqueness, (Greene 1998, p. 317)." In the KJV bible book of Matthew chapter 5 verses 10-12; the Messiah Yashu'a (Jesus) said: "Blessed are they which are persecuted for righteousness' sake: for theirs is the kingdom of heaven. Blessed are ye, when men shall revile you, and persecute you, and shall say all manner of evil against you falsely, for my sake. Rejoice, and be exceeding glad: for great is your reward in heaven: for so persecuted they the prophets which were before you."

232

Yashu'a (Jesus) said: "A new commandment I give unto you, that ye love one another; as I have loved you, that ye also love one another."

ASSASSINS of DISOBEDIENCE!
Invoking the Power of the Most High Through Obedience, is the Key to Living Your Best Life
as the Supreme Ingredient!
Heaven or Hell?

CHILDREN OF THE MOST HIGH:
PRISTINE YOUTH AND FAMILY SOLUTIONS, LLC.
SONS AND DAUGHTERS OF THE MOST HIGH PUBLISHERS ®

Oh, Gracious Most High Heavenly father, Holy is your name,
Your Will Be Done Now and Forever!
Yashu'a (Jesus) said: "Thou shalt love the Most High Heavenly Father, thy Sustainer with all
thy heart, and with all thy soul, and with all thy mind. Thou shalt love
thy neighbour as thyself."

Sanctify them through thy truth: thy word is truth, KJV John 17:17." "Lying lips [are] abomination to the LORD: but they that deal truly [are] his delight, KJV Proverbs 12:22." In the KJV bible book of Proverbs chapter 23 verse 7; it states: "For as he thinketh in his heart, so is he: Eat and drink, saith he to thee; but his heart is not with thee." In the KJV bible book of Romans chapter 12 verse 2; it states: "And be not conformed to this world: but be ye transformed by the renewing of your mind, that ye may prove what is that good, and acceptable, and perfect, will of God."

233

Yashu'a (Jesus) said: "A new commandment I give unto you, that ye love one another; as I have loved you, that ye also love one another."

ASSASSINS of DISOBEDIENCE!
Invoking the Power of the Most High Through Obedience, is the Key to Living Your Best Life
as the Supreme Ingredient!
Heaven or Hell?

CHILDREN OF THE MOST HIGH:
PRISTINE YOUTH AND FAMILY SOLUTIONS, LLC.
SONS AND DAUGHTERS OF THE MOST HIGH PUBLISHERS ®

Oh, Gracious Most High Heavenly father, Holy is your name,
Your Will Be Done Now and Forever!
Yashu'a (Jesus) said: "Thou shalt love the Most High Heavenly Father, thy Sustainer with all
thy heart, and with all thy soul, and with all thy mind. Thou shalt love
thy neighbour as thyself."

"The **thirty-nineth (39) out of 48 Laws of Power** is: **STIR UP WATERS TO CATCH FISH.** Anger and emotion are strategically counterproductive. You must always stay calm and objective. But if you can make your enemies angry while staying calm yourself, you gain a decided advantage. Put your enemies off-balance: Find the chink in their vanity through which you can rattle them and you hold the strings, (Greene 1998, p. 325)." In the KJV bible book of Hebrew chapter 10 verse 24; it states: "And let us consider one another to provoke unto love and to good works." In the KJV bible book of James chapter 1 verse 19; it states: "Wherefore, my beloved brethren, let every man be swift to hear, slow to speak, slow to wrath." "Hatred stirreth up strifes: but love covereth all sins (KJV Proverbs chapter 10 verse 12)." In the KJV bible book of Proverbs chapter 15 verse 1; it states: "A soft answer turneth away wrath: but grievous words stir up anger." "It is an honour for a man to cease from strife: but every fool will be meddling (KJV bible book of Proverbs chapter 20 verse 3)." In the KJV bible book of Colossians chapter 3 verse 21; it states: "Fathers, provoke not your children to anger, lest they be discouraged." "And, ye fathers, provoke not your children to wrath: but bring them up in the nurture and admonition of the Lord (KJV bible book of Ephesians chapter 6 verse 4)."

Yashu'a (Jesus) said: "A new commandment I give unto you, that ye love one another; as I have loved you, that ye also love one another."

ASSASSINS of DISOBEDIENCE!
Invoking the Power of the Most High Through Obedience, is the Key to Living Your Best Life
as the Supreme Ingredient!
Heaven or Hell?

CHILDREN OF THE MOST HIGH:
PRISTINE YOUTH AND FAMILY SOLUTIONS, LLC.
SONS AND DAUGHTERS OF THE MOST HIGH PUBLISHERS ®

Oh, Gracious Most High Heavenly father, Holy is your name,
Your Will Be Done Now and Forever!
Yashu'a (Jesus) said: *"Thou shalt love the Most High Heavenly Father, thy Sustainer with all thy heart, and with all thy soul, and with all thy mind. Thou shalt love thy neighbour as thyself."*

"The **fortieth (40) out of 48 Laws of Power** is: **DESPISE THE FREE LUNCH.** What is offered for free is dangerous-it usually involves either a trick or a hidden obligation. What has worth is worth paying for. By paying your own way you stay clear of gratitude, guilt, and deceit. It is also often wise to pay the full price—there is no cutting corners with excellence. Be lavish with your money and keep it circulating, for generosity is a sign and a magnet for power, (Greene 1998, p. 333)." In the KJV bible book of Acts chapter 20 verse 35; it states: "I have shewed you all things, how that so laboring ye ought to support the weak, and to remember the words of the Lord Jesus, how he said, It is more blessed to give than to receive."

Yashu'a (Jesus) said: *"A new commandment I give unto you, that ye love one another; as I have loved you, that ye also love one another."*

ASSASSINS of DISOBEDIENCE!
Invoking the Power of the Most High Through Obedience, is the Key to Living Your Best Life
as the Supreme Ingredient!
Heaven or Hell?

CHILDREN OF THE MOST HIGH:
PRISTINE YOUTH AND FAMILY SOLUTIONS, LLC.
SONS AND DAUGHTERS OF THE MOST HIGH PUBLISHERS ®

Oh, Gracious Most High Heavenly father, Holy is your name,
Your Will Be Done Now and Forever!
Yashu'a (Jesus) said: *"Thou shalt love the Most High Heavenly Father, thy Sustainer with all*
thy heart, and with all thy soul, and with all thy mind. Thou shalt love
thy neighbour as thyself."

"The **forty-first (41) out of 48 Laws of Power** is: <u>AVOID STEPPING INTO A GREAT MAN'S SHOES.</u> What happens first always appears better and more original than what comes after. If you succeed a great man or have a famous parent, you will have to accomplish double their achievements to outshine them. Do not get lost in their shadow, or stuck in a past not of your own making: Establish your own name and identity by changing course. Slay the overbearing father, disparage his legacy, and gain power by shining in your own way, (Greene 1998, p. 347)." In the KJV bible book of John chapter 13 verses 13-17; **the Messiah Yashu'a (Jesus) said**: "Ye call me Master and Lord: and ye say well; for [so] I am. If I then, [your] Lord and Master, have washed your feet; ye also ought to wash one another's feet."

236

Yashu'a (Jesus) said: "A new commandment I give unto
you, that ye love one another; as I have loved you,
that ye also love one another."

ASSASSINS of DISOBEDIENCE!
Invoking the Power of the Most High Through Obedience, is the Key to Living Your Best Life
as the Supreme Ingredient!
Heaven or Hell?

CHILDREN OF THE MOST HIGH:
PRISTINE YOUTH AND FAMILY SOLUTIONS, LLC.
SONS AND DAUGHTERS OF THE MOST HIGH PUBLISHERS ®

Oh, Gracious Most High Heavenly father, Holy is your name,
Your Will Be Done Now and Forever!
Yashu'a (Jesus) said: "Thou shalt love the Most High Heavenly Father, thy Sustainer with all
thy heart, and with all thy soul, and with all thy mind. Thou shalt love
thy neighbour as thyself."

"For I have given you an example, that ye should do as I have done to you. Verily, verily, I say unto you, the servant is not greater than his lord; neither he that is sent greater than he that sent him. If ye know these things, happy are ye if ye do them." "He that saith he abideth in **him (the Messiah Yashu'a, Jesus)** ought himself also so to walk, even as he walked, KJV 1 John 2:6."

237

Yashu'a (Jesus) said: "A new commandment I give unto you, that ye love one another; as I have loved you, that ye also love one another."

ASSASSINS of DISOBEDIENCE!
Invoking the Power of the Most High Through Obedience, is the Key to Living Your Best Life
as the Supreme Ingredient!
Heaven or Hell?

CHILDREN OF THE MOST HIGH:
PRISTINE YOUTH AND FAMILY SOLUTIONS, LLC.
SONS AND DAUGHTERS OF THE MOST HIGH PUBLISHERS ®

Oh, Gracious Most High Heavenly father, Holy is your name,
Your Will Be Done Now and Forever!
Yashu'a (Jesus) said: *"Thou shalt love the Most High Heavenly Father, thy Sustainer with all*
thy heart, and with all thy soul, and with all thy mind. Thou shalt love
thy neighbour as thyself."

"The forty-second **(42) out of 48 Laws of Power** is: <u>**STRIKE THE SHEPHERD AND THE SHEEP WILL SCATTER.**</u> Trouble can often be traced to a single strong individual —the stirrer, the arrogant underling, the poisoner of goodwill. If you allow such people room to operate, others will succumb to their influence. Do not wait for the troubles they cause to multiply, do not try to negotiate with them—they are irredeemable. Neutralize their influence by isolating or banishing them. Strike at the source of the trouble and the sheep will scatter, (Greene 1998, p. 358)."

238

Yashu'a (Jesus) said: *"A new commandment I give unto you, that ye love one another; as I have loved you, that ye also love one another."*

ASSASSINS of DISOBEDIENCE!
Invoking the Power of the Most High Through Obedience, is the Key to Living Your Best Life
as the Supreme Ingredient!
Heaven or Hell?

CHILDREN OF THE MOST HIGH:
PRISTINE YOUTH AND FAMILY SOLUTIONS, LLC.
SONS AND DAUGHTERS OF THE MOST HIGH PUBLISHERS ®

Oh, Gracious Most High Heavenly father, Holy is your name,
Your Will Be Done Now and Forever!
Yashu'a (Jesus) said: "Thou shalt love the Most High Heavenly Father, thy Sustainer with all
thy heart, and with all thy soul, and with all thy mind. Thou shalt love
thy neighbour as thyself."

In the KJV bible book of John chapter 10 verses 7-18; the Messiah Yashu'a (Jesus) said: "Verily, verily, I say unto you, I am the door of the sheep. All that ever came before me are thieves and robbers: but the sheep did not hear them. I am the door: by me if any man enters in, he shall be saved, and shall go in and out, and find pasture. The thief cometh not, but for to steal, and to kill, and to destroy: I am come that they might have life, and that they might have it more abundantly. <u>I am the good shepherd</u>: <u>the good shepherd giveth his life for the sheep</u>. But he that is a hireling, and not the shepherd, who's own the sheep are not, seeth the wolf coming, and leaveth the sheep, and fleeth: and the wolf catcheth them, and scattereth the sheep. The hireling fleeth, because he is a hireling, and careth not for the sheep."

239

Yashu'a (Jesus) said: "A new commandment I give unto
you, that ye love one another; as I have loved you,
that ye also love one another."

ASSASSINS of DISOBEDIENCE!
Invoking the Power of the Most High Through Obedience, is the Key to Living Your Best Life
as the Supreme Ingredient!
Heaven or Hell?

CHILDREN OF THE MOST HIGH:
PRISTINE YOUTH AND FAMILY SOLUTIONS, LLC.
SONS AND DAUGHTERS OF THE MOST HIGH PUBLISHERS ®

Oh, Gracious Most High Heavenly father, Holy is your name,
Your Will Be Done Now and Forever!
Yashu'a (Jesus) said: *"Thou shalt love the Most High Heavenly Father, thy Sustainer with all thy heart, and with all thy soul, and with all thy mind. Thou shalt love thy neighbour as thyself."*

"I am the good shepherd, and know my sheep, and am known of mine. As the Father knoweth me, even so know I the Father: and I lay down my life for the sheep. And other sheep I have, which are not of this fold: them also I must bring, and they shall hear my voice; and there shall be one-fold, and one shepherd. Therefore; doth my Father love me, because I lay down my life, that I might take it again. No man taketh it from me, but I lay it down of myself. I have power to lay it down, and I have power to take it again. This commandment have I received of my Father."

240

Yashu'a (Jesus) said: *"A new commandment I give unto you, that ye love one another; as I have loved you, that ye also love one another."*

CHILDREN OF THE MOST HIGH:
PRISTINE YOUTH AND FAMILY SOLUTIONS, LLC.
SONS AND DAUGHTERS OF THE MOST HIGH PUBLISHERS ®

Oh, Gracious Most High Heavenly father, Holy is your name,
Your Will Be Done Now and Forever!
Yashu'a (Jesus) said: *"Thou shalt love the Most High Heavenly Father, thy Sustainer with all thy heart, and with all thy soul, and with all thy mind. Thou shalt love thy neighbour as thyself."*

"The **forty-third (43) out of 48 Laws of Power** is: <u>**WORK ON THE HEARTS AND MINDS OF OTHERS.**</u> Coercion creates a reaction that will eventually work against you. You must <u>**seduce**</u> others into wanting to move in your direction. <u>**A person you have seduced becomes your loyal pawn**</u>. And <u>**the way to seduce others is to operate on their individual psychologies and weaknesses**</u>. Soften up the resistant by working on their emotions, playing on what they hold dear and what they fear. Ignore the hearts and minds of others and they will grow to hate you, (Greene 1998, p. 376)."

241

Yashu'a (Jesus) said: *"A new commandment I give unto you, that ye love one another; as I have loved you, that ye also love one another."*

ASSASSINS of DISOBEDIENCE!
Invoking the Power of the Most High Through Obedience, is the Key to Living Your Best Life
as the Supreme Ingredient!
Heaven or Hell?

CHILDREN OF THE MOST HIGH:
PRISTINE YOUTH AND FAMILY SOLUTIONS, LLC.
SONS AND DAUGHTERS OF THE MOST HIGH PUBLISHERS ®

Oh, Gracious Most High Heavenly father, Holy is your name,
Your Will Be Done Now and Forever!
Yashu'a (Jesus) said: "Thou shalt love the Most High Heavenly Father, thy Sustainer with all
thy heart, and with all thy soul, and with all thy mind. Thou shalt love
thy neighbour as thyself."

The Online American Heritage Dictionary (2020) defines "__seduce__" as: "**To attract or lead (someone) away from proper behavior or thinking; To induce (someone) to engage in sexual activity, as by flirting or persuasion. To entice into a different state or position. [Middle English seduisen, from Old French seduire, seduis-, alteration (influenced by Medieval Latin sēdūcere, to lead astray) of suduire, to seduce, from Latin subdūcere, to withdraw: sub-, sub- + dūcere, to lead; see deuk- in the Appendix of Indo-European roots].**"

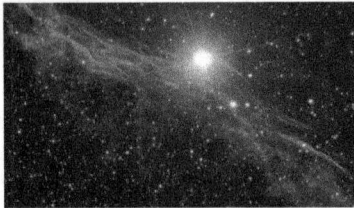

242

Yashu'a (Jesus) said: "A new commandment I give unto you, that ye love one another; as I have loved you, that ye also love one another."

ASSASSINS of DISOBEDIENCE!
Invoking the Power of the Most High Through Obedience, is the Key to Living Your Best Life
as the Supreme Ingredient!
Heaven or Hell?

CHILDREN OF THE MOST HIGH:
PRISTINE YOUTH AND FAMILY SOLUTIONS, LLC.
SONS AND DAUGHTERS OF THE MOST HIGH PUBLISHERS ®

Oh, Gracious Most High Heavenly father, Holy is your name,
Your Will Be Done Now and Forever!
Yashu'a (Jesus) said: *"Thou shalt love the Most High Heavenly Father, thy Sustainer with all*
thy heart, and with all thy soul, and with all thy mind. Thou shalt love
thy neighbour as thyself."

In the KJV bible book of 1st Timothy chapter 4 verse 1; it states: "Now the Spirit speaketh expressly, that in the latter times some shall depart from the faith, giving heed to **seducing spirits**, and **doctrines of devils**; **Speaking lies in hypocrisy**; **having their conscience seared with a hot iron**." In the KJV bible Greek Strong's Concordance#**4108** word for "**seducing**" is: πλάνος **Plános**, **Plan'-os**; **of uncertain affinity**; roving (as a tramp), i.e. (by implication), **leading into error**, a vagabond, **an impostor** or **misleader**; **universally a corrupter**, **deceiver**, **seducing**."

243

Yashu'a (Jesus) said: *"A new commandment I give unto you, that ye love one another; as I have loved you, that ye also love one another."*

ASSASSINS of DISOBEDIENCE!
Invoking the Power of the Most High Through Obedience, is the Key to Living Your Best Life
as the Supreme Ingredient!
Heaven or Hell?

CHILDREN OF THE MOST HIGH:
PRISTINE YOUTH AND FAMILY SOLUTIONS, LLC.
SONS AND DAUGHTERS OF THE MOST HIGH PUBLISHERS ®

Oh, Gracious Most High Heavenly father, Holy is your name,
Your Will Be Done Now and Forever!
Yashu'a (Jesus) said: "Thou shalt love the Most High Heavenly Father, thy Sustainer with all
thy heart, and with all thy soul, and with all thy mind. Thou shalt love
thy neighbour as thyself."

So, according to the aforementioned verse, **seducers** and **the art of seduction** are **empowered**, and **influenced** by **seducing spirits that are: universally corrupt, and deceiving spirits that lead people into error through their disobedience to the Most High's Laws and Commandments and the Doctrine of the Most High that the Messiah Yashu'a (Jesus) taught.**

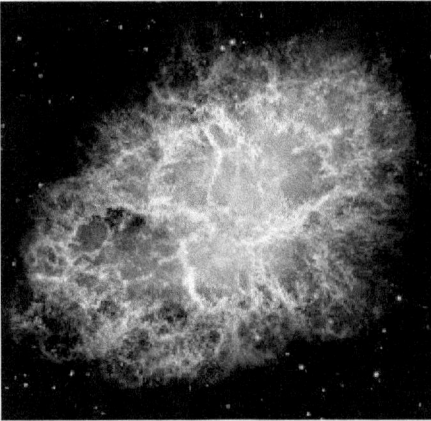

244

Yashu'a (Jesus) said: "A new commandment I give unto you, that ye love one another; as I have loved you, that ye also love one another."

ASSASSINS of DISOBEDIENCE!
Invoking the Power of the Most High Through Obedience, is the Key to Living Your Best Life
as the Supreme Ingredient!
Heaven or Hell?

CHILDREN OF THE MOST HIGH:
PRISTINE YOUTH AND FAMILY SOLUTIONS, LLC.
SONS AND DAUGHTERS OF THE MOST HIGH PUBLISHERS ®

Oh, Gracious Most High Heavenly father, Holy is your name,
Your Will Be Done Now and Forever!
Yashu'a (Jesus) said: "Thou shalt love the Most High Heavenly Father, thy Sustainer with all
thy heart, and with all thy soul, and with all thy mind. Thou shalt love
thy neighbour as thyself."

For more information about what are spirits, and what is the difference between soul and spirit; seek out the book entitled: "Spiritual Trillionaire: Cherishing the Breath of Life While Simultaneously Preparing for the Blow of Death!

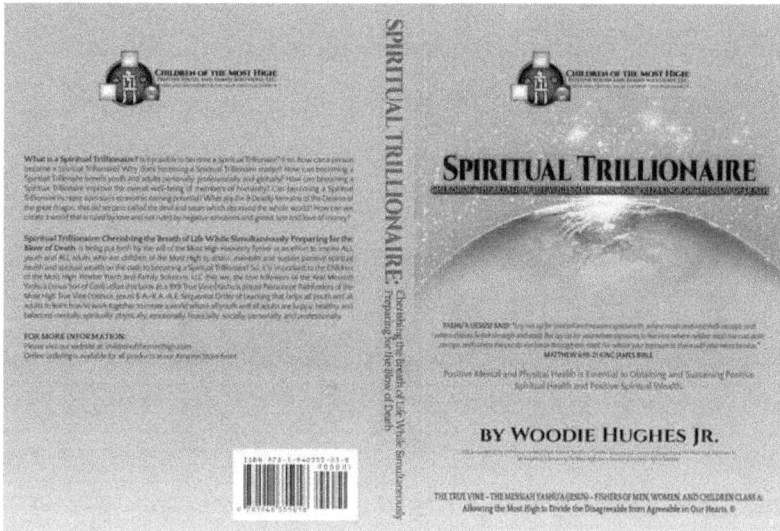

245

Yashu'a (Jesus) said: "A new commandment I give unto
you, that ye love one another; as I have loved you,
that ye also love one another."

ASSASSINS of DISOBEDIENCE!
Invoking the Power of the Most High Through Obedience, is the Key to Living Your Best Life
as the Supreme Ingredient!
Heaven or Hell?

CHILDREN OF THE MOST HIGH:
PRISTINE YOUTH AND FAMILY SOLUTIONS, LLC.
SONS AND DAUGHTERS OF THE MOST HIGH PUBLISHERS ®

Oh, Gracious Most High Heavenly father, Holy is your name,
Your Will Be Done Now and Forever!
Yashu'a (Jesus) said: "Thou shalt love the Most High Heavenly Father, thy Sustainer with all
thy heart, and with all thy soul, and with all thy mind. Thou shalt love
thy neighbour as thyself."

"The **forty-fourth (44)** out of **48 Laws of Power** is: <u>**DISARM**</u>

<u>**AND INFURIATE WITH THE MIRROR EFFECT**</u>. The

mirror reflects reality, but it is also the **perfect tool for**

deception: When you mirror your enemies, doing exactly as

they do, they cannot figure out your strategy. The Mirror Effect

mocks and humiliates them, making them overreact. By holding

up a mirror to their psyches, **you seduce them with the illusion**

that you share their values; by holding up a mirror to their

actions, you teach them a lesson. Few can resist the power of

the Mirror Effect, (Greene 1998, p. 376)."

246

Yashu'a (Jesus) said: "A new commandment I give unto
you, that ye love one another; as I have loved you,
that ye also love one another."

ASSASSINS of DISOBEDIENCE!
Invoking the Power of the Most High Through Obedience, is the Key to Living Your Best Life
as the Supreme Ingredient!
Heaven or Hell?

CHILDREN OF THE MOST HIGH:
PRISTINE YOUTH AND FAMILY SOLUTIONS, LLC.
SONS AND DAUGHTERS OF THE MOST HIGH PUBLISHERS ®

Oh, Gracious Most High Heavenly father, Holy is your name,
Your Will Be Done Now and Forever!
Yashu'a (Jesus) said: "Thou shalt love the Most High Heavenly Father, thy Sustainer with all
thy heart, and with all thy soul, and with all thy mind. Thou shalt love
thy neighbour as thyself."

In the KJV bible book of Job chapter 15 verse 35; it states: "**They [the wicked] conceive mischief**, and bring forth vanity, **and their belly prepareth deceit**." "**His mouth is full of cursing and deceit and fraud**: under his tongue [is] mischief and vanity, KJV Psalms 10:7." "And for this cause **God shall send them strong delusion, that they should believe a lie**, KJV 2nd Timothy chapter 2 verse 11."

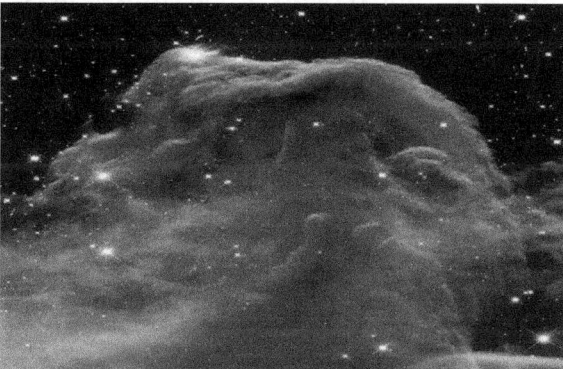

247

Yashu'a (Jesus) said: "A new commandment I give unto
you, that ye love one another; as I have loved you,
that ye also love one another."

ASSASSINS of DISOBEDIENCE!
Invoking the Power of the Most High Through Obedience, is the Key to Living Your Best Life
as the Supreme Ingredient!
Heaven or Hell?

CHILDREN OF THE MOST HIGH:
PRISTINE YOUTH AND FAMILY SOLUTIONS, LLC.
SONS AND DAUGHTERS OF THE MOST HIGH PUBLISHERS ®

Oh, Gracious Most High Heavenly father, Holy is your name,
Your Will Be Done Now and Forever!
Yashu'a (Jesus) said: *"Thou shalt love the Most High Heavenly Father, thy Sustainer with all*
thy heart, and with all thy soul, and with all thy mind. Thou shalt love
thy neighbour as thyself."

In the KJV bible book of 1st Timothy chapter 4 verse 1; it states: "Now the Spirit speaketh expressly, that in the latter times some shall depart from the faith, giving heed to **seducing spirits**, and **doctrines of devils**; **Speaking lies in hypocrisy**; **having their conscience seared with a hot iron**." In the KJV bible Greek Strong's Concordance#**4108** word for "**seducing**" is: πλάνος **Plános**, **Plan'-os**; **of uncertain affinity; roving (as a tramp)**, i.e. (by implication), **leading into error**, a vagabond, **an impostor** or **misleader**; **universally a corrupter**, **deceiver**, **seducing**."

248

Yashu'a (Jesus) said: "A new commandment I give unto
you, that ye love one another; as I have loved you,
that ye also love one another."

ASSASSINS of DISOBEDIENCE!
Invoking the Power of the Most High Through Obedience, is the Key to Living Your Best Life
as the Supreme Ingredient!
Heaven or Hell?

CHILDREN OF THE MOST HIGH:
PRISTINE YOUTH AND FAMILY SOLUTIONS, LLC.
SONS AND DAUGHTERS OF THE MOST HIGH PUBLISHERS ®

Oh, Gracious Most High Heavenly father, Holy is your name,
Your Will Be Done Now and Forever!
Yashu'a (Jesus) said: "Thou shalt love the Most High Heavenly Father, thy Sustainer with all
thy heart, and with all thy soul, and with all thy mind. Thou shalt love
thy neighbour as thyself."

"The **forty-fifth (45)** out of **48 Laws of Power** is: **PREACH THE NEED FOR CHANGE, BUT NEVER REFORM TOO MUCH AT ONCE**. Everyone understands the need for change in the abstract, but on the day-to-day level people are creatures of habit. Too much innovation is traumatic, and will lead to revolt. If you are new to a position of power, or an outsider trying to build a power base, make a show of respecting the old way of doing things. If change is necessary, make it feel like a gentle improvement on the past, (Greene 1998, p. 392)."

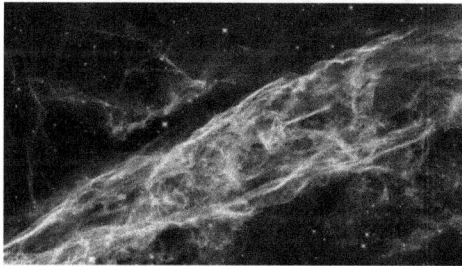

249

Yashu'a (Jesus) said: "A new commandment I give unto you, that ye love one another; as I have loved you, that ye also love one another."

ASSASSINS of DISOBEDIENCE!
Invoking the Power of the Most High Through Obedience, is the Key to Living Your Best Life
as the Supreme Ingredient!
Heaven or Hell?

CHILDREN OF THE MOST HIGH:
PRISTINE YOUTH AND FAMILY SOLUTIONS, LLC.
SONS AND DAUGHTERS OF THE MOST HIGH PUBLISHERS ®

Oh, Gracious Most High Heavenly father, Holy is your name,
Your Will Be Done Now and Forever!
Yashu'a (Jesus) said: *"Thou shalt love the Most High Heavenly Father, thy Sustainer with all thy heart, and with all thy soul, and with all thy mind. Thou shalt love thy neighbour as thyself."*

In the KJV bible book of Matthew chapter 24 verse 24; the Messiah Yashu'a (Jesus) said: "**For there shall arise false Christs, and false prophets, and shall shew great signs and wonders; insomuch that, if it were possible, they shall deceive the very elect.**" Therefore; if any man [be] in Christ, [he is] a new creature: old things are passed away; behold, all things are become new, KJV 2 Corinthians 5:17." In the KJV bible book of Job chapter 15 verse 35; it states: "**They [the wicked] conceive mischief**, and bring forth vanity, **and their belly prepareth deceit**."

250

Yashu'a (Jesus) said: *"A new commandment I give unto you, that ye love one another; as I have loved you, that ye also love one another."*

ASSASSINS of DISOBEDIENCE!
Invoking the Power of the Most High Through Obedience, is the Key to Living Your Best Life
as the Supreme Ingredient!
Heaven or Hell?

CHILDREN OF THE MOST HIGH:
PRISTINE YOUTH AND FAMILY SOLUTIONS, LLC.
SONS AND DAUGHTERS OF THE MOST HIGH PUBLISHERS ®

Oh, Gracious Most High Heavenly father, Holy is your name,
Your Will Be Done Now and Forever!
Yashu'a (Jesus) said: "Thou shalt love the Most High Heavenly Father, thy Sustainer with all
thy heart, and with all thy soul, and with all thy mind. Thou shalt love
thy neighbour as thyself."

The **forty-sixth (46)** out of **48 Laws of Power** is: "**NEVER APPEAR TOO PERFECT**. Appearing better than others is always dangerous, but most dangerous of all is to appear to have no faults or weaknesses. Envy creates silent enemies. It is smart to occasionally display defects, and admit to harmless vices, in order to deflect envy and appear more human and approachable. Only gods and the dead can seem perfect with impunity, (Greene 1998, p. 400)." The Online American Heritage Dictionary defines the word "**perfect**" as: "**adj.** 1. **Lacking nothing essential to the whole**; **complete of its nature or kind**. 2. **Being without defect** or blemish: a perfect specimen. 3. Thoroughly skilled or talented in a certain field or area; proficient.4. Completely suited for a particular purpose or situation: 5. a. Completely corresponding to a description,"

251

Yashu'a (Jesus) said: "A new commandment I give unto
you, that ye love one another; as I have loved you,
that ye also love one another."

ASSASSINS of DISOBEDIENCE!
Invoking the Power of the Most High Through Obedience, is the Key to Living Your Best Life
as the Supreme Ingredient!
Heaven or Hell?

CHILDREN OF THE MOST HIGH:
PRISTINE YOUTH AND FAMILY SOLUTIONS, LLC.
SONS AND DAUGHTERS OF THE MOST HIGH PUBLISHERS ®

Oh, Gracious Most High Heavenly father, Holy is your name,
Your Will Be Done Now and Forever!
Yashu'a (Jesus) said: "Thou shalt love the Most High Heavenly Father, thy Sustainer with all thy heart, and with all thy soul, and with all thy mind. Thou shalt love thy neighbour as thyself."

"Standard, or type: b. Accurately reproducing an original: a perfect copy of the painting. 6. **Complete**; 7. **Pure**; **undiluted**; **unmixed**. To bring to perfection or **completion**: [Middle English perfit, from Old French parfit, from Latin perfectus, past participle of perficere, to finish: per-, per- + facere, to do; see dhē- in the Appendix of Indo-European roots.] The KJV bible book of Genesis chapter 6 verse 9; it states that: "These are the generations of Noah: Noah was a just man and **perfect** in his generations, and Noah walked with God." The KJV bible Hebrew Strong's Concordance#8549 for the word: "**perfect**" is תָּמִים **Tamiym** and means: **upright, uprightly, undiluted; complete, whole, entire, sound, wholesome, unimpaired, innocent, having integrity, what is complete or entirely in accord with truth and fact.**"

Yashu'a (Jesus) said: "A new commandment I give unto you, that ye love one another; as I have loved you, that ye also love one another."

CHILDREN OF THE MOST HIGH:
PRISTINE YOUTH AND FAMILY SOLUTIONS, LLC.
SONS AND DAUGHTERS OF THE MOST HIGH PUBLISHERS ®

Oh, Gracious Most High Heavenly father, Holy is your name,
Your Will Be Done Now and Forever!
Yashu'a (Jesus) said: "Thou shalt love the Most High Heavenly Father, thy Sustainer with all thy heart, and with all thy soul, and with all thy mind. Thou shalt love thy neighbour as thyself."

"Entire (literally, figuratively or morally); integrity, <u>Pure</u>; truth: —without blemish, full, perfect, sincerely (-ity), without spot, <u>undefiled</u>, <u>unmixed</u>: upright(-ly), whole. In the KJV bible book of Matthew chapter 5 verse 48; the Messiah Yashu'a (Jesus) said: "Be ye therefore <u>perfect</u>, even as your Father which is in heaven is <u>perfect</u>." The KJV bible Greek Strong's Concordance#5046 for the word: "<u>perfect</u>" is τέλειος <u>Teleios</u> and means: <u>complete (in various applications of labor, growth, mental and moral character</u>, etc.); neuter (as noun, with G3588) <u>completeness</u>: —of full age, man, perfect; <u>balanced</u>, consummate human integrity and virtue; brought to its end, finished."

253

ASSASSINS of DISOBEDIENCE!
Invoking the Power of the Most High Through Obedience, is the Key to Living Your Best Life
as the Supreme Ingredient!
Heaven or Hell?

CHILDREN OF THE MOST HIGH:
PRISTINE YOUTH AND FAMILY SOLUTIONS, LLC.
SONS AND DAUGHTERS OF THE MOST HIGH PUBLISHERS ®

Oh, Gracious Most High Heavenly father, Holy is your name,
Your Will Be Done Now and Forever!
Yashu'a (Jesus) said: *"Thou shalt love the Most High Heavenly Father, thy Sustainer with all*
thy heart, and with all thy soul, and with all thy mind. Thou shalt love
thy neighbour as thyself."

"The **forty-seventh (47)** out of **48 Laws of Power** is: <u>**DO NOT**</u> <u>**GO PAST THE MARK YOU AIMED FOR; IN VICTORY,**</u> <u>**LEARN WHEN TO STOP**</u>. The moment of victory is often the moment of greatest peril. In the heat of victory, arrogance and overconfidence can push you past the goal you had aimed for, and by going too far, you make more enemies than you defeat. Do not allow success to go to your head. There is no substitute for strategy and careful planning. Set a goal, and when you reach it, stop, (Greene 1998, p. 410)."

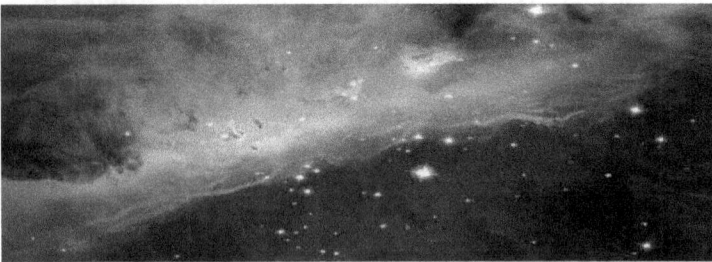

254

Yashu'a (Jesus) said: *"A new commandment I give unto you, that ye love one another; as I have loved you, that ye also love one another."*

ASSASSINS of DISOBEDIENCE!
Invoking the Power of the Most High Through Obedience, is the Key to Living Your Best Life
as the Supreme Ingredient!
Heaven or Hell?

CHILDREN OF THE MOST HIGH:
PRISTINE YOUTH AND FAMILY SOLUTIONS, LLC.
SONS AND DAUGHTERS OF THE MOST HIGH PUBLISHERS ®

Oh, Gracious Most High Heavenly father, Holy is your name,
Your Will Be Done Now and Forever!
Yashu'a (Jesus) said: "Thou shalt love the Most High Heavenly Father, thy Sustainer with all
thy heart, and with all thy soul, and with all thy mind. Thou shalt love
thy neighbour as thyself."

In the KJV bible book of Matthew chapter 6 verse 33; the Messiah Yashu'a (Jesus) said: "**But seek ye first the kingdom of God, and his righteousness; and all these things shall be added unto you.**" The Messiah Yashu'a (Jesus) also said: "**I am the way, the truth, and the life: no man cometh unto the Father, but by me, KJV John 14:6.**" In the KJV bible book of Matthew chapter 22 verses 37-39; the Messiah Yashu'a (Jesus) said: "**Thou shalt love the Lord thy God with all thy heart, and with all thy soul, and with all thy mind. This is the first and great commandment. And the second is like unto it, Thou shalt love thy neighbour as thyself.**"

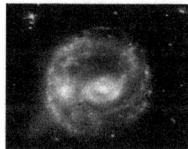

255

Yashu'a (Jesus) said: "A new commandment I give unto
you, that ye love one another; as I have loved you,
that ye also love one another."

ASSASSINS of DISOBEDIENCE!
Invoking the Power of the Most High Through Obedience, is the Key to Living Your Best Life
as the Supreme Ingredient!
Heaven or Hell?

CHILDREN OF THE MOST HIGH:
PRISTINE YOUTH AND FAMILY SOLUTIONS, LLC.
SONS AND DAUGHTERS OF THE MOST HIGH PUBLISHERS ®

Oh, Gracious Most High Heavenly father, Holy is your name,
Your Will Be Done Now and Forever!
Yashu'a (Jesus) said: "Thou shalt love the Most High Heavenly Father, thy Sustainer with all
thy heart, and with all thy soul, and with all thy mind. Thou shalt love
thy neighbour as thyself."

"The **forty-eighth (48)** out of **48 Laws of Power** is: <u>ASSUME</u>

<u>FORMLESSNESS</u>. By taking a shape, by having a visible

plan, you open yourself to attack. Instead of taking a form for

your enemy to grasp, keep yourself adaptable and on the move.

Accept the fact that nothing is certain and no law is fixed. The

best way to protect yourself is to be as fluid and formless as

water; never bet on stability or lasting order. Everything

changes, (Greene 1998, p. 419)." In the KJV bible book of 1st

Corinthians chapter 15 verses 51-54; it states: "Behold, I shew

you a mystery; We shall not all sleep, but we shall all be

changed. In a moment, in the twinkling of an eye, at the last

trump: for the trumpet shall sound, and the dead shall be raised

incorruptible, and we shall be changed."

Yashu'a (Jesus) said: "A new commandment I give unto
you, that ye love one another; as I have loved you,
that ye also love one another."

ASSASSINS of DISOBEDIENCE!
Invoking the Power of the Most High Through Obedience, is the Key to Living Your Best Life
as the Supreme Ingredient!
Heaven or Hell?

CHILDREN OF THE MOST HIGH:
PRISTINE YOUTH AND FAMILY SOLUTIONS, LLC.
SONS AND DAUGHTERS OF THE MOST HIGH PUBLISHERS ®

Oh, Gracious Most High Heavenly father, Holy is your name,
Your Will Be Done Now and Forever!
Yashu'a (Jesus) said: "Thou shalt love the Most High Heavenly Father, thy Sustainer with all
thy heart, and with all thy soul, and with all thy mind. Thou shalt love
thy neighbour as thyself."

"For this corruptible must put on incorruption, and this mortal must put on immortality. So, when this corruptible shall have put on incorruption, and this mortal shall have put on immortality, then shall be brought to pass the saying that is written, Death is swallowed up in victory." In the KJV bible book of John chapter 7 verse 16; the Messiah Yashu'a said: "My doctrine is not mine, but his that sent me." **After examining and reviewing the 48 Laws of Power**, the children of the Most High **have to decide**; **Remember: The Messiah Yashu'a (Jesus) said:** "no person can serve two masters, for either a person will hate the one, and love the other; or else he will hold to the one, and despise the other." In conclusion, **will you** choose to follow **the 48 Laws of Power**, or **will you** choose your Most High preordained obligation to **obey God's (אֱלֹהִים 'Elohiym) Commandments and Laws;** and the **Doctrine of the Most High that the Messiah Yashu'a** (Jesus) **taught**?

Yashu'a (Jesus) said: "A new commandment I give unto you, that ye love one another; as I have loved you, that ye also love one another."

ASSASSINS of DISOBEDIENCE!
Invoking the Power of the Most High Through Obedience, is the Key to Living Your Best Life
as the Supreme Ingredient!
Heaven or Hell?

CHILDREN OF THE MOST HIGH:
PRISTINE YOUTH AND FAMILY SOLUTIONS, LLC.
SONS AND DAUGHTERS OF THE MOST HIGH PUBLISHERS ®

Oh, Gracious Most High Heavenly father, Holy is your name,
Your Will Be Done Now and Forever!
Yashu'a (Jesus) said: *"Thou shalt love the Most High Heavenly Father, thy Sustainer with all*
thy heart, and with all thy soul, and with all thy mind. Thou shalt love
thy neighbour as thyself."

Chapter 8: Poison Breathing, Dreadful Day of the Lord (יְהֹוָה Yahayyu, Yahuwa or Yehovah)!

The Most High Heavenly Father is "The Mighty."

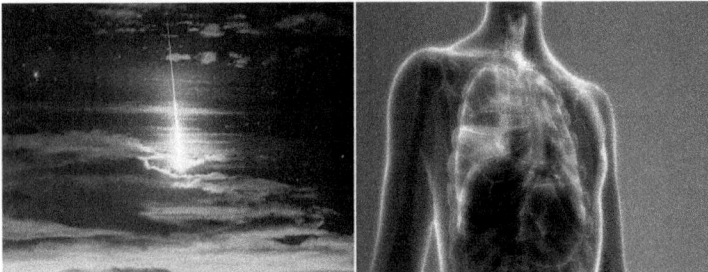

"If my people, which are called by my name, shall humble
themselves, and pray, and seek my face, and turn from their
wicked ways; then will I hear from heaven, and will forgive
their sin, and will heal their land, KJV 2 Chronicles 7:14."

Yashu'a (Jesus) said: "A new commandment I give unto
you, that ye love one another; as I have loved you,
that ye also love one another."

ASSASSINS of DISOBEDIENCE!
Invoking the Power of the Most High Through Obedience, is the Key to Living Your Best Life
as the Supreme Ingredient!
Heaven or Hell?

CHILDREN OF THE MOST HIGH:
PRISTINE YOUTH AND FAMILY SOLUTIONS, LLC.
SONS AND DAUGHTERS OF THE MOST HIGH PUBLISHERS ®

Oh, Gracious Most High Heavenly father, Holy is your name,
Your Will Be Done Now and Forever!
Yashu'a (Jesus) said: "Thou shalt love the Most High Heavenly Father, thy Sustainer with all
thy heart, and with all thy soul, and with all thy mind. Thou shalt love
thy neighbour as thyself."

In the KJV bible book of Malachi chapter 4 verses 4-6; it states: **"For, behold, the day cometh, that shall burn as an oven; and all the proud, yea, and all that do wickedly, shall be stubble: and the day that cometh shall burn them up, saith the Lord of hosts, that it shall leave them neither root nor branch.** Behold, I will send you Elijah the prophet before the coming of the **great and dreadful day of the Lord**: And he shall turn the heart of the fathers to the children, and the heart of the children to their fathers, **lest I come and smite the earth with a curse."**

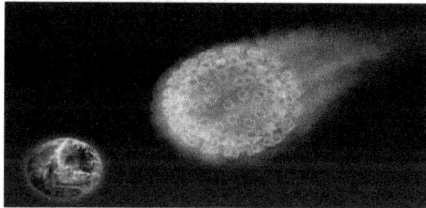

259

Yashu'a (Jesus) said: "A new commandment I give unto you, that ye love one another; as I have loved you, that ye also love one another."

ASSASSINS of DISOBEDIENCE!
Invoking the Power of the Most High Through Obedience, is the Key to Living Your Best Life
as the Supreme Ingredient!
Heaven or Hell?

CHILDREN OF THE MOST HIGH:
PRISTINE YOUTH AND FAMILY SOLUTIONS, LLC.
SONS AND DAUGHTERS OF THE MOST HIGH PUBLISHERS ®

Oh, Gracious Most High Heavenly father, Holy is your name,
Your Will Be Done Now and Forever!
Yashu'a (Jesus) said: *"Thou shalt love the Most High Heavenly Father, thy Sustainer with all*
thy heart, and with all thy soul, and with all thy mind. Thou shalt love
thy neighbour as thyself."

Oh, children of the Most High; be in the world and not of the world! According to the aforementioned KJV bible book of Malachi chapter 4 verses 4-6; a day of reckoning referred to as **"the dreadful day of the Lord"** is coming to the planet earth, to punish wicked people and disobedient people on the planet earth. Is today the day and time of **"the dreadful day of the Lord**?" In the KJV bible book of Revelation chapter 11 verses 8-9; it states: **"And their dead bodies shall lie in the street of the great city, which spiritually is called Sodom and Egypt, where also our Lord was crucified**. And they of the people and kindreds and tongues and nations **shall see their dead bodies** three days and a half, and **shall not suffer their dead bodies to be put in graves**."

Yashu'a (Jesus) said: *"A new commandment I give unto you, that ye love one another; as I have loved you, that ye also love one another."*

ASSASSINS of DISOBEDIENCE!
Invoking the Power of the Most High Through Obedience, is the Key to Living Your Best Life
as the Supreme Ingredient!
Heaven or Hell?

CHILDREN OF THE MOST HIGH:
PRISTINE YOUTH AND FAMILY SOLUTIONS, LLC.
SONS AND DAUGHTERS OF THE MOST HIGH PUBLISHERS ®

Oh, Gracious Most High Heavenly father, Holy is your name,
Your Will Be Done Now and Forever!
Yashu'a (Jesus) said: *"Thou shalt love the Most High Heavenly Father, thy Sustainer with all*
thy heart, and with all thy soul, and with all thy mind. Thou shalt love
thy neighbour as thyself."

In 2020 in the month of April in the state of New York, due to the thousands of dead bodies of people who died by the hundreds per day from the **Coronavirus (COVID-19)**; the city ordered semi-trucks to stack the bodies as the above verse mentioned "**shall not suffer their dead bodies to be put in graves**." This is another one of the Yashu'a (Jesus) book of Revelation prophesies fulfilled.

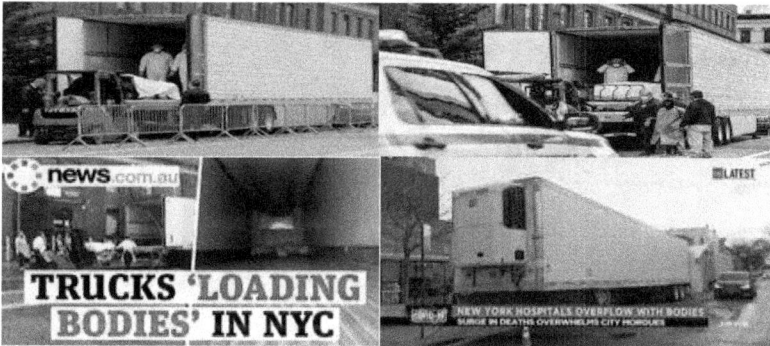

261

Yashu'a (Jesus) said: "A new commandment I give unto
you, that ye love one another; as I have loved you,
that ye also love one another."

ASSASSINS of DISOBEDIENCE!
Invoking the Power of the Most High Through Obedience, is the Key to Living Your Best Life
as the Supreme Ingredient!
Heaven or Hell?

CHILDREN OF THE MOST HIGH:
PRISTINE YOUTH AND FAMILY SOLUTIONS, LLC.
SONS AND DAUGHTERS OF THE MOST HIGH PUBLISHERS ®

Oh, Gracious Most High Heavenly father, Holy is your name,
Your Will Be Done Now and Forever!
Yashu'a (Jesus) said: *"Thou shalt love the Most High Heavenly Father, thy Sustainer with all thy heart, and with all thy soul, and with all thy mind. Thou shalt love thy neighbour as thyself."*

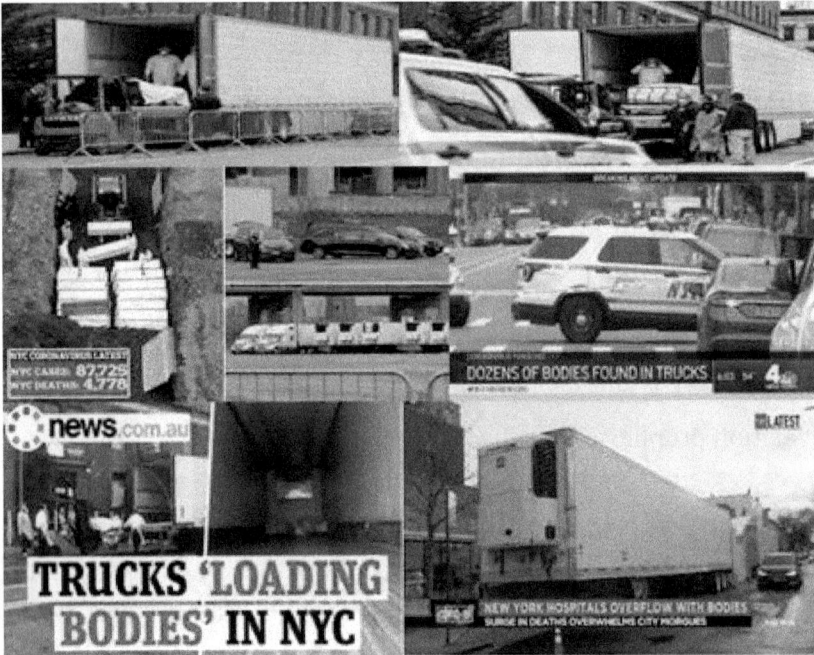

262

Yashu'a (Jesus) said: *"A new commandment I give unto you, that ye love one another; as I have loved you, that ye also love one another."*

ASSASSINS of DISOBEDIENCE!
Invoking the Power of the Most High Through Obedience, is the Key to Living Your Best Life
as the Supreme Ingredient!
Heaven or Hell?

CHILDREN OF THE MOST HIGH:
PRISTINE YOUTH AND FAMILY SOLUTIONS, LLC.
SONS AND DAUGHTERS OF THE MOST HIGH PUBLISHERS ®

Oh, Gracious Most High Heavenly father, Holy is your name,
Your Will Be Done Now and Forever!
Yashu'a (Jesus) said: "Thou shalt love the Most High Heavenly Father, thy Sustainer with all
thy heart, and with all thy soul, and with all thy mind. Thou shalt love
thy neighbour as thyself."

Is it possible that in the KJV bible book of Revelation chapter 11 verse 8; where it states: "**And their dead bodies shall lie in the street of the great city, which spiritually is called Sodom and Egypt, where also our Lord was crucified**," that; **the great city** is in reference to **New York City**? If so, what does the KJV bible book of Revelation chapter 11 verse 8 mean when it states: "**the great city, which spiritually is called Sodom and Egypt, where also our Lord was crucified**?" It means that the same **sins** that went against **God's (אֱלֹהִים 'Elohiym) Commandments** in **Sodom and Egypt,** are the same **sins that** occur all around the world; inclusive of **the great city (New York City**).

263

Yashu'a (Jesus) said: "A new commandment I give unto
you, that ye love one another; as I have loved you,
that ye also love one another."

ASSASSINS of DISOBEDIENCE!
Invoking the Power of the Most High Through Obedience, is the Key to Living Your Best Life
as the Supreme Ingredient!
Heaven or Hell?

CHILDREN OF THE MOST HIGH:
PRISTINE YOUTH AND FAMILY SOLUTIONS, LLC.
SONS AND DAUGHTERS OF THE MOST HIGH PUBLISHERS ®

Oh, Gracious Most High Heavenly father, Holy is your name,
Your Will Be Done Now and Forever!
Yashu'a (Jesus) said: "Thou shalt love the Most High Heavenly Father, thy Sustainer with all
thy heart, and with all thy soul, and with all thy mind. Thou shalt love
thy neighbour as thyself."

The great city (New York City) is a part of **the great country of America** which is **a Christian nation**, inclusive of many other denominations; where we predominately teach that **God sent Jesus to earth to be the Messiah and Savior to the world that was crucified on the cross** for our sins. America's forefathers **like Thomas Jefferson, George Washington, and 12 out of 18 of the first presidents of the United States of America owned African-American slaves** according to the Smithsonian Magazine article entitled: "**Founding Fathers and Slaveholders**, 2002" and "**African Slave Trade, The Cruelest Commerce** (1992). So, America's forefathers who were also Christians acknowledged God and Jesus Christ as their Lord and Savior **in their words** while simultaneously, **they committed ungodly actions through such acts as slave profiteering from their African American slaves that they owned!**

264

CHILDREN OF THE MOST HIGH:
PRISTINE YOUTH AND FAMILY SOLUTIONS, LLC.
SONS AND DAUGHTERS OF THE MOST HIGH PUBLISHERS ®

Oh, Gracious Most High Heavenly father, Holy is your name,
Your Will Be Done Now and Forever!
Yashu'a (Jesus) said: "Thou shalt love the Most High Heavenly Father, thy Sustainer with all thy heart, and with all thy soul, and with all thy mind. Thou shalt love thy neighbour as thyself."

This was made possible through **the kidnapping of Africans** from **different parts of Africa** **that were brought to America to be enslaved and to work for free against their will for Caucasian (White) People**. **Many of the African American slaves were beaten, killed, raped, separated from their families, humiliated, and physically tortured at any time** (Clarke, 1998). So, ask yourself; do the Caucasian (White) American forefathers who were Christians, while **simultaneously owning slaves, and committed actions of cruelty against African American slaves; reflect the evil works of "that great dragon that was cast out of heaven, that old serpent, called the Devil, and Satan, which deceiveth the whole world**? Or do their actions of owning **African American slaves** reflect the works of God and our Lord and Savior Jesus Christ, who the Caucasian (White) American forefathers acknowledged as their Lord and Savior?

265

Yashu'a (Jesus) said: "A new commandment I give unto you, that ye love one another; as I have loved you, that ye also love one another."

ASSASSINS of DISOBEDIENCE!
Invoking the Power of the Most High Through Obedience, is the Key to Living Your Best Life
as the Supreme Ingredient!
Heaven or Hell?

CHILDREN OF THE MOST HIGH:
PRISTINE YOUTH AND FAMILY SOLUTIONS, LLC.
SONS AND DAUGHTERS OF THE MOST HIGH PUBLISHERS ®

Oh, Gracious Most High Heavenly father, Holy is your name,
Your Will Be Done Now and Forever!
Yashu'a (Jesus) said: "Thou shalt love the Most High Heavenly Father, thy Sustainer with all
thy heart, and with all thy soul, and with all thy mind. Thou shalt love
thy neighbour as thyself."

So, the descendants of African American slaves in America in the 21st century, in the year 2020 <u>are being killed by each other (other-African Americans)</u>, and <u>are still being killed by the descendants of American forefathers who were owners of African American slaves</u>!

"Hearing set for 3 Georgia White men charged in Ahmaud Arbery killing. Arbery, 25, was shot and killed February 23, 2020 as he was jogging through the Satilla Shores, Georgia, neighborhood, but charges weren't filed until last month, May 21, 2020."

266

Yashu'a (Jesus) said: "A new commandment I give unto
you, that ye love one another; as I have loved you,
that ye also love one another."

ASSASSINS of DISOBEDIENCE!
Invoking the Power of the Most High Through Obedience, is the Key to Living Your Best Life
as the Supreme Ingredient!
Heaven or Hell?

CHILDREN OF THE MOST HIGH:
PRISTINE YOUTH AND FAMILY SOLUTIONS, LLC.
SONS AND DAUGHTERS OF THE MOST HIGH PUBLISHERS ®

Oh, Gracious Most High Heavenly father, Holy is your name,
Your Will Be Done Now and Forever!
Yashu'a (Jesus) said: "Thou shalt love the Most High Heavenly Father, thy Sustainer with all
thy heart, and with all thy soul, and with all thy mind. Thou shalt love
thy neighbour as thyself."

"Breonna Taylor: White Police officers killed black woman after storming home in hunt for suspect already in custody, lawsuit says US News."

The murder of an African American man, Mr. George Floyd at the hands of White police officer on May 25, 2020.

267

Yashu'a (Jesus) said: "A new commandment I give unto
you, that ye love one another; as I have loved you,
that ye also love one another."

ASSASSINS of DISOBEDIENCE!
Invoking the Power of the Most High Through Obedience, is the Key to Living Your Best Life
as the Supreme Ingredient!
Heaven or Hell?

CHILDREN OF THE MOST HIGH:
PRISTINE YOUTH AND FAMILY SOLUTIONS, LLC.
SONS AND DAUGHTERS OF THE MOST HIGH PUBLISHERS ®

Oh, Gracious Most High Heavenly father, Holy is your name,
Your Will Be Done Now and Forever!
Yashu'a (Jesus) said: "Thou shalt love the Most High Heavenly Father, thy Sustainer with all
thy heart, and with all thy soul, and with all thy mind. Thou shalt love
thy neighbour as thyself."

In the KJV bible book of Job chapter 4 verse 8; it states: "Even as I have seen, **they that plow iniquity, and sow wickedness, reap the same**." "He made a pit, and digged it, and is fallen into the ditch which he made. His mischief shall return upon his own head, and his violent dealing shall come down upon his own **pate** (קָדְקֹד Qādĕqōd-means **the top or crown of a person's head**), KJV Psalms 7:15-16."

268

Yashu'a (Jesus) said: "A new commandment I give unto you, that ye love one another; as I have loved you, that ye also love one another."

ASSASSINS of DISOBEDIENCE!
Invoking the Power of the Most High Through Obedience, is the Key to Living Your Best Life
as the Supreme Ingredient!
Heaven or Hell?

CHILDREN OF THE MOST HIGH:
PRISTINE YOUTH AND FAMILY SOLUTIONS, LLC.
SONS AND DAUGHTERS OF THE MOST HIGH PUBLISHERS ®

Oh, Gracious Most High Heavenly father, Holy is your name,
Your Will Be Done Now and Forever!
Yashu'a (Jesus) said: "Thou shalt love the Most High Heavenly Father, thy Sustainer with all
thy heart, and with all thy soul, and with all thy mind. Thou shalt love
thy neighbour as thyself."

"Be not deceived; God is not mocked: <u>for whatsoever a man soweth, that shall he also reap. For he that soweth to his flesh shall of the flesh reap corruption</u>; but he that soweth to the Spirit shall of the Spirit reap life everlasting. And let us not be weary in well doing: for in due season we shall reap, if we faint not, KJV Galatians 6:7-9." The Messiah Yashu'a (Jesus) said: "And, behold, I come quickly; and my reward is with me, to give every man according as his work shall be, KJV Revelation 22:12." The Messiah Yashu'a (Jesus) also said to the people during his life time that disobeyed **God's** (אֱלֹהִים 'Elohiym), commandments: "<u>Ye are of your father the devil</u>, and the lusts of your father ye will do. <u>He was a murderer from the beginning, and abode not in the truth, because there is no truth in him. When he speaketh a lie, he speaketh of his own: for he is a liar, and the father of it</u>, KJV John 8:44."

269

Yashu'a (Jesus) said: "A new commandment I give unto you, that ye love one another; as I have loved you, that ye also love one another."

ASSASSINS of DISOBEDIENCE!
Invoking the Power of the Most High Through Obedience, is the Key to Living Your Best Life
as the Supreme Ingredient!
Heaven or Hell?

CHILDREN OF THE MOST HIGH:
PRISTINE YOUTH AND FAMILY SOLUTIONS, LLC.
SONS AND DAUGHTERS OF THE MOST HIGH PUBLISHERS ®

Oh, Gracious Most High Heavenly father, Holy is your name,
Your Will Be Done Now and Forever!
Yashu'a (Jesus) said: "Thou shalt love the Most High Heavenly Father, thy Sustainer with all
thy heart, and with all thy soul, and with all thy mind. Thou shalt love
thy neighbour as thyself."

Nature puts humanity in check when chaos and wickedness are most rampant upon the earth! Nature intercedes on behalf of the preservation of the planet earth, and on behalf of the obedient children of the Most High during those sacred moments of time when all the foundations of the earth are out of course. **However; this occurs in the most noticeable way when nature's power of balance is felt on the planet earth where the foundation of global inequities, violates moral integrity!** Human beings can't suppress Nature and they can't stop Nature! Human beings can't push the sun away from the earth, nor can they stop the sun from coming closer to the planet earth!!! Nature is the great Equalizer of global inequities, mistreatment of the poor, and oppression of marginalized members of humanity!

270

Yashu'a (Jesus) said: "A new commandment I give unto you, that ye love one another; as I have loved you, that ye also love one another."

ASSASSINS of DISOBEDIENCE!
Invoking the Power of the Most High Through Obedience, is the Key to Living Your Best Life
as the Supreme Ingredient!
Heaven or Hell?

CHILDREN OF THE MOST HIGH:
PRISTINE YOUTH AND FAMILY SOLUTIONS, LLC.
SONS AND DAUGHTERS OF THE MOST HIGH PUBLISHERS ®

Oh, Gracious Most High Heavenly father, Holy is your name,
Your Will Be Done Now and Forever!
Yashu'a (Jesus) said: *"Thou shalt love the Most High Heavenly Father, thy Sustainer with all thy heart, and with all thy soul, and with all thy mind. Thou shalt love thy neighbour as thyself."*

Is the Coronavirus, COVID-19; the biblical global pandemic plague of the 21st century? Is the Coronavirus, COVID-19 the invisible assassin?

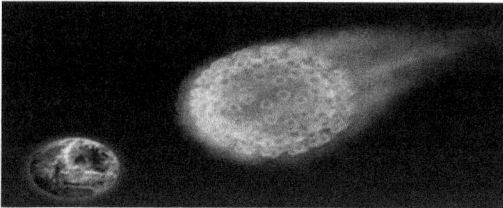

What is Poison Breathing for the children of the Most High?
Improper breathing of: inhaling cigarette smoke, inhaling cigar smoke, inhaling marijuana smoke, inhaling cocaine, inhaling meth, inhaling vaping smoke, inhaling the Coronavirus (COVID-19), and inhaling anything that is toxic to your body is: **"Poison Breathing!" Poison Breathing can lead to not Breathing!**

271

Yashu'a (Jesus) said: *"A new commandment I give unto you, that ye love one another; as I have loved you, that ye also love one another."*

ASSASSINS of DISOBEDIENCE!
Invoking the Power of the Most High Through Obedience, is the Key to Living Your Best Life
as the Supreme Ingredient!
Heaven or Hell?

CHILDREN OF THE MOST HIGH:
PRISTINE YOUTH AND FAMILY SOLUTIONS, LLC.
SONS AND DAUGHTERS OF THE MOST HIGH PUBLISHERS ®

Oh, Gracious Most High Heavenly father, Holy is your name,
Your Will Be Done Now and Forever!
Yashu'a (Jesus) said: *"Thou shalt love the Most High Heavenly Father, thy Sustainer with all*
thy heart, and with all thy soul, and with all thy mind. Thou shalt love
thy neighbour as thyself."

"If my people, which are called by my name, shall humble themselves, and pray, and seek my face, and turn from their wicked ways; then will I hear from heaven, and will forgive their sin, and will heal their land, KJV 2 Chronicles 7:14."

"This is the covenant that I will make with them after those days, saith the Lord, I will put my laws into their hearts, and in their minds will I write them, Hebrews 10:16."

272

Yashu'a (Jesus) said: *"A new commandment I give unto you, that ye love one another; as I have loved you, that ye also love one another."*

ASSASSINS of DISOBEDIENCE!
Invoking the Power of the Most High Through Obedience, is the Key to Living Your Best Life
as the Supreme Ingredient!
Heaven or Hell?

CHILDREN OF THE MOST HIGH:
PRISTINE YOUTH AND FAMILY SOLUTIONS, LLC.
SONS AND DAUGHTERS OF THE MOST HIGH PUBLISHERS ®

Oh, Gracious Most High Heavenly father, Holy is your name,
Your Will Be Done Now and Forever!
Yashu'a (Jesus) said: "Thou shalt love the Most High Heavenly Father, thy Sustainer with all
thy heart, and with all thy soul, and with all thy mind. Thou shalt love
thy neighbour as thyself."

Chapter 9: The Laws that Yashu'a (Jesus) followed are the same Laws that We who have Accepted him as our Savior are Commanded to Follow Today!

The Most High Heavenly Father is
"The Majestic."

"Blessed are they that do his commandments, that they may have right
to the tree of life, and may enter in through the gates into the city,
KJV Revelation 22:14."

273

Yashu'a (Jesus) said: "A new commandment I give unto
you, that ye love one another; as I have loved you,
that ye also love one another."

ASSASSINS of DISOBEDIENCE!
Invoking the Power of the Most High Through Obedience, is the Key to Living Your Best Life
as the Supreme Ingredient!
Heaven or Hell?

CHILDREN OF THE MOST HIGH:
PRISTINE YOUTH AND FAMILY SOLUTIONS, LLC.
SONS AND DAUGHTERS OF THE MOST HIGH PUBLISHERS ®

Oh, Gracious Most High Heavenly father, Holy is your name,
Your Will Be Done Now and Forever!
Yashu'a (Jesus) said: "Thou shalt love the Most High Heavenly Father, thy Sustainer with all
thy heart, and with all thy soul, and with all thy mind. Thou shalt love
thy neighbour as thyself."

In the KJV bible book of John chapter 14 verse 21; the Messiah **Yashu'a (Jesus) said**: "He [or she] that hath my commandments, and keepeth them, he [or she] it is that loveth me: and he [or she] that loveth me shall be loved of my Father, and I will love him [or her], and will manifest myself to him [or her]." **How financially wealthy would prosperity gospel preachers be if they practiced what the Messiah Yashu'a** (Jesus) **said:** "There shall be no moneychangers in my Father's house?"

274

Yashu'a (Jesus) said: "A new commandment I give unto you, that ye love one another; as I have loved you, that ye also love one another."

CHILDREN OF THE MOST HIGH:
PRISTINE YOUTH AND FAMILY SOLUTIONS, LLC.
SONS AND DAUGHTERS OF THE MOST HIGH PUBLISHERS ®

Oh, Gracious Most High Heavenly father, Holy is your name,
Your Will Be Done Now and Forever!
Yashu'a (Jesus) said: "Thou shalt love the Most High Heavenly Father, thy Sustainer with all thy heart, and with all thy soul, and with all thy mind. Thou shalt love thy neighbour as thyself."

In the KJV bible book of Matthew chapter 21 verses 12-13; it states: "And Jesus went into the temple of God, and cast out all them that sold and bought in the temple, and overthrew the tables of the **moneychangers**, and the seats of them that sold doves, And [the Messiah Yashu'a, Jesus] said unto them, It is written, My house shall be called the house of prayer; but ye have made it a den of thieves." "In the aforementioned verse, the KJV bible Greek Strong's Concordance#**2855** κολλυβιστής **Kollybistēs** for the word: "**moneychangers**" and means: **a money-changer, banker; One that exchanges money, as from one currency to another**." In the KJV bible book of John chapter 14 verse 6; the Messiah Yashu'a (Jesus) said: "I am the way, the truth, and the life: no man cometh unto the Father, but by me."

275

Yashu'a (Jesus) said: "A new commandment I give unto you, that ye love one another; as I have loved you, that ye also love one another."

ASSASSINS of DISOBEDIENCE!
Invoking the Power of the Most High Through Obedience, is the Key to Living Your Best Life
as the Supreme Ingredient!
Heaven or Hell?

CHILDREN OF THE MOST HIGH:
PRISTINE YOUTH AND FAMILY SOLUTIONS, LLC.
SONS AND DAUGHTERS OF THE MOST HIGH PUBLISHERS ®

Oh, Gracious Most High Heavenly father, Holy is your name,
Your Will Be Done Now and Forever!
Yashu'a (Jesus) said: "Thou shalt love the Most High Heavenly Father, thy Sustainer with all
thy heart, and with all thy soul, and with all thy mind. Thou shalt love
thy neighbour as thyself."

So, the Messiah Yashu'a (Jesus) is not only the way to the Most High Heavenly Father, he is also the example of the way the children of the Most High should think, speak and do. "**He that saith he abideth in him ought himself also so to walk, even as he walked**, KJV 1st John 2:6." The Messiah Yashu'a (Jesus) said: "If ye love me, keep my commandments, KJV John 14:15." The Messiah Yashu'a didn't ever take money or offerings from his congregation, he didn't passed around a basket or tray to receive pledges and donations at the end of each sermon, he didn't ever ask for a payment after he gave a sermon; and the Messiah Yashu'a (Jesus) told his disciples to not take or accept money or gifts for teaching or preaching the doctrine of the Most High.

Yashu'a (Jesus) said: "A new commandment I give unto
you, that ye love one another; as I have loved you,
that ye also love one another."

ASSASSINS of DISOBEDIENCE!
Invoking the Power of the Most High Through Obedience, is the Key to Living Your Best Life
as the Supreme Ingredient!
Heaven or Hell?

CHILDREN OF THE MOST HIGH:
PRISTINE YOUTH AND FAMILY SOLUTIONS, LLC.
SONS AND DAUGHTERS OF THE MOST HIGH PUBLISHERS ®

Oh, Gracious Most High Heavenly father, Holy is your name,
Your Will Be Done Now and Forever!
Yashu'a (Jesus) said: *"Thou shalt love the Most High Heavenly Father, thy Sustainer with all*
thy heart, and with all thy soul, and with all thy mind. Thou shalt love
thy neighbour as thyself."

In the KJV bible book of Mathew chapter 10 verse 5-10; the Messiah Yashu'a (Jesus) said: "These twelve Jesus sent forth, and commanded them, saying, **Go not into the way of the Gentiles**, and into any city of the Samaritans enter ye not. **But go rather to the lost sheep of the house of Israel**. And as ye go, preach, saying, the kingdom of heaven is at hand. Heal the sick, cleanse the lepers, raise the dead, cast out devils: **freely ye have received, freely give**. **Provide neither gold, nor silver, nor brass in your purses, (The only money at that time was gold, silver, and brass. In other words, don't take any MONEY!)** <u>Nor for scrip for your journey, neither two coats, neither shoes, nor yet staves</u>: for the workman is worthy of his meat (In other words, don't take any gifts either)."

Yashu'a (Jesus) said: "A new commandment I give unto
you, that ye love one another; as I have loved you,
that ye also love one another."

ASSASSINS of DISOBEDIENCE!
Invoking the Power of the Most High Through Obedience, is the Key to Living Your Best Life
as the Supreme Ingredient!
Heaven or Hell?

CHILDREN OF THE MOST HIGH:
PRISTINE YOUTH AND FAMILY SOLUTIONS, LLC.
SONS AND DAUGHTERS OF THE MOST HIGH PUBLISHERS ®

Oh, Gracious Most High Heavenly father, Holy is your name,
Your Will Be Done Now and Forever!
Yashu'a (Jesus) said: *"Thou shalt love the Most High Heavenly Father, thy Sustainer with all*
thy heart, and with all thy soul, and with all thy mind. Thou shalt love
thy neighbour as thyself."

In the KJV bible book of John chapter 5 verses 30-43; the Messiah Yashu'a (Jesus) said: "I can of mine own self do nothing: as I hear, I judge: and my judgment is just; because I seek not mine own will, but the will of the Father which hath sent me. If I bear witness of myself, my witness is not true. There is another that beareth witness of me; and I know that the witness which he witnessed of me is true. Ye sent unto John, and he bare witness unto the truth. But I receive not testimony from man: but these things I say, that ye might be saved. He was a burning and a shining light: and ye were willing for a season to rejoice in his light. But I have greater witness than that of John: for the works which the Father hath given me to finish, the same works that I do, bear witness of me, that the Father hath sent me."

278

Yashu'a (Jesus) said: *"A new commandment I give unto you, that ye love one another; as I have loved you, that ye also love one another."*

ASSASSINS of DISOBEDIENCE!
Invoking the Power of the Most High Through Obedience, is the Key to Living Your Best Life
as the Supreme Ingredient!
Heaven or Hell?

CHILDREN OF THE MOST HIGH:
PRISTINE YOUTH AND FAMILY SOLUTIONS, LLC.
SONS AND DAUGHTERS OF THE MOST HIGH PUBLISHERS ®

Oh, Gracious Most High Heavenly father, Holy is your name,
Your Will Be Done Now and Forever!
Yashu'a (Jesus) said: *"Thou shalt love the Most High Heavenly Father, thy Sustainer with all thy heart, and with all thy soul, and with all thy mind. Thou shalt love thy neighbour as thyself."*

"And the Father himself, which hath sent me, hath borne witness of me. Ye have neither heard his voice at any time, nor seen his shape. And ye have not his word abiding in you: for whom he hath sent, him ye believe not. Search the scriptures; for in them ye think ye have eternal life: and they are they which testify of me. And ye will not come to me, that ye might have life. I receive not honour from men. But I know you, that ye have not the love of God in you. I am come in my Father's name, and ye receive me not: if another shall come in his own name (**Speaking in the 1ˢᵗ person as "I"**), him ye will receive."

279

Yashu'a (Jesus) said: *"A new commandment I give unto you, that ye love one another; as I have loved you, that ye also love one another."*

ASSASSINS of DISOBEDIENCE!
Invoking the Power of the Most High Through Obedience, is the Key to Living Your Best Life
as the Supreme Ingredient!
Heaven or Hell?

CHILDREN OF THE MOST HIGH:
PRISTINE YOUTH AND FAMILY SOLUTIONS, LLC.
SONS AND DAUGHTERS OF THE MOST HIGH PUBLISHERS ®

Oh, Gracious Most High Heavenly father, Holy is your name,
Your Will Be Done Now and Forever!
Yashu'a (Jesus) said: "Thou shalt love the Most High Heavenly Father, thy Sustainer with all
thy heart, and with all thy soul, and with all thy mind. Thou shalt love
thy neighbour as thyself."

The Messiah Yashu'a (Jesus) <u>taught the Doctrine of the</u>
<u>Most High on the foundation of love (God is Love) without</u>
<u>money in the name of the Most High</u>; and <u>the ministers of</u>
<u>satan built a foundation on another gospel, another spirit,</u>
<u>and another Jesus out of the love of money in Jesus name</u>.
In the KJV bible book of 2nd Corinthians chapter 11 verses 1-
21; **Paul said**: "Would to God ye could bear with me a little **in**
my folly (**foolishness**): and indeed, bear with me. **For I am**
jealous over you with godly jealousy: for **I** have espoused you
to one husband, that **I** may present you as a chaste virgin to
Christ. But **I** fear, lest by any means, as the serpent beguiled
Eve through his subtilty, <u>so your minds should be corrupted</u>
<u>from the simplicity that is in Christ</u>."

280

Yashu'a (Jesus) said: "A new commandment I give unto
you, that ye love one another; as I have loved you,
that ye also love one another."

ASSASSINS of DISOBEDIENCE!
Invoking the Power of the Most High Through Obedience, is the Key to Living Your Best Life
as the Supreme Ingredient!
Heaven or Hell?

CHILDREN OF THE MOST HIGH:
PRISTINE YOUTH AND FAMILY SOLUTIONS, LLC.
SONS AND DAUGHTERS OF THE MOST HIGH PUBLISHERS ®

Oh, Gracious Most High Heavenly father, Holy is your name,
Your Will Be Done Now and Forever!
Yashu'a (Jesus) said: "Thou shalt love the Most High Heavenly Father, thy Sustainer with all
thy heart, and with all thy soul, and with all thy mind. Thou shalt love
thy neighbour as thyself."

"For if he that cometh preacheth **another Jesus**, whom we have not preached, or if ye receive **another spirit**, which ye have not received, or **another gospel**, which ye have not accepted, **ye might well bear with him**. (**I (the Messiah Yashu'a, Jesus) am come in my Father's name, and ye receive me not: if another shall come in his own name, him ye will receive**, KJV John 5:43)." For **I** suppose **I** was not a whit behind the very chiefest apostles. But though **I be rude in speech**, yet not in knowledge; but we have been throughly made manifest among you in all things. **Have I committed an offence in abasing myself that ye might be exalted, because I have preached to you the gospel of God freely?**"

Yashu'a (Jesus) said: "A new commandment I give unto
you, that ye love one another; as I have loved you,
that ye also love one another."

ASSASSINS of DISOBEDIENCE!
Invoking the Power of the Most High Through Obedience, is the Key to Living Your Best Life
as the Supreme Ingredient!
Heaven or Hell?

CHILDREN OF THE MOST HIGH:
PRISTINE YOUTH AND FAMILY SOLUTIONS, LLC.
SONS AND DAUGHTERS OF THE MOST HIGH PUBLISHERS ®

Oh, Gracious Most High Heavenly father, Holy is your name,
Your Will Be Done Now and Forever!
Yashu'a (Jesus) said: "Thou shalt love the Most High Heavenly Father, thy Sustainer with all
thy heart, and with all thy soul, and with all thy mind. Thou shalt love
thy neighbour as thyself."

"**I robbed other churches, taking wages of them, to do you service**. And when **I** was present with you, and wanted, **I was chargeable to no man**: for that which was lacking to me the brethren which came from Macedonia supplied. And in all things, **I** have kept myself from being burdensome unto you, and so will **I** keep myself. As the truth of Christ is in me, **no man shall stop me of this boasting** ("**Boast not thyself of tomorrow; for thou knowest not what a day may bring forth. Let another man praise thee, and not thine own mouth; a stranger, and not thine own lips**, KJV Proverbs 27:1-2." "**But now ye rejoice in your boastings: all such rejoicing is evil**, KJV James 4:16.") in the regions of Achaia. Wherefore? **because I love you not**? **God knoweth**."

282

Yashu'a (Jesus) said: "A new commandment I give unto
you, that ye love one another; as I have loved you,
that ye also love one another."

ASSASSINS of DISOBEDIENCE!
Invoking the Power of the Most High Through Obedience, is the Key to Living Your Best Life
as the Supreme Ingredient!
Heaven or Hell?

CHILDREN OF THE MOST HIGH:
PRISTINE YOUTH AND FAMILY SOLUTIONS, LLC.
SONS AND DAUGHTERS OF THE MOST HIGH PUBLISHERS ®

Oh, Gracious Most High Heavenly father, Holy is your name,
Your Will Be Done Now and Forever!
Yashu'a (Jesus) said: *"Thou shalt love the Most High Heavenly Father, thy Sustainer with all*
thy heart, and with all thy soul, and with all thy mind. Thou shalt love
thy neighbour as thyself."

"But what **I** do, that **I** will do, that **I** may cut off occasion from them which desire occasion; that wherein they glory, they may be found even as we. **For such are false apostles, deceitful workers, transforming themselves into the apostles of Christ**. **And no marvel; for Satan himself is transformed into an angel of light**. **Therefore, it is no great thing if his ministers also be transformed as the ministers of righteousness**; whose end shall be according to their works. **I** say again, **let no man think me a fool; if otherwise, yet as a fool receive me, that I may boast myself a little. That which I speak, I speak it not after the Lord**, **but as it were foolishly, in this confidence of boasting. Seeing that many glory after the flesh, I will glory also**. For ye suffer fools gladly, seeing ye yourselves are wise."

Yashu'a (Jesus) said: *"A new commandment I give unto you, that ye love one another; as I have loved you, that ye also love one another."*

ASSASSINS of DISOBEDIENCE!
Invoking the Power of the Most High Through Obedience, is the Key to Living Your Best Life
as the Supreme Ingredient!
Heaven or Hell?

CHILDREN OF THE MOST HIGH:
PRISTINE YOUTH AND FAMILY SOLUTIONS, LLC.
SONS AND DAUGHTERS OF THE MOST HIGH PUBLISHERS ®

Oh, Gracious Most High Heavenly father, Holy is your name,
Your Will Be Done Now and Forever!
Yashu'a (Jesus) said: *"Thou shalt love the Most High Heavenly Father, thy Sustainer with all*
thy heart, and with all thy soul, and with all thy mind. Thou shalt love
thy neighbour as thyself."

"For ye suffer, if a man brings you into bondage, if a man devours you, if a man takes of you, if a man exalt himself, if a man smites you on the face. **I** speak as concerning reproach, as though we had been weak. Howbeit wheresoever any is bold, (**I speak foolishly**) **I am bold also**." "Yea, **so have I strived to preach the gospel, not where Christ was named**, lest **I** should build upon another man's foundation, KJV Romans 15:20." "For if the truth of God hath more abounded through **my lie** unto his glory; why yet am **I** also judged as a sinner? KJV Romans 3:7." In the KJV bible book of Jeremiah, chapter 23 verses 1-3; it states: "**Woe be unto the pastors that destroy and scatter the sheep of my pasture! saith the LORD**."

284

Yashu'a (Jesus) said: *"A new commandment I give unto you, that ye love one another; as I have loved you, that ye also love one another."*

ASSASSINS of DISOBEDIENCE!
Invoking the Power of the Most High Through Obedience, is the Key to Living Your Best Life
as the Supreme Ingredient!
Heaven or Hell?

CHILDREN OF THE MOST HIGH:
PRISTINE YOUTH AND FAMILY SOLUTIONS, LLC.
SONS AND DAUGHTERS OF THE MOST HIGH PUBLISHERS ®

Oh, Gracious Most High Heavenly father, Holy is your name,
Your Will Be Done Now and Forever!
Yashu'a (Jesus) said: "Thou shalt love the Most High Heavenly Father, thy Sustainer with all
thy heart, and with all thy soul, and with all thy mind. Thou shalt love
thy neighbour as thyself."

"<u>Therefore, thus saith the LORD God of Israel against the pastors that feed my people; Ye have scattered my flock, and driven them away</u>, and have not visited them: behold, <u>I will visit upon you the evil of your doings, saith the LORD. And I will gather the remnant of my flock out of all countries whither I have driven them, and will bring them again to their folds; and they shall be fruitful and increase</u>.

285

Yashu'a (Jesus) said: "A new commandment I give unto you, that ye love one another; as I have loved you, that ye also love one another."

ASSASSINS of DISOBEDIENCE!
Invoking the Power of the Most High Through Obedience, is the Key to Living Your Best Life
as the Supreme Ingredient!
Heaven or Hell?

CHILDREN OF THE MOST HIGH:
PRISTINE YOUTH AND FAMILY SOLUTIONS, LLC.
SONS AND DAUGHTERS OF THE MOST HIGH PUBLISHERS ®

Oh, Gracious Most High Heavenly father, Holy is your name,
Your Will Be Done Now and Forever!
Yashu'a (Jesus) said: "Thou shalt love the Most High Heavenly Father, thy Sustainer with all
thy heart, and with all thy soul, and with all thy mind. Thou shalt love
thy neighbour as thyself."

In the KJV bible book of Romans chapter 7 verses 7-24; Paul said: "What shall we say then? Is the law sin? God forbid. **Nay, I had not known sin, but by the law: for I had not known lust, except the law had said**, Thou shalt not covet. But sin, taking occasion by the commandment, wrought in me all manner of concupiscence. For without the law sin was dead." "For **I** was alive without the law once: but when the commandment came, sin revived, and **I** died. And the commandment, which was ordained to life, **I** found to be unto death. For sin, taking occasion by the commandment, deceived me, and by it slew me. **Wherefore the law is holy, and the commandment holy, and just, and good**. Was then that which is good made death unto me? God forbid."

286

Yashu'a (Jesus) said: "A new commandment I give unto
you, that ye love one another; as I have loved you,
that ye also love one another."

ASSASSINS of DISOBEDIENCE!
Invoking the Power of the Most High Through Obedience, is the Key to Living Your Best Life
as the Supreme Ingredient!
Heaven or Hell?

CHILDREN OF THE MOST HIGH:
PRISTINE YOUTH AND FAMILY SOLUTIONS, LLC.
SONS AND DAUGHTERS OF THE MOST HIGH PUBLISHERS ®

Oh, Gracious Most High Heavenly father, Holy is your name,
Your Will Be Done Now and Forever!
Yashu'a (Jesus) said: *"Thou shalt love the Most High Heavenly Father, thy Sustainer with all*
thy heart, and with all thy soul, and with all thy mind. Thou shalt love
thy neighbour as thyself."

"But sin, that it might appear sin, working death in me by that which is good; that sin by the commandment might become exceeding sinful. For we know that the law is spiritual: but I am carnal, sold under sin. **For that which I do I allow not: for what I would, that do I not; but what I hate, that do I. If then I do that which I would not, I consent unto the law that it is good. Now then it is no more I that do it, but sin that dwelleth in me.** "For **I** know that in me (that is, in my flesh,) dwelleth no good thing: for to will is present with me; **but how to perform that which is good I find not. For the good that I would I do not: but the evil which I would not, that I do. Now if I do that I would not, it is no more I that do it, but sin that dwelleth in me. I find then a law, that, when I would do good, evil is present with me.**"

287

Yashu'a (Jesus) said: *"A new commandment I give unto you, that ye love one another; as I have loved you, that ye also love one another."*

ASSASSINS of DISOBEDIENCE!
Invoking the Power of the Most High Through Obedience, is the Key to Living Your Best Life
as the Supreme Ingredient!
Heaven or Hell?

CHILDREN OF THE MOST HIGH:
PRISTINE YOUTH AND FAMILY SOLUTIONS, LLC.
SONS AND DAUGHTERS OF THE MOST HIGH PUBLISHERS ®

Oh, Gracious Most High Heavenly father, Holy is your name,
Your Will Be Done Now and Forever!
Yashu'a (Jesus) said: *"Thou shalt love the Most High Heavenly Father, thy Sustainer with all thy heart, and with all thy soul, and with all thy mind. Thou shalt love thy neighbour as thyself."*

"For I delight in the law of God after the inward man. **But I see another law in my members, warring against the law of my mind, and bringing me into captivity to the law of sin which is in my members. O wretched man that I am**! who shall deliver me from the body of this death?" The Messiah Yashu'a (Jesus) said: "I am come in my Father's name, and ye receive me not: if another shall come in his own name, him ye will receive, KJV John 5:43)."

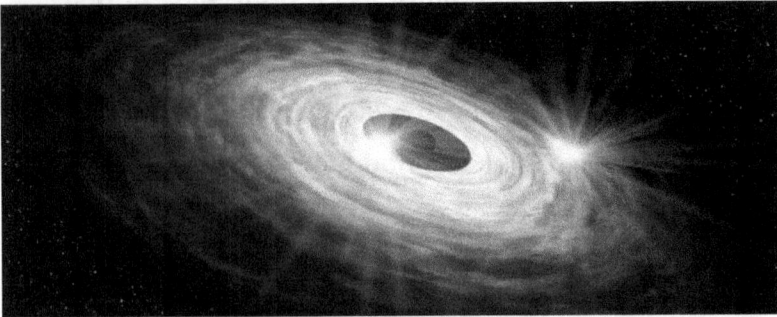

288

Yashu'a (Jesus) said: *"A new commandment I give unto you, that ye love one another; as I have loved you, that ye also love one another."*

ASSASSINS of DISOBEDIENCE!
Invoking the Power of the Most High Through Obedience, is the Key to Living Your Best Life
as the Supreme Ingredient!
Heaven or Hell?

CHILDREN OF THE MOST HIGH:
PRISTINE YOUTH AND FAMILY SOLUTIONS, LLC.
SONS AND DAUGHTERS OF THE MOST HIGH PUBLISHERS ®

Oh, Gracious Most High Heavenly father, Holy is your name,
Your Will Be Done Now and Forever!
Yashu'a (Jesus) said: "Thou shalt love the Most High Heavenly Father, thy Sustainer with all thy heart, and with all thy soul, and with all thy mind. Thou shalt love thy neighbour as thyself."

In the KJV bible book of Revelation chapter 22 verses 12-16; the Messiah Yashu'a said: "And, behold, I come quickly; and my reward is with me, to give every man according as his work shall be. I am Alpha and Omega, the beginning and the end, the first and the last. <u>Blessed are they that do his commandments, that they may have right to the tree of life, and may enter in through the gates into the city</u>. "For without are dogs, and sorcerers, and whoremongers, and murderers, and idolaters, and whosoever loveth and maketh a lie. <u>I Jesus have sent mine angel to testify unto you these things in the churches</u>. I am the root and the offspring of David, and the bright and morning star."

Yashu'a (Jesus) said: "A new commandment I give unto you, that ye love one another; as I have loved you, that ye also love one another."

ASSASSINS of DISOBEDIENCE!
Invoking the Power of the Most High Through Obedience, is the Key to Living Your Best Life
as the Supreme Ingredient!
Heaven or Hell?

CHILDREN OF THE MOST HIGH:
PRISTINE YOUTH AND FAMILY SOLUTIONS, LLC.
SONS AND DAUGHTERS OF THE MOST HIGH PUBLISHERS ®

Oh, Gracious Most High Heavenly father, Holy is your name,
Your Will Be Done Now and Forever!
Yashu'a (Jesus) said: "Thou shalt love the Most High Heavenly Father, thy Sustainer with all
thy heart, and with all thy soul, and with all thy mind. Thou shalt love
thy neighbour as thyself."

The Messiah Yashu'a (Jesus) said: "If ye love me, keep my commandments, KJV John 14:15." **Assassins of Disobedience must only quench their thirst with the <u>Living Waters</u>** in order to keep the Messiah Yashu'a (Jesus) commandments!

According to the bible, what are the <u>Living Waters</u>?

In the KJV bible book of John chapter 7 verse 38; the Messiah Yashu'a (Jesus) said: "He that believeth on me, as the scripture hath said, out of his belly shall flow rivers of <u>living water</u>. "In the aforementioned verse, the word "**living**" is the KJV bible Greek Strong's Concordance#**2198** is the word: ζάω **Záō**, pronounced as: **dzah'-o**; and means: a primary verb;

Yashu'a (Jesus) said: "A new commandment I give unto you, that ye love one another; as I have loved you, that ye also love one another."

ASSASSINS of DISOBEDIENCE!
Invoking the Power of the Most High Through Obedience, is the Key to Living Your Best Life
as the Supreme Ingredient!
Heaven or Hell?

CHILDREN OF THE MOST HIGH:
PRISTINE YOUTH AND FAMILY SOLUTIONS, LLC.
SONS AND DAUGHTERS OF THE MOST HIGH PUBLISHERS ®

Oh, Gracious Most High Heavenly father, Holy is your name,
Your Will Be Done Now and Forever!
Yashu'a (Jesus) said: *"Thou shalt love the Most High Heavenly Father, thy Sustainer with all*
thy heart, and with all thy soul, and with all thy mind. Thou shalt love
thy neighbour as thyself."

"To live (literally or figuratively):—life(-time), (a-)live(-ly), quick; to live, breathe, be among the living (not lifeless, not dead); to enjoy real life, to have true life and worthy of the name, active, blessed, endless in the kingdom of God, to live i.e. pass life, in the manner of the living and acting of mortals or character, living water, having vital power in itself and exerting the same upon the soul, metaph. to be in full vigor, to be fresh, strong, efficient, as adj. active, powerful, efficacious." "In the aforementioned verse, the word "**water**" is the KJV bible Greek Strong's Concordance#**5204** is the word: ὕδωρ **Hydōr** and means: **water (as if rainy) literally or figuratively: of water in rivers, in pools, of the water of the deluge, of water in any of the earth's repositories, of water as the primary element, fig. used of many peoples.**"

291

Yashu'a (Jesus) said: *"A new commandment I give unto you, that ye love one another; as I have loved you, that ye also love one another."*

CHILDREN OF THE MOST HIGH:
PRISTINE YOUTH AND FAMILY SOLUTIONS, LLC.
SONS AND DAUGHTERS OF THE MOST HIGH PUBLISHERS ®

Oh, Gracious Most High Heavenly father, Holy is your name,
Your Will Be Done Now and Forever!
Yashu'a (Jesus) said: "Thou shalt love the Most High Heavenly Father, thy Sustainer with all thy heart, and with all thy soul, and with all thy mind. Thou shalt love thy neighbour as thyself."

In the KJV bible book of Jeremiah chapter 2 verse 13: it states; "For my people have committed two evils; they have forsaken me the fountain of **living waters**, [and] hewed them out cisterns, broken cisterns, that can hold no water." "In the aforementioned verse, the word "**living**" is the KJV bible Hebrew Strong's Concordance#2416 is the word: **Khah-Ee חי** (**Khay** or **Chay**) and means **living**, **alive**. In the aforementioned verse, the word "**water**" is the KJV bible Greek Strong's Concordance#4325 is the word: **מַיִם Mayim** and means: **water, waters, watering**." In the KJV bible book of Revelation chapter 1 verses 14-15; it states: "His head and his hairs were white like **wool**, as white as snow; and his eyes were as a flame of fire; And his **feet like unto fine brass, as if they burned in a furnace**; and **his voice as the sound of many waters (ὕδωρ Hydōr).**"

Yashu'a (Jesus) said: "A new commandment I give unto you, that ye love one another; as I have loved you, that ye also love one another."

ASSASSINS of DISOBEDIENCE!
Invoking the Power of the Most High Through Obedience, is the Key to Living Your Best Life
as the Supreme Ingredient!
Heaven or Hell?

CHILDREN OF THE MOST HIGH:
PRISTINE YOUTH AND FAMILY SOLUTIONS, LLC.
SONS AND DAUGHTERS OF THE MOST HIGH PUBLISHERS ®

Oh, Gracious Most High Heavenly father, Holy is your name,
Your Will Be Done Now and Forever!
Yashu'a (Jesus) said: *"Thou shalt love the Most High Heavenly Father, thy Sustainer with all*
thy heart, and with all thy soul, and with all thy mind. Thou shalt love
thy neighbour as thyself."

So, the **"Living Waters"** are the true rejuvenating energy that the Messiah Yashu'a (Jesus) gives those sincere-hearted and devout children of the Most High who only seek to obey the Most High Heavenly Father. Those who only have divine love for the Most High Heavenly Father, and those who sacrifice their limited time to study and teach others the Most High's scriptures from the original languages that they were revealed in order to learn and know the truth about the Most High's Doctrine that will make their hearts, minds, spirits and souls free from that great dragon; that old serpent, called the devil, and satan, which deceiveth the whole world! **How does a child of the Most High arrive at the point of growth that you speak of?** Only by the **"Will"** of the Most High Heavenly Father, does a child of the Most High become aware with the inspirational thought of: **"there is more to know!"**

293

Yashu'a (Jesus) said: *"A new commandment I give unto you, that ye love one another; as I have loved you, that ye also love one another."*

ASSASSINS of DISOBEDIENCE!
Invoking the Power of the Most High Through Obedience, is the Key to Living Your Best Life
as the Supreme Ingredient!
Heaven or Hell?

CHILDREN OF THE MOST HIGH:
PRISTINE YOUTH AND FAMILY SOLUTIONS, LLC.
SONS AND DAUGHTERS OF THE MOST HIGH PUBLISHERS ®

Oh, Gracious Most High Heavenly father, Holy is your name,
Your Will Be Done Now and Forever!
Yashu'a (Jesus) said: "Thou shalt love the Most High Heavenly Father, thy Sustainer with all
thy heart, and with all thy soul, and with all thy mind. Thou shalt love
thy neighbour as thyself."

This thought initiates the next thought: **A.S.K**: "**what do I need to know?**" **NOW** is the **TIME, and CHANGE** is the **MOTIVE**! In the KJV bible book of John chapter 4 verses 23-24; the Messiah Yashu'a (Jesus) said: "**But the hour cometh, and now is, when the true worshippers shall worship the Father in spirit and in truth: for the Father seeketh such to worship him. God is a Spirit: and they that worship him must worship him in spirit and in truth.**" In the KJV bible book of Matthew chapter 7 verses 6-10; the Messiah Yashu'a (Jesus) said: "**Give not that which is holy unto the dogs, neither cast ye your pearls before swine, lest they trample them under their feet, and turn again and rend you. Ask, and it shall be given you; seek, and ye shall find; knock, and it shall be opened unto you.**"

294

Yashu'a (Jesus) said: "A new commandment I give unto
you, that ye love one another; as I have loved you,
that ye also love one another."

ASSASSINS of DISOBEDIENCE!
Invoking the Power of the Most High Through Obedience, is the Key to Living Your Best Life
as the Supreme Ingredient!
Heaven or Hell?

CHILDREN OF THE MOST HIGH:
PRISTINE YOUTH AND FAMILY SOLUTIONS, LLC.
SONS AND DAUGHTERS OF THE MOST HIGH PUBLISHERS ®

Oh, Gracious Most High Heavenly father, Holy is your name,
Your Will Be Done Now and Forever!
Yashu'a (Jesus) said: *"Thou shalt love the Most High Heavenly Father, thy Sustainer with all*
thy heart, and with all thy soul, and with all thy mind. Thou shalt love
thy neighbour as thyself."

"For every one that asketh receiveth; and he that seeketh findeth; and to him that knocketh it shall be opened. Or what man is there of you, whom if his son ask bread, will he give him a stone? Or if he asks a fish, will he give him a serpent?" So, a person may acquire the "**Living Waters**" if they have true-faith in the Most High Heavenly Father and true-faith in the Messiah Yashu'a; who are those sincere-hearted and devout children of the Most High who only seek to obey the Most High Heavenly Father. Those who only have divine love for the Most High Heavenly Father! In the KJV bible book of John chapter 7 verse 38; the Messiah Yashu'a (Jesus) said: "He that believeth on me, as the scripture hath said, out of his belly shall flow rivers of <u>living water</u>."

295

Yashu'a (Jesus) said: *"A new commandment I give unto you, that ye love one another; as I have loved you, that ye also love one another."*

ASSASSINS of DISOBEDIENCE!
Invoking the Power of the Most High Through Obedience, is the Key to Living Your Best Life
as the Supreme Ingredient!
Heaven or Hell?

CHILDREN OF THE MOST HIGH:
PRISTINE YOUTH AND FAMILY SOLUTIONS, LLC.
SONS AND DAUGHTERS OF THE MOST HIGH PUBLISHERS ®

Oh, Gracious Most High Heavenly father, Holy is your name,
Your Will Be Done Now and Forever!
Yashu'a (Jesus) said: *"Thou shalt love the Most High Heavenly Father, thy Sustainer with all*
thy heart, and with all thy soul, and with all thy mind. Thou shalt love
thy neighbour as thyself."

For more information about the **Living Waters**, seek out the book below: **"Mind Gardening in the Creative Garden of Will (Your Mind) to Grow a Living Water Mentality."** Authored by: Woodie Hughes Jr.

Yashu'a (Jesus) said: *"A new commandment I give unto you, that ye love one another; as I have loved you, that ye also love one another."*

ASSASSINS of DISOBEDIENCE!
Invoking the Power of the Most High Through Obedience, is the Key to Living Your Best Life
as the Supreme Ingredient!
Heaven or Hell?

CHILDREN OF THE MOST HIGH:
PRISTINE YOUTH AND FAMILY SOLUTIONS, LLC.
SONS AND DAUGHTERS OF THE MOST HIGH PUBLISHERS &

Oh, Gracious Most High Heavenly father, Holy is your name,
Your Will Be Done Now and Forever!
Yashu'a (Jesus) said: "Thou shalt love the Most High Heavenly Father, thy Sustainer with all
thy heart, and with all thy soul, and with all thy mind. Thou shalt love
thy neighbour as thyself."

If the children of the Most High at some point in time were obeying the Most High, and doing the Most High's "Will" on earth as it is in heaven; what did we do, or didn't do that we are now experiencing the great and dreadful day of the LORD as is mentioned in the KJV bible book of Malachi chapter 4 verses 1-6?

That's a great question! The answer to that question is the KJV bible book of Romans chapter 1 verses 18-34; and in KJV bible book of Malachi chapter 4 verses 1-6.

297

Yashu'a (Jesus) said: "A new commandment I give unto you, that ye love one another; as I have loved you, that ye also love one another."

ASSASSINS of DISOBEDIENCE!
Invoking the Power of the Most High Through Obedience, is the Key to Living Your Best Life
as the Supreme Ingredient!
Heaven or Hell?

CHILDREN OF THE MOST HIGH:
PRISTINE YOUTH AND FAMILY SOLUTIONS, LLC.
SONS AND DAUGHTERS OF THE MOST HIGH PUBLISHERS ®

Oh, Gracious Most High Heavenly father, Holy is your name,
Your Will Be Done Now and Forever!
Yashu'a (Jesus) said: "Thou shalt love the Most High Heavenly Father, thy Sustainer with all
thy heart, and with all thy soul, and with all thy mind. Thou shalt love
thy neighbour as thyself."

According to the KJV bible book of Romans chapter 1 verses 18-32; it states: "**For the wrath of God is revealed from heaven against all ungodliness and unrighteousness** of men (people), **who hold the truth in unrighteousness**; Because that which may be **known of God is manifest in them**; **for God hath shewed it unto them**. For the invisible things of him from the creation of the world are clearly seen, being understood by the things that are made, even his eternal power and Godhead; **so that they are without excuse**: **Because that, when they knew God, they glorified him not as God, neither were thankful; but became vain in their imaginations, and their foolish heart was darkened. Professing themselves to be wise, they became fools**."

Yashu'a (Jesus) said: "A new commandment I give unto you, that ye love one another; as I have loved you, that ye also love one another."

ASSASSINS of DISOBEDIENCE!
Invoking the Power of the Most High Through Obedience, is the Key to Living Your Best Life
as the Supreme Ingredient!
Heaven or Hell?

CHILDREN OF THE MOST HIGH:
PRISTINE YOUTH AND FAMILY SOLUTIONS, LLC.
SONS AND DAUGHTERS OF THE MOST HIGH PUBLISHERS ®

Oh, Gracious Most High Heavenly father, Holy is your name,
Your Will Be Done Now and Forever!
Yashu'a (Jesus) said: *"Thou shalt love the Most High Heavenly Father, thy Sustainer with all*
thy heart, and with all thy soul, and with all thy mind. Thou shalt love
thy neighbour as thyself."

"And changed the glory of the **uncorruptible God** into an image made like to **corruptible man**, and to birds, and four-footed beasts, and creeping things. Wherefore **God also gave them up to uncleanness through the lusts of their own hearts, to dishonor their own bodies between themselves.** Who changed the truth of God into a lie, and worshipped and served the creature more than the Creator, who is blessed forever. Amen."

299

Yashu'a (Jesus) said: "A new commandment I give unto you, that ye love one another; as I have loved you, that ye also love one another."

ASSASSINS of DISOBEDIENCE!
Invoking the Power of the Most High Through Obedience, is the Key to Living Your Best Life
as the Supreme Ingredient!
Heaven or Hell?

CHILDREN OF THE MOST HIGH:
PRISTINE YOUTH AND FAMILY SOLUTIONS, LLC.
SONS AND DAUGHTERS OF THE MOST HIGH PUBLISHERS ®

Oh, Gracious Most High Heavenly father, Holy is your name,
Your Will Be Done Now and Forever!
Yashu'a (Jesus) said: "Thou shalt love the Most High Heavenly Father, thy Sustainer with all
thy heart, and with all thy soul, and with all thy mind. Thou shalt love
thy neighbour as thyself."

"For this cause God gave them up unto **vile** (KJV bible Greek Strong's Concordance **#819** for the word: **ἀτιμία** Atimia-means: **dishonor, ignominy, disgrace, shame**:) **affections** (KJV bible Greek Strong's Concordance **#3806** for the word: πάθος Pathos-means: **suffering in a bad sense, depraved passion** (**especially concupiscence**):—(**inordinate**) **lust, whatever befalls one, whether it be sad or joyous; spec. a calamity, mishap, evil, affliction, a feeling which the mind suffers; an affliction of the mind, emotion, passion**), for even their women did change the natural use into that which is against nature."

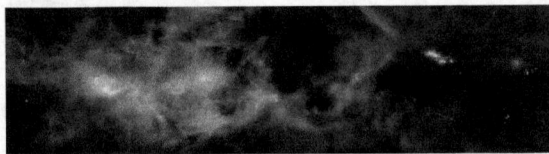

300

Yashu'a (Jesus) said: "A new commandment I give unto you, that ye love one another; as I have loved you, that ye also love one another."

ASSASSINS of DISOBEDIENCE!
Invoking the Power of the Most High Through Obedience, is the Key to Living Your Best Life
as the Supreme Ingredient!
Heaven or Hell?

CHILDREN OF THE MOST HIGH:
PRISTINE YOUTH AND FAMILY SOLUTIONS, LLC.
SONS AND DAUGHTERS OF THE MOST HIGH PUBLISHERS ®

Oh, Gracious Most High Heavenly father, Holy is your name,
Your Will Be Done Now and Forever!
Yashu'a (Jesus) said: *"Thou shalt love the Most High Heavenly Father, thy Sustainer with all*
thy heart, and with all thy soul, and with all thy mind. Thou shalt love
thy neighbour as thyself."

"And likewise, also the men, leaving the natural use of the woman, burned in their lust one toward another; men with men working that which is unseemly, and receiving in themselves that **recompence** (KJV bible Greek Strong's Concordance **#489** for the word: ἀντιμισθία Antimisthia-means: **a reward given in compensation, requital, recompense**) of their error which was meet. **And even as they did not like to retain God in their knowledge, <u>God gave them over to a</u> reprobate** (KJV bible Greek Strong's Concordance **#96** for the word: ἀδόκιμος **Adokimos**-means: <u>**unapproved**</u>, <u>**rejected**</u>; <u>**worthless**</u> (<u>**literally or morally**</u>, <u>**not standing the test, not approved, that which does not prove itself such as it ought, unfit for, unproved**</u>,) <u>**mind**</u>, to do those things which are not convenient."

301

Yashu'a (Jesus) said: "A new commandment I give unto
you, that ye love one another; as I have loved you,
that ye also love one another."

ASSASSINS of DISOBEDIENCE!
Invoking the Power of the Most High Through Obedience, is the Key to Living Your Best Life
as the Supreme Ingredient!
Heaven or Hell?

CHILDREN OF THE MOST HIGH:
PRISTINE YOUTH AND FAMILY SOLUTIONS, LLC.
SONS AND DAUGHTERS OF THE MOST HIGH PUBLISHERS *

Oh, Gracious Most High Heavenly father, Holy is your name,
Your Will Be Done Now and Forever!
Yashu'a (Jesus) said: *"Thou shalt love the Most High Heavenly Father, thy Sustainer with all thy heart, and with all thy soul, and with all thy mind. Thou shalt love thy neighbour as thyself."*

Being filled with all unrighteousness, <u>fornication</u> (KJV bible Greek Strong's Concordance **#4202** for the word: πορνεία Porneia-pronounced as: **<u>Por-na'-ä</u>** means: **<u>illicit sexual intercourse, fornication, homosexuality, lesbianism, intercourse with animals, sexual intercourse with close relatives; harlotry (including adultery and incest)</u>**, wickedness, **<u>covetousness</u>** (KJV bible Greek Strong's Concordance **#4124** for the word: πλεονεξία Pleonexia-means: **<u>greedy desire to have more</u>**, **<u>covetousness</u>**, **<u>avarice</u>**, **<u>greediness</u>**), **<u>maliciousness</u>** (KJV bible Greek Strong's Concordance **#2549** for the word: κακία Kakia-means: **<u>badness, depravity, malignity, malice(-iousness), naughtiness</u>**, **<u>malice, ill-will, desire to injure, wickedness that is not ashamed to break laws, evil, trouble</u>**)."

302

Yashu'a (Jesus) said: *"A new commandment I give unto you, that ye love one another; as I have loved you, that ye also love one another."*

ASSASSINS of DISOBEDIENCE!
Invoking the Power of the Most High Through Obedience, is the Key to Living Your Best Life
as the Supreme Ingredient!
Heaven or Hell?

CHILDREN OF THE MOST HIGH:
PRISTINE YOUTH AND FAMILY SOLUTIONS, LLC.
SONS AND DAUGHTERS OF THE MOST HIGH PUBLISHERS ®

Oh, Gracious Most High Heavenly father, Holy is your name,
Your Will Be Done Now and Forever!
Yashu'a (Jesus) said: "Thou shalt love the Most High Heavenly Father, thy Sustainer with all
thy heart, and with all thy soul, and with all thy mind. Thou shalt love
thy neighbour as thyself."

"**Full of envy, murder, debate** (KJV bible Greek Strong's Concordance #**2054** for the word: ἔρις Eris-means: **of uncertain affinity; a quarrel, wrangling, contention, debate, strife, variance**), **deceit** (KJV bible Greek Strong's Concordance #**1388** for the word: δόλος Dolos-means: (**probably meaning to decoy; a trick (bait), craft, deceit, guile, subtilty**), **malignity** (KJV bible Greek Strong's Concordance #**2550** for the word: κακοήθεια Kakoëtheia-means: **mischievousness, bad character, depravity of heart and life, malignant subtlety, malicious craftiness**) **whisperers** (KJV bible Greek Strong's Concordance #**5588** for the word: ψιθυριστής Psithyristēs-means: **a whisperer, secret slanderer, detractor**)."

303

Yashu'a (Jesus) said: "A new commandment I give unto
you, that ye love one another; as I have loved you,
that ye also love one another."

ASSASSINS of DISOBEDIENCE!
Invoking the Power of the Most High Through Obedience, is the Key to Living Your Best Life
as the Supreme Ingredient!
Heaven or Hell?

Oh, Gracious Most High Heavenly father, Holy is your name,
Your Will Be Done Now and Forever!
Yashu'a (Jesus) said: *"Thou shalt love the Most High Heavenly Father, thy Sustainer with all thy heart, and with all thy soul, and with all thy mind. Thou shalt love thy neighbour as thyself."*

"**Backbiters** (KJV bible Greek Strong's Concordance **#2637** for the word: κατάλαλος Katalalos-means: **a defamer**, **evil speaker**, **talkative against**, **a slanderer**, **backbiter**), **haters of God** (KJV bible Greek Strong's Concordance **#2319** for the word: θεοστυγής Theostygēs-means: **hater of God**, **hateful to God**, **exceptionally impious and wicked**), **despiteful**, proud (KJV bible Greek Strong's Concordance **#5244** for the word: ὑπερήφανος Hyperēphanos-means: **showing one's self above others**, **overtopping**, **proud**, **conspicuous above others**, **preeminent with an overweening estimate of one's means or merits**, **despising others or even treating them with contempt**, **haughty**), **boasters** (KJV bible Greek Strong's Concordance **#213** for the word: ἀλαζών Alazōn-means: **an empty pretender**, **a boaster**, **vagrancy**, **braggart**)."

304

Yashu'a (Jesus) said: *"A new commandment I give unto you, that ye love one another; as I have loved you, that ye also love one another."*

ASSASSINS of DISOBEDIENCE!
Invoking the Power of the Most High Through Obedience, is the Key to Living Your Best Life
as the Supreme Ingredient!
Heaven or Hell?

CHILDREN OF THE MOST HIGH:
PRISTINE YOUTH AND FAMILY SOLUTIONS, LLC.
SONS AND DAUGHTERS OF THE MOST HIGH PUBLISHERS ®

Oh, Gracious Most High Heavenly father, Holy is your name,
Your Will Be Done Now and Forever!
Yashu'a (Jesus) said: "Thou shalt love the Most High Heavenly Father, thy Sustainer with all
thy heart, and with all thy soul, and with all thy mind. Thou shalt love
thy neighbour as thyself."

Inventors of evil things, disobedient to parents, without understanding, covenant breakers, without natural affection, implacable (KJV bible Greek Strong's Concordance **#786** for the word: ἄσπονδος **Aspondos**-means: **trucebreakers**, **truceless**, **that cannot be persuaded to enter into a covenant**, **implacable**, **literally**, **without libation (which usually accompanied a treaty)**, **unmerciful**. Who knowing the judgment of God, that they which commit such things are worthy of death, not only do the same, but have pleasure in them that do them."

305

Yashu'a (Jesus) said: "A new commandment I give unto
you, that ye love one another; as I have loved you,
that ye also love one another."

ASSASSINS of DISOBEDIENCE!
Invoking the Power of the Most High Through Obedience, is the Key to Living Your Best Life
as the Supreme Ingredient!
Heaven or Hell?

CHILDREN OF THE MOST HIGH:
PRISTINE YOUTH AND FAMILY SOLUTIONS, LLC.
SONS AND DAUGHTERS OF THE MOST HIGH PUBLISHERS ®

Oh, Gracious Most High Heavenly father, Holy is your name,
Your Will Be Done Now and Forever!
Yashu'a (Jesus) said: *"Thou shalt love the Most High Heavenly Father, thy Sustainer with all*
thy heart, and with all thy soul, and with all thy mind. Thou shalt love
thy neighbour as thyself."

According to the KJV bible book of Malachi chapter 4 verses 1-6; it states: "For, behold, the day cometh, that shall burn as an oven; and all the proud, yea, and all that do wickedly, shall be stubble: and the day that cometh shall burn them up, saith the LORD of hosts, that it shall leave them neither root nor branch. But unto you that fear my name shall the Sun of righteousness arise with healing in his wings; and ye shall go forth, and grow up as calves of the stall. And ye shall tread down the wicked. For they shall be ashes under the soles of your feet in the day that I shall do this, saith the LORD of hosts. Remember ye the law of Moses my servant, which I commanded unto him in Horeb for all Israel, with the statutes and judgments. Behold, I will send you Elijah the prophet **before the coming of the great and dreadful day of the LORD**."

306

Yashu'a (Jesus) said: "A new commandment I give unto you, that ye love one another; as I have loved you, that ye also love one another."

ASSASSINS of DISOBEDIENCE!
Invoking the Power of the Most High Through Obedience, is the Key to Living Your Best Life
as the Supreme Ingredient!
Heaven or Hell?

CHILDREN OF THE MOST HIGH:
PRISTINE YOUTH AND FAMILY SOLUTIONS, LLC.
SONS AND DAUGHTERS OF THE MOST HIGH PUBLISHERS ®

Oh, Gracious Most High Heavenly father, Holy is your name,
Your Will Be Done Now and Forever!
Yashu'a (Jesus) said: "Thou shalt love the Most High Heavenly Father, thy Sustainer with all
thy heart, and with all thy soul, and with all thy mind. Thou shalt love
thy neighbour as thyself."

"And he shall turn the heart of the fathers to the children, and the heart of the children to their fathers, **lest I come and smite the earth with a curse**."

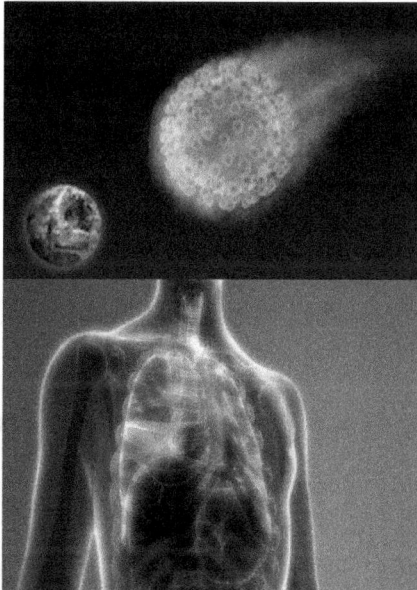

307

Yashu'a (Jesus) said: "A new commandment I give unto you, that ye love one another; as I have loved you, that ye also love one another."

ASSASSINS of DISOBEDIENCE!
Invoking the Power of the Most High Through Obedience, is the Key to Living Your Best Life
as the Supreme Ingredient!
Heaven or Hell?

CHILDREN OF THE MOST HIGH:
PRISTINE YOUTH AND FAMILY SOLUTIONS, LLC.
SONS AND DAUGHTERS OF THE MOST HIGH PUBLISHERS ®

Oh, Gracious Most High Heavenly father, Holy is your name,
Your Will Be Done Now and Forever!
Yashu'a (Jesus) said: *"Thou shalt love the Most High Heavenly Father, thy Sustainer with all*
thy heart, and with all thy soul, and with all thy mind. Thou shalt love
thy neighbour as thyself."

Was the tribe of Judah the only remnant left of Israel when Yashu'a was born?

According to the KJV bible book of 2 Kings chapter 17 verse 18; it states: "Therefore, the LORD was very angry with Israel, **and removed them out of his sight: there was none left but the tribe of Judah only**."

What happened to the remnant of the tribe of Judah?

According to the KJV bible book of 2 Kings chapter 19 verses 30-31; it states: "And the **remnant** that is escaped of the house of **Judah** shall yet again take root downward, and bear fruit upward. For out of Jerusalem shall go forth a **remnant**, and they that escape out of mount Zion: the zeal of **the LORD of hosts shall do this**."

Yashu'a (Jesus) said: *"A new commandment I give unto you, that ye love one another; as I have loved you, that ye also love one another."*

ASSASSINS of DISOBEDIENCE!
Invoking the Power of the Most High Through Obedience, is the Key to Living Your Best Life
as the Supreme Ingredient!
Heaven or Hell?

CHILDREN OF THE MOST HIGH:
PRISTINE YOUTH AND FAMILY SOLUTIONS, LLC.
SONS AND DAUGHTERS OF THE MOST HIGH PUBLISHERS ®

Oh, Gracious Most High Heavenly father, Holy is your name,
Your Will Be Done Now and Forever!
Yashu'a (Jesus) said: "Thou shalt love the Most High Heavenly Father, thy Sustainer with all
thy heart, and with all thy soul, and with all thy mind. Thou shalt love
thy neighbour as thyself."

According to Yashu'a (Jesus), who did he say he was sent to? According to the KJV bible book of Matthew chapter 15 verse 24; Yashu'a (Jesus) said: "I am not sent but unto the lost sheep of the house of Israel." **"If my people, which are called by my name, shall humble themselves, and pray, and seek my face, and turn from their wicked ways; then will I hear from heaven, and will forgive their sin, and will heal their land, KJV 2 Chronicles 7:14."**

Who raised the Messiah Yashu'a (Jesus) as a child? And what Laws did they follow?

According to the KJV bible book of Matthew chapter 1 verses 18-25; the Messiah Yashu'a (Jesus) was raised by his adopted father Joseph and mother Mary.

309

Yashu'a (Jesus) said: "A new commandment I give unto you, that ye love one another; as I have loved you, that ye also love one another."

ASSASSINS of DISOBEDIENCE!
Invoking the Power of the Most High Through Obedience, is the Key to Living Your Best Life
as the Supreme Ingredient!
Heaven or Hell?

CHILDREN OF THE MOST HIGH:
PRISTINE YOUTH AND FAMILY SOLUTIONS, LLC.
SONS AND DAUGHTERS OF THE MOST HIGH PUBLISHERS ®

Oh, Gracious Most High Heavenly father, Holy is your name,
Your Will Be Done Now and Forever!
Yashu'a (Jesus) said: "Thou shalt love the Most High Heavenly Father, thy Sustainer with all
thy heart, and with all thy soul, and with all thy mind. Thou shalt love
thy neighbour as thyself."

Mary and Joseph were both learnt in the Laws of Moses. After the birth of the Messiah Yashu'a (Jesus), he was brought to the temple by his parents according to the customs of the laws of Moses. According to the KJV bible book of Luke chapter 2 verses 27 and 39; it states: "And he came by the Spirit into the temple: and when the parents brought in the child Jesus, to do for him **after the custom of the law**. **And when they had performed all things according to the law of the Lord**, they returned into Galilee, to their own city Nazareth." "And it shall be for a sign unto thee upon thine hand, and for a memorial between thine eyes, that the LORD'S law may be in thy mouth: for with a strong hand hath the LORD brought thee out of Egypt. Thou shalt therefore keep this ordinance in his season from year to year, KJV Exodus 13:9-10."

310

Yashu'a (Jesus) said: "A new commandment I give unto
you, that ye love one another; as I have loved you,
that ye also love one another."

ASSASSINS of DISOBEDIENCE!
Invoking the Power of the Most High Through Obedience, is the Key to Living Your Best Life
as the Supreme Ingredient!
Heaven or Hell?

CHILDREN OF THE MOST HIGH:
PRISTINE YOUTH AND FAMILY SOLUTIONS, LLC.
SONS AND DAUGHTERS OF THE MOST HIGH PUBLISHERS ®

Oh, Gracious Most High Heavenly father, Holy is your name,
Your Will Be Done Now and Forever!
Yashu'a (Jesus) said: "Thou shalt love the Most High Heavenly Father, thy Sustainer with all
thy heart, and with all thy soul, and with all thy mind. Thou shalt love
thy neighbour as thyself."

"Now his parents went to Jerusalem every year at the feast of the **Passover** (πάσχα Pascha), KJV Luke 2:41." "And when a stranger shall sojourn with thee, and will keep the **Passover** (פֶּסַח **Pecach**) to the LORD, let all his males be circumcised, and then let him come near and keep it; and he shall be as one that is born in the land: for no uncircumcised person shall eat thereof, KJV Exodus 12:48." "And when **eight days were accomplished for the circumcising of the child**, his name **was called JESUS**, which was so named of the angel before he was conceived in the womb, KJV Luke 2:21." "And **in the eighth day the flesh of his foreskin shall be circumcised**, KJV Leviticus 12:3."

Yashu'a (Jesus) said: "A new commandment I give unto you, that ye love one another; as I have loved you, that ye also love one another."

ASSASSINS of DISOBEDIENCE!
Invoking the Power of the Most High Through Obedience, is the Key to Living Your Best Life
as the Supreme Ingredient!
Heaven or Hell?

CHILDREN OF THE MOST HIGH:
PRISTINE YOUTH AND FAMILY SOLUTIONS, LLC.
SONS AND DAUGHTERS OF THE MOST HIGH PUBLISHERS ®

Oh, Gracious Most High Heavenly father, Holy is your name,
Your Will Be Done Now and Forever!
Yashu'a (Jesus) said: "Thou shalt love the Most High Heavenly Father, thy Sustainer with all
thy heart, and with all thy soul, and with all thy mind. Thou shalt love
thy neighbour as thyself."

"This is my covenant, which ye shall keep, between me and you and thy seed after thee; Every man child among you shall be circumcised. And ye shall circumcise the flesh of your foreskin; and it shall be a token of the covenant between me and you. And **he that is eight days old shall be circumcised among you**, every man child in your generations, he that is born in the house, or bought with money of any stranger, which is not of thy seed. He that is born in thy house, and he that is bought with thy money, must needs be circumcised: and my covenant shall be in your flesh for an everlasting covenant. **And the uncircumcised man child whose flesh of his foreskin is not circumcised, that soul shall be cut off from his people; he hath broken my covenant**, KJV Genesis 17:10-14."

Yashu'a (Jesus) said: "A new commandment I give unto you, that ye love one another; as I have loved you, that ye also love one another."

ASSASSINS of DISOBEDIENCE!
Invoking the Power of the Most High Through Obedience, is the Key to Living Your Best Life
as the Supreme Ingredient!
Heaven or Hell?

CHILDREN OF THE MOST HIGH:
PRISTINE YOUTH AND FAMILY SOLUTIONS, LLC.
SONS AND DAUGHTERS OF THE MOST HIGH PUBLISHERS ®

Oh, Gracious Most High Heavenly father, Holy is your name,
Your Will Be Done Now and Forever!
Yashu'a (Jesus) said: "Thou shalt love the Most High Heavenly Father, thy Sustainer with all
thy heart, and with all thy soul, and with all thy mind. Thou shalt love
thy neighbour as thyself."

The aforementioned verses also show how Joseph and Mary followed the **Law of Abraham**. "And when the days of her purification **according to the law of Moses** were accomplished, they brought him to Jerusalem, to present him to the Lord. As it is written in the **law of the Lord**, every male that openeth the womb shall be called holy to the Lord, KJV Luke 2:22-23." The aforementioned verses show how Joseph and Mary followed the **Laws of Moses. How do we know?** According to the KJV bible book of John chapter 7 verse 19; the Messiah Yashu'a (Jesus) said: "Did not Moses give you the law, and yet none of you keepeth the law? Why go ye about to kill me?" "These are the words which I spake unto you, while I was yet with you, that all things must be fulfilled,

313

Yashu'a (Jesus) said: "A new commandment I give unto
you, that ye love one another; as I have loved you,
that ye also love one another."

ASSASSINS of DISOBEDIENCE!
Invoking the Power of the Most High Through Obedience, is the Key to Living Your Best Life
as the Supreme Ingredient!
Heaven or Hell?

CHILDREN OF THE MOST HIGH:
PRISTINE YOUTH AND FAMILY SOLUTIONS, LLC.
SONS AND DAUGHTERS OF THE MOST HIGH PUBLISHERS ®

Oh, Gracious Most High Heavenly father, Holy is your name,
Your Will Be Done Now and Forever!
Yashu'a (Jesus) said: *"Thou shalt love the Most High Heavenly Father, thy Sustainer with all*
thy heart, and with all thy soul, and with all thy mind. Thou shalt love
thy neighbour as thyself."

"which were written in the law of Moses, and in the prophets, and in the psalms, concerning me, KJV Luke 24:44." "I have done one work, and ye all marvel. Moses therefore gave unto you circumcision; (not because it is of Moses, but of the fathers;) and ye on the sabbath day circumcise a man. If a man on the sabbath day receive circumcision, that the law of Moses should not be broken; are ye angry at me, because I have made a man every whit whole on the sabbath day? Judge not according to the appearance, but judge righteous judgment, KJV John 7:21-24."

Yashu'a (Jesus) said: *"A new commandment I give unto you, that ye love one another; as I have loved you, that ye also love one another."*

ASSASSINS of DISOBEDIENCE!
Invoking the Power of the Most High Through Obedience, is the Key to Living Your Best Life
as the Supreme Ingredient!
Heaven or Hell?

CHILDREN OF THE MOST HIGH:
PRISTINE YOUTH AND FAMILY SOLUTIONS, LLC.
SONS AND DAUGHTERS OF THE MOST HIGH PUBLISHERS ®

Oh, Gracious Most High Heavenly father, Holy is your name,
Your Will Be Done Now and Forever!
Yashu'a (Jesus) said: "Thou shalt love the Most High Heavenly Father, thy Sustainer with all
thy heart, and with all thy soul, and with all thy mind. Thou shalt love
thy neighbour as thyself."

"For the law was given by Moses, but grace and truth came by Jesus Christ. Philip findeth Nathanael, and saith unto him, we have found him, of whom Moses in the law, and the prophets, did write, Jesus of Nazareth, the son of Joseph, KJV John 1:17;45." In the KJV bible book of John chapter 7 verse 16; the Messiah Yashu'a (Jesus) said: "My doctrine is not mine, but his that sent me." So, the Messiah Yashu'a (Jesus) taught, followed practiced, and obeyed **God's (אֱלֹהִים 'Elohiym) Commandments**.

315

Yashu'a (Jesus) said: "A new commandment I give unto
you, that ye love one another; as I have loved you,
that ye also love one another."

ASSASSINS of DISOBEDIENCE!
Invoking the Power of the Most High Through Obedience, is the Key to Living Your Best Life
as the Supreme Ingredient!
Heaven or Hell?

CHILDREN OF THE MOST HIGH:
PRISTINE YOUTH AND FAMILY SOLUTIONS, LLC.
SONS AND DAUGHTERS OF THE MOST HIGH PUBLISHERS ®

Oh, Gracious Most High Heavenly father, Holy is your name,
Your Will Be Done Now and Forever!
Yashu'a (Jesus) said: "Thou shalt love the Most High Heavenly Father, thy Sustainer with all
thy heart, and with all thy soul, and with all thy mind. Thou shalt love
thy neighbour as thyself."

Since Yashu'a (Jesus) did not eat pork (swine/pig), what did God's (אֱלֹהִים 'Elohiym), commandments and laws that Yashu'a (Jesus) followed say about eating swine? "They that sanctify themselves, and purify themselves in the gardens behind one tree in the midst, **eating swine's flesh, and the abomination, and the mouse, shall be consumed together, saith the LORD**, KJV Isaiah 66:17." "And **the swine**, though he divide the hoof, and be clovenfooted, yet he cheweth not the cud; he **[is] unclean to you**, KJV Leviticus 11:7." "And **the swine**, because it divideth the hoof, yet cheweth not the cud, **it is unclean unto you**: **ye shall not eat of their flesh, nor touch their dead carcase**, KJV Deuteronomy 14:8."

Yashu'a (Jesus) said: "A new commandment I give unto
you, that ye love one another; as I have loved you,
that ye also love one another."

ASSASSINS of DISOBEDIENCE!
Invoking the Power of the Most High Through Obedience, is the Key to Living Your Best Life
as the Supreme Ingredient!
Heaven or Hell?

CHILDREN OF THE MOST HIGH:
PRISTINE YOUTH AND FAMILY SOLUTIONS, LLC.
SONS AND DAUGHTERS OF THE MOST HIGH PUBLISHERS ®

Oh, Gracious Most High Heavenly father, Holy is your name,
Your Will Be Done Now and Forever!
Yashu'a (Jesus) said: "Thou shalt love the Most High Heavenly Father, thy Sustainer with all
thy heart, and with all thy soul, and with all thy mind. Thou shalt love
thy neighbour as thyself."

After reading these verses, how did Paul justify eating pork? Paul justified eating pork by the KJV verses listed below: "For one believeth that he may eat all things: another, who is weak, eateth herbs, KJV Romans 14:2." And, the Messiah Yashu'a (Jesus) said: "Not that which goeth into the mouth defileth a man; but that which cometh out of the mouth, this defileth a man, KJV Matthew 15:11." **If the KJV bible book of Matthew chapter 15 verse 11 is not referring to food, what is it referring to**? This is another great question! **This verse is not referring to food, it is referring God's (אֱלֹהִים 'Elohiym), Laws coming out of your mouth, and the law going into your heart in your body.**

317

ASSASSINS of DISOBEDIENCE!
Invoking the Power of the Most High Through Obedience, is the Key to Living Your Best Life
as the Supreme Ingredient!
Heaven or Hell?

CHILDREN OF THE MOST HIGH:
PRISTINE YOUTH AND FAMILY SOLUTIONS, LLC.
SONS AND DAUGHTERS OF THE MOST HIGH PUBLISHERS ®

Oh, Gracious Most High Heavenly father, Holy is your name,
Your Will Be Done Now and Forever!
Yashu'a (Jesus) said: "Thou shalt love the Most High Heavenly Father, thy Sustainer with all
thy heart, and with all thy soul, and with all thy mind. Thou shalt love
thy neighbour as thyself."

In the KJV bible book of Jeremiah chapter 31 verse 33; it states: "**But this shall be the covenant that I will make with the house of Israel; After those days, <u>saith the LORD, I will put my law in their inward parts, and write it in their hearts; and will be their God, and they shall be my people.</u>**" In the KJV bible book of Hebrews chapter 10 verse 16; it states: "**This is the covenant that I will make with them after those days, <u>saith the Lord, I will put my laws into their hearts, and in their minds will I write them</u>.**" "Receive, I pray thee, **<u>the law from his mouth, and lay up his words in thine heart</u>**, KJV Job 22:22." "**<u>The law of thy mouth</u>** is better unto me than thousands of gold and silver, KJV Psalms 119:72."

Yashu'a (Jesus) said: "A new commandment I give unto
you, that ye love one another; as I have loved you,
that ye also love one another."

ASSASSINS of DISOBEDIENCE!
Invoking the Power of the Most High Through Obedience, is the Key to Living Your Best Life
as the Supreme Ingredient!
Heaven or Hell?

CHILDREN OF THE MOST HIGH:
PRISTINE YOUTH AND FAMILY SOLUTIONS, LLC.
SONS AND DAUGHTERS OF THE MOST HIGH PUBLISHERS ®

Oh, Gracious Most High Heavenly father, Holy is your name,
Your Will Be Done Now and Forever!
Yashu'a (Jesus) said: "Thou shalt love the Most High Heavenly Father, thy Sustainer with all
thy heart, and with all thy soul, and with all thy mind. Thou shalt love
thy neighbour as thyself."

"**For the priest's lips should keep knowledge**, **and they should seek the law at his mouth**: for he is the messenger of the LORD of hosts, KJV Malachi 2:7." In the KJV bible book of John chapter 10 verse 34; the Messiah Yashu'a (Jesus) said: "Is it not written in your law, I said, Ye are gods?" "It is written, Man shall not live by bread alone, but by every word that proceedeth out of the mouth of God, KJV Matthew 4:4." "It is written, that man shall not live by bread alone, but by every word of God, KJV Luke 4:4." "**And I went unto the angel, and said unto him, Give me the little book. And he said unto me, take it, and eat it up; and it shall make thy belly bitter, but it shall be in thy mouth sweet as honey**, KJV Revelation 10:9."

319

Yashu'a (Jesus) said: "A new commandment I give unto you, that ye love one another; as I have loved you, that ye also love one another."

CHILDREN OF THE MOST HIGH:
PRISTINE YOUTH AND FAMILY SOLUTIONS, LLC.
SONS AND DAUGHTERS OF THE MOST HIGH PUBLISHERS ®

Oh, Gracious Most High Heavenly father, Holy is your name,
Your Will Be Done Now and Forever!
Yashu'a (Jesus) said: *"Thou shalt love the Most High Heavenly Father, thy Sustainer with all thy heart, and with all thy soul, and with all thy mind. Thou shalt love thy neighbour as thyself."*

In the KJV bible book of Galatians chapter 3 verses 10-11; Paul says: "For as many as are of the works of the law are under the curse: **for it is written, cursed is every one that continueth not in all things which are written in the book of the law to do them**. But that no man is justified by the law in the sight of God, it is evident: for, **the just shall live by faith**." The aforementioned KJV bible verses show that the Messiah Yashu'a (Jesus) teaching of the Most Doctrine is based on obedience to him and the Most High Heavenly Father, and obedience to **God's (אֱלֹהִים 'Elohiym), Commandments and Laws**; and **Paul's Gospel is based by living by faith and the ending of the laws**.

Yashu'a (Jesus) said: "A new commandment I give unto you, that ye love one another; as I have loved you, that ye also love one another."

ASSASSINS of DISOBEDIENCE!
Invoking the Power of the Most High Through Obedience, is the Key to Living Your Best Life
as the Supreme Ingredient!
Heaven or Hell?

CHILDREN OF THE MOST HIGH:
PRISTINE YOUTH AND FAMILY SOLUTIONS, LLC.
SONS AND DAUGHTERS OF THE MOST HIGH PUBLISHERS ®

Oh, Gracious Most High Heavenly father, Holy is your name,
Your Will Be Done Now and Forever!
Yashu'a (Jesus) said: "Thou shalt love the Most High Heavenly Father, thy Sustainer with all
thy heart, and with all thy soul, and with all thy mind. Thou shalt love
thy neighbour as thyself."

How does Paul justify abolishing the law? "<u>**For Christ is the**</u> <u>**end of the law for righteousness to everyone that believeth**</u>, KJV Romans 10:4." "For the woman which hath an husband is bound by the law to her husband so long as he liveth; but if the husband be dead, she is loosed from the law of her husband. Wherefore, my brethren, ye also are become dead to the law by the body of Christ; that ye should be married to another, even to him who is raised from the dead, that we should bring forth fruit unto God, KJV Romans 7:2 and 4." In these verses, Paul is comparing the Messiah Yashu'a (Jesus) to a widowed woman. Stating that since the Messiah Yashu'a (Jesus) is dead, then the law died with him. However; the children of the Most High that adheres to the **Doctrine of the Most High** that Yasu'a (Yashu'a/Jesus) taught; knows that Yashu'a (Jesus) is not dead.

Yashu'a (Jesus) said: "A new commandment I give unto
you, that ye love one another; as I have loved you,
that ye also love one another."

ASSASSINS of DISOBEDIENCE!
Invoking the Power of the Most High Through Obedience, is the Key to Living Your Best Life
as the Supreme Ingredient!
Heaven or Hell?

CHILDREN OF THE MOST HIGH:
PRISTINE YOUTH AND FAMILY SOLUTIONS, LLC.
SONS AND DAUGHTERS OF THE MOST HIGH PUBLISHERS ®

Oh, Gracious Most High Heavenly father, Holy is your name,
Your Will Be Done Now and Forever!
Yashu'a (Jesus) said: "Thou shalt love the Most High Heavenly Father, thy Sustainer with all
thy heart, and with all thy soul, and with all thy mind. Thou shalt love
thy neighbour as thyself."

Did the Messiah Yashu'a (Jesus) ever say the law ended with him? No! Nowhere in the scriptures did the Messiah Yashu'a (Jesus) ever say that. However; in the book of Revelation chapter 22 verse 14; it states: "**Blessed are they that do his commandments**, that they may have right to the tree of life, and may enter in through the gates into the city." The Messiah Yashu'a (Jesus) said: "Think not that I am come to destroy the law, or the prophets: I am not come to destroy, but to fulfil. For verily I say unto you, till heaven and earth pass, one jot or one tittle shall in no wise pass from the law, till all be fulfilled, KJV Mathew 5:17-18." **Did heaven and earth pass away? No.**

Yashu'a (Jesus) said: "A new commandment I give unto you, that ye love one another; as I have loved you, that ye also love one another."

ASSASSINS of DISOBEDIENCE!
Invoking the Power of the Most High Through Obedience, is the Key to Living Your Best Life
as the Supreme Ingredient!
Heaven or Hell?

CHILDREN OF THE MOST HIGH:
PRISTINE YOUTH AND FAMILY SOLUTIONS, LLC.
SONS AND DAUGHTERS OF THE MOST HIGH PUBLISHERS ®

Oh, Gracious Most High Heavenly father, Holy is your name,
Your Will Be Done Now and Forever!
Yashu'a (Jesus) said: "Thou shalt love the Most High Heavenly Father, thy Sustainer with all
thy heart, and with all thy soul, and with all thy mind. Thou shalt love
thy neighbour as thyself."

According to the KJV bible, **when is all fulfilled** according to what the Messiah Yashu'a (Jesus) said? **All is fulfilled** at the end of chapter 22 in the Book of Revelation. According to the KJV bible, **when does heaven and earth pass away? Heaven and earth don't pass away** until the KJV bible book of Revelation chapter 21 verse 1; it states: "And I saw a new heaven and a new earth: for the first heaven and the first earth were passed away; and there was no more sea." <u>So, according to the aforementioned KJV bible verses about God's (אֱלֹהִים 'Elohiym), commandments; since Yashu'a (Jesus) did not put pork (swine/pig) in his body, it is imperative that the children of the Most High follow the Messiah Yashu'a (Jesus) example by not putting pork in our bodies if we are in the body of Christ!</u>

323

Yashu'a (Jesus) said: "A new commandment I give unto you, that ye love one another; as I have loved you, that ye also love one another."

ASSASSINS of DISOBEDIENCE!
Invoking the Power of the Most High Through Obedience, is the Key to Living Your Best Life
as the Supreme Ingredient!
Heaven or Hell?

CHILDREN OF THE MOST HIGH:
PRISTINE YOUTH AND FAMILY SOLUTIONS, LLC.
SONS AND DAUGHTERS OF THE MOST HIGH PUBLISHERS ®

Oh, Gracious Most High Heavenly father, Holy is your name,
Your Will Be Done Now and Forever!
Yashu'a (Jesus) said: "Thou shalt love the Most High Heavenly Father, thy Sustainer with all
thy heart, and with all thy soul, and with all thy mind. Thou shalt love
thy neighbour as thyself."

Did the Messiah Yashu'a (Jesus) ever say that he loved the church? **No. Nowhere in the scriptures did the Messiah Yashu'a (Jesus) ever say that**. **Paul said that**, (**the Messiah Yashu'a (Jesus) and the Most High Heavenly Father; did not ever say, that Christ loved the church, that was already existing in Antioch before the disciples arrived in Antioch**). **Paul said**: "Husbands, love your wives, **even as Christ also loved the church**, and gave himself for it; That he might sanctify and cleanse it with the washing of water by the word, KJV Ephesians 5:25-25." However; the Messiah Yashu'a (Jesus) said: "And I say also unto thee, That thou art Peter, and upon this rock I will build my church; and the gates of hell shall not prevail against it, but **he** (**Yashu'a/Jesus**) turned, and **said unto Peter**, **Get thee behind me, Satan**:"

324

Yashu'a (Jesus) said: "A new commandment I give unto you, that ye love one another; as I have loved you, that ye also love one another."

ASSASSINS of DISOBEDIENCE!
Invoking the Power of the Most High Through Obedience, is the Key to Living Your Best Life
as the Supreme Ingredient!
Heaven or Hell?

CHILDREN OF THE MOST HIGH:
PRISTINE YOUTH AND FAMILY SOLUTIONS, LLC.
SONS AND DAUGHTERS OF THE MOST HIGH PUBLISHERS ®

Oh, Gracious Most High Heavenly father, Holy is your name,
Your Will Be Done Now and Forever!
Yashu'a (Jesus) said: "Thou shalt love the Most High Heavenly Father, thy Sustainer with all
thy heart, and with all thy soul, and with all thy mind. Thou shalt love
thy neighbour as thyself."

"**thou art an offence unto me**: **for thou savourest not the things that be of God, but those that be of men**, KJV Matthew 16: 18 and 23.**"** In the aforementioned verse, the Messiah Yashu'a (Jesus) called **Peter, Satan. Did the Messiah Yashu'a (Jesus) finish or complete teaching the Doctrine of the Most High**? **No**. In the KJV bible book of John chapter 16 verses 12-16; the Messiah Yashu'a (Jesus) said: "I have yet many things to say unto you, but ye cannot bear them now." Howbeit when he, the Spirit of truth, is come, he will guide you into all truth. "For he shall not speak of himself; but whatsoever he shall hear, that shall he speak: and he will shew you things to come. He shall glorify me: for he shall receive of mine, and shall shew it unto you."

Yashu'a (Jesus) said: "A new commandment I give unto you, that ye love one another; as I have loved you, that ye also love one another."

ASSASSINS of DISOBEDIENCE!
Invoking the Power of the Most High Through Obedience, is the Key to Living Your Best Life
as the Supreme Ingredient!
Heaven or Hell?

CHILDREN OF THE MOST HIGH:
PRISTINE YOUTH AND FAMILY SOLUTIONS, LLC.
SONS AND DAUGHTERS OF THE MOST HIGH PUBLISHERS ®

Oh, Gracious Most High Heavenly father, Holy is your name,
Your Will Be Done Now and Forever!
Yashu'a (Jesus) said: *"Thou shalt love the Most High Heavenly Father, thy Sustainer with all*
thy heart, and with all thy soul, and with all thy mind. Thou shalt love
thy neighbour as thyself."

"All things that the Father hath are mine: therefore; said I, that he shall take of mine, and shall shew it unto you. A little while, and ye shall not see me: and again, a little while, and ye shall see me, because I go to the Father." **What Laws did Yashu'a (Jesus) follow? And are the Laws that Yashu'a (Jesus) followed the same Laws that we who have Accepted him as our Savior are Commanded to Follow Today? Those are great questions**! Therefore; we will list the KJV bible New Testament Torah Laws of Moses with the KJV bible Old Testament Torah Laws of Moses, side by side that Yashu'a (Jesus) followed below:

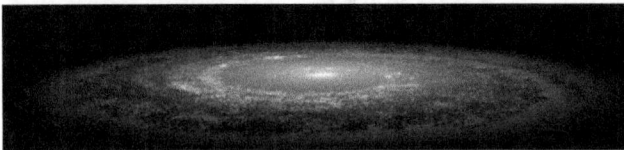

326

Yashu'a (Jesus) said: "A new commandment I give unto you, that ye love one another; as I have loved you, that ye also love one another."

ASSASSINS of DISOBEDIENCE!
Invoking the Power of the Most High Through Obedience, is the Key to Living Your Best Life
as the Supreme Ingredient!
Heaven or Hell?

CHILDREN OF THE MOST HIGH:
PRISTINE YOUTH AND FAMILY SOLUTIONS, LLC.
SONS AND DAUGHTERS OF THE MOST HIGH PUBLISHERS ®

Oh, Gracious Most High Heavenly father, Holy is your name,
Your Will Be Done Now and Forever!
Yashu'a (Jesus) said: *"Thou shalt love the Most High Heavenly Father, thy Sustainer with all thy heart, and with all thy soul, and with all thy mind. Thou shalt love thy neighbour as thyself."*

Law of Circumcision: Luke 2:21 and Leviticus 12:1-3.

In the KJV bible book of Luke 2 verse 21; it states: "And when eight days were accomplished for the circumcising of the child, his name was called JESUS, which was so named of the angel before he was conceived in the womb." "**And the LORD spake unto Moses, saying**: Speak unto the children of Israel, saying, if a woman has conceived seed, and born a man child: then she shall be unclean seven days; according to the days of the separation for her infirmity shall she be unclean. And in the eighth day the flesh of his foreskin shall be circumcised, KJV Leviticus 12:1-3."

Yashu'a (Jesus) said: "A new commandment I give unto you, that ye love one another; as I have loved you, that ye also love one another."

ASSASSINS of DISOBEDIENCE!
Invoking the Power of the Most High Through Obedience, is the Key to Living Your Best Life
as the Supreme Ingredient!
Heaven or Hell?

CHILDREN OF THE MOST HIGH:
PRISTINE YOUTH AND FAMILY SOLUTIONS, LLC.
SONS AND DAUGHTERS OF THE MOST HIGH PUBLISHERS ®

Oh, Gracious Most High Heavenly father, Holy is your name,
Your Will Be Done Now and Forever!
Yashu'a (Jesus) said: "Thou shalt love the Most High Heavenly Father, thy Sustainer with all
thy heart, and with all thy soul, and with all thy mind. Thou shalt love
thy neighbour as thyself."

What did Paul preach about circumcision? "For in Jesus Christ neither circumcision availeth anything, nor uncircumcision; but faith which worketh by love, KJV Galatians 5:6." "**Therefore; we conclude** that a man is justified by faith without the deeds of the law, KJV Romans 3:28." So, according to Paul, (**Not the Messiah Yashu'a (Jesus) or the Most High Heavenly Father**), he (Paul) said: "**Therefore; we conclude that a man is justified by faith without the deeds of the law**." "For do I now persuade men, or God? or do I seek to please men? for if I yet pleased men, I should not be the servant of Christ, KJV Galatians 1:10."

328

Yashu'a (Jesus) said: "A new commandment I give unto you, that ye love one another; as I have loved you, that ye also love one another."

ASSASSINS of DISOBEDIENCE!
Invoking the Power of the Most High Through Obedience, is the Key to Living Your Best Life
as the Supreme Ingredient!
Heaven or Hell?

CHILDREN OF THE MOST HIGH:
PRISTINE YOUTH AND FAMILY SOLUTIONS, LLC.
SONS AND DAUGHTERS OF THE MOST HIGH PUBLISHERS ®

Oh, Gracious Most High Heavenly father, Holy is your name,
Your Will Be Done Now and Forever!
Yashu'a (Jesus) said: "Thou shalt love the Most High Heavenly Father, thy Sustainer with all
thy heart, and with all thy soul, and with all thy mind. Thou shalt love
thy neighbour as thyself."

Law of keeping the Sabbath: Luke 4:16 and Exodus 31:15.

Law against Associating images with the Creator: Matthew 4:10 and Exodus 20:3.

Obeying Laws: Matthew 5:17-18, and Exodus 13:9-10.

Law about Anointing: John 9:6,11 and Exodus 40:13.

Law about not Tempting the Lord: Matthew 4:7 and Deuteronomy 6:16.

Law about Honoring Thy Father and Mother: Matthew 15:4 and Exodus 20:14.

Fasting: Matthew 4:2 and Judges 20:26.

Prostrating in Prayer: Matthew 26:39 and Numbers 20:6.

Intoxication is a Sin: Luke 1:15 and Leviticus 10:9.

329

Yashu'a (Jesus) said: "A new commandment I give unto
you, that ye love one another; as I have loved you,
that ye also love one another."

ASSASSINS of DISOBEDIENCE!
Invoking the Power of the Most High Through Obedience, is the Key to Living Your Best Life
as the Supreme Ingredient!
Heaven or Hell?

CHILDREN OF THE MOST HIGH:
PRISTINE YOUTH AND FAMILY SOLUTIONS, LLC.
SONS AND DAUGHTERS OF THE MOST HIGH PUBLISHERS ®

Oh, Gracious Most High Heavenly father, Holy is your name,
Your Will Be Done Now and Forever!
Yashu'a (Jesus) said: "Thou shalt love the Most High Heavenly Father, thy Sustainer with all
thy heart, and with all thy soul, and with all thy mind. Thou shalt love
thy neighbour as thyself."

Passover: Matthew 26:18-19 and Exodus 12:48. So, according to the aforementioned verses; we have identified some of the Laws of Moses that the Messiah Yashu'a (Jesus) followed to establish clear evidence, that the Messiah Yashu'a (Jesus) did not come to destroy the laws as he said, he came to fulfill the laws. This is why the Messiah Yashu'a (Jesus) said: "Think not that I am come to destroy the law, or the prophets: I am not come to destroy, but to fulfill. For verily I say unto you, till heaven and earth pass, one jot or one tittle shall in no wise pass from the law, till all be fulfilled." Did heaven and earth pass? No. Therefore; according to the Messiah Yashu'a (Jesus), Till heaven and earth pass (which occurs in Revelation 21:1), one jot or one tittle shall in no wise pass from the law, till all be fulfilled (which occurs in Revelation 22:21)."

"Whosoever therefore shall break one of these least commandments, and shall teach men so, he shall be called the least in the kingdom of heaven: but whosoever shall do

Yashu'a (Jesus) said: "A new commandment I give unto
you, that ye love one another; as I have loved you,
that ye also love one another."

ASSASSINS of DISOBEDIENCE!
Invoking the Power of the Most High Through Obedience, is the Key to Living Your Best Life
as the Supreme Ingredient!
Heaven or Hell?

CHILDREN OF THE MOST HIGH:
PRISTINE YOUTH AND FAMILY SOLUTIONS, LLC.
SONS AND DAUGHTERS OF THE MOST HIGH PUBLISHERS ®

Oh, Gracious Most High Heavenly father, Holy is your name,
Your Will Be Done Now and Forever!
Yashu'a (Jesus) said: "Thou shalt love the Most High Heavenly Father, thy Sustainer with all
thy heart, and with all thy soul, and with all thy mind. Thou shalt love
thy neighbour as thyself."

and teach them, the same shall be called great in the
kingdom of heaven, KJV Matthew 5:17-19."

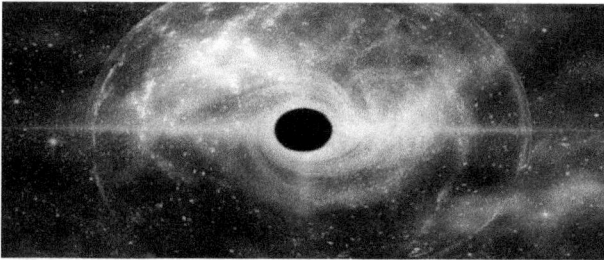

So, the Messiah Yashu'a (Jesus) taught, followed practiced, and
obeyed **God's (אֱלֹהִים 'Elohiym) Commandments** which are
the same Laws that we who have accepted him as our Savior
are commanded to follow today!

This is why the Messiah Yashu'a (Jesus) said: "And, behold,
I come quickly; and my reward is with me, to give every

331

Yashu'a (Jesus) said: "A new commandment I give unto
you, that ye love one another; as I have loved you,
that ye also love one another."

ASSASSINS of DISOBEDIENCE!
Invoking the Power of the Most High Through Obedience, is the Key to Living Your Best Life
as the Supreme Ingredient!
Heaven or Hell?

CHILDREN OF THE MOST HIGH:
PRISTINE YOUTH AND FAMILY SOLUTIONS, LLC.
SONS AND DAUGHTERS OF THE MOST HIGH PUBLISHERS ®

Oh, Gracious Most High Heavenly father, Holy is your name,
Your Will Be Done Now and Forever!
Yashu'a (Jesus) said: *"Thou shalt love the Most High Heavenly Father, thy Sustainer with all*
thy heart, and with all thy soul, and with all thy mind. Thou shalt love
thy neighbour as thyself."

man according as his work shall be. I am Alpha and Omega, the beginning and the end, the first and the last. **Blessed are they that do his commandments**, that they may have right to the tree of life, and may enter in through the gates into the city, KJV Revelation 22:12-14."

In conclusion, the KJV bible book of Jeremiah chapter 29 verse 11; it states: **"For I know the plans I have for you,"** declares

Yashu'a (Jesus) said: *"A new commandment I give unto you, that ye love one another; as I have loved you, that ye also love one another."*

ASSASSINS of DISOBEDIENCE!
Invoking the Power of the Most High Through Obedience, is the Key to Living Your Best Life
as the Supreme Ingredient!
Heaven or Hell?

CHILDREN OF THE MOST HIGH:
PRISTINE YOUTH AND FAMILY SOLUTIONS, LLC.
SONS AND DAUGHTERS OF THE MOST HIGH PUBLISHERS ®

Oh, Gracious Most High Heavenly father, Holy is your name,
Your Will Be Done Now and Forever!
Yashu'a (Jesus) said: "Thou shalt love the Most High Heavenly Father, thy Sustainer with all
thy heart, and with all thy soul, and with all thy mind. Thou shalt love
thy neighbour as thyself."

the LORD, "plans to prosper you and not to harm you, plans to give you hope and a future." "This is the covenant that I will make with them after those days, saith the Lord, I will put my laws into their hearts, and in their minds will I write them, Hebrews 10:16." In the KJV bible book of John chapter 14 verse 21; the Messiah **Yashu'a (Jesus) said:** "He [or she] that hath my commandments, and keepeth them, he [or she] it is that loveth me: and he [or she] that loveth me shall be loved of my Father, and I will love him [or her], and will manifest myself to him [or her]."

In the KJV bible book of Revelation chapter 22 verses 11-19; it states: "And he saith unto me, Seal not the sayings of the

333

Yashu'a (Jesus) said: "A new commandment I give unto you, that ye love one another; as I have loved you, that ye also love one another."

ASSASSINS of DISOBEDIENCE!
*Invoking the Power of the Most High Through Obedience, is the Key to Living Your Best Life
as the Supreme Ingredient!
Heaven or Hell?*

CHILDREN OF THE MOST HIGH:
PRISTINE YOUTH AND FAMILY SOLUTIONS, LLC.
SONS AND DAUGHTERS OF THE MOST HIGH PUBLISHERS ®

*Oh, Gracious Most High Heavenly father, Holy is your name,
Your Will Be Done Now and Forever!*
*Yashu'a (Jesus) said: "Thou shalt love the Most High Heavenly Father, thy Sustainer with all
thy heart, and with all thy soul, and with all thy mind. Thou shalt love
thy neighbour as thyself."*

prophecy of this book: for the time is at hand. **He that is unjust, let him be unjust still: and he which is filthy, let him be filthy still: and he that is righteous, let him be righteous still: and he that is holy, let him be holy still**. And, behold, I come quickly; and my reward is with me, to give every man according as his work shall be. I am Alpha and Omega, the beginning and the end, the first and the last. **Blessed are they that do his commandments, that they may have right to the tree of life, and may enter in through the gates into the city. For without are dogs, and sorcerers, and whoremongers, and murderers, and idolaters, and whosoever loveth and maketh a lie.**"

"I Jesus have sent mine angel to testify unto you these things in the churches. I am the root and the offspring of David,

334

Yashu'a (Jesus) said: "A new commandment I give unto you, that ye love one another; as I have loved you, that ye also love one another."

ASSASSINS of DISOBEDIENCE!
Invoking the Power of the Most High Through Obedience, is the Key to Living Your Best Life
as the Supreme Ingredient!
Heaven or Hell?

CHILDREN OF THE MOST HIGH:
PRISTINE YOUTH AND FAMILY SOLUTIONS, LLC.
SONS AND DAUGHTERS OF THE MOST HIGH PUBLISHERS ®

Oh, Gracious Most High Heavenly father, Holy is your name,
Your Will Be Done Now and Forever!
Yashu'a (Jesus) said: "Thou shalt love the Most High Heavenly Father, thy Sustainer with all thy heart, and with all thy soul, and with all thy mind. Thou shalt love thy neighbour as thyself."

and the bright and morning star. And the Spirit and the bride say, Come. And let him that heareth say, Come. And let him that is athirst come. **And whosoever will, let him take the water of life freely**. For I testify unto every man (τις tis, **means a person**) that heareth the words of the prophecy of this book, if any man (τις tis, **means a person**) shall add unto these things, God shall add unto him [or her] the plagues that are written in this book. And if any man (τις tis, **means a person**) shall take away from the words of the book of this prophecy, God shall take away his [or her] part out of the book of life, and out of the holy city, and from the things which are written in this book."

"If my people, which are called by my name, shall humble themselves, and pray, and seek my face, and turn from their

335

Yashu'a (Jesus) said: "A new commandment I give unto you, that ye love one another; as I have loved you, that ye also love one another."

ASSASSINS of DISOBEDIENCE!
Invoking the Power of the Most High Through Obedience, is the Key to Living Your Best Life
as the Supreme Ingredient!
Heaven or Hell?

CHILDREN OF THE MOST HIGH:
PRISTINE YOUTH AND FAMILY SOLUTIONS, LLC.
SONS AND DAUGHTERS OF THE MOST HIGH PUBLISHERS ®

Oh, Gracious Most High Heavenly father, Holy is your name,
Your Will Be Done Now and Forever!
Yashu'a (Jesus) said: "Thou shalt love the Most High Heavenly Father, thy Sustainer with all
thy heart, and with all thy soul, and with all thy mind. Thou shalt love
thy neighbour as thyself."

wicked ways; then will I hear from heaven, and will forgive

their sin, and will heal their land, KJV 2 Chronicles 7:14."

So, for the Children of the Most High: Pristine Youth and Family

Solutions, LLC., the title of this book: "**ASSASSINS of**

Yashu'a (Jesus) said: "A new commandment I give unto
you, that ye love one another; as I have loved you,
that ye also love one another."

ASSASSINS of DISOBEDIENCE!
Invoking the Power of the Most High Through Obedience, is the Key to Living Your Best Life
as the Supreme Ingredient!
Heaven or Hell?

CHILDREN OF THE MOST HIGH:
PRISTINE YOUTH AND FAMILY SOLUTIONS, LLC.
SONS AND DAUGHTERS OF THE MOST HIGH PUBLISHERS ®

Oh, Gracious Most High Heavenly father, Holy is your name,
Your Will Be Done Now and Forever!
Yashu'a (Jesus) said: *"Thou shalt love the Most High Heavenly Father, thy Sustainer with all thy heart, and with all thy soul, and with all thy mind. Thou shalt love thy neighbour as thyself."*

DISOBEDIENCE! Invoking the Power of the Most High Through Obedience, is the Key to Living Your Best Life as the Supreme Ingredient! Heaven or Hell?" means the children of the Most High peacemakers (KJV Matthew 5:9) will rigorously work on improving their character through the Messiah Yashu'a (Jesus) by **eliminating (assassinating) disobedience** to **God's** (אֱלֹהִים **'Elohiym**), commandments. This is done through the Messiah Yashu'a (Jesus) by **Invoking the Power of the Most High Through Obedience** (being obedient to **the Most High Heavenly Father (ELYOWN עֶלְיוֹן EL אֵל**) and the Messiah Yashu'a (Jesus) commandments which is **the KEY ingredient** to **the children of the Most High living their best life!**

Appendix

Below is a Prayer of Repentance:

337

Yashu'a (Jesus) said: *"A new commandment I give unto you, that ye love one another; as I have loved you, that ye also love one another."*

ASSASSINS of DISOBEDIENCE!
Invoking the Power of the Most High Through Obedience, is the Key to Living Your Best Life
as the Supreme Ingredient!
Heaven or Hell?

CHILDREN OF THE MOST HIGH:
PRISTINE YOUTH AND FAMILY SOLUTIONS, LLC.
SONS AND DAUGHTERS OF THE MOST HIGH PUBLISHERS ®

Oh, Gracious Most High Heavenly father, Holy is your name,
Your Will Be Done Now and Forever!
Yashu'a (Jesus) said: "Thou shalt love the Most High Heavenly Father, thy Sustainer with all
thy heart, and with all thy soul, and with all thy mind. Thou shalt love
thy neighbour as thyself."

In the KJV bible book of Psalms chapter 51 verses 1-19; it states: "51 Have mercy upon me, O God, according to thy lovingkindness: according unto the multitude of thy tender mercies blot out my transgressions. ²Wash me throughly from mine iniquity, and cleanse me from my sin. ³For I acknowledge my transgressions: and my sin is ever before me. ⁴Against thee, thee only, have I sinned, and done this evil in thy sight: that thou mightest be justified when thou speakest, and be clear when thou judgest. ⁵Behold, I was shapen in iniquity; and in sin did my mother conceive me. ⁶Behold, thou desirest truth in the inward parts: and in the hidden part thou shalt make me to know wisdom."

"⁷Purge me with hyssop, and I shall be clean: wash me, and I shall be whiter than snow. ⁸Make me to hear joy and

Yashu'a (Jesus) said: "A new commandment I give unto you, that ye love one another; as I have loved you, that ye also love one another."

ASSASSINS of DISOBEDIENCE!
Invoking the Power of the Most High Through Obedience, is the Key to Living Your Best Life
as the Supreme Ingredient!
Heaven or Hell?

CHILDREN OF THE MOST HIGH:
PRISTINE YOUTH AND FAMILY SOLUTIONS, LLC.
SONS AND DAUGHTERS OF THE MOST HIGH PUBLISHERS ®

Oh, Gracious Most High Heavenly father, Holy is your name,
Your Will Be Done Now and Forever!
Yashu'a (Jesus) said: "Thou shalt love the Most High Heavenly Father, thy Sustainer with all
thy heart, and with all thy soul, and with all thy mind. Thou shalt love
thy neighbour as thyself."

gladness; that the bones which thou hast broken may rejoice. [9] Hide thy face from my sins, and blot out all mine iniquities. [10] Create in me a clean heart, O God; and renew a right spirit within me. [11] Cast me not away from thy presence; and take not thy holy spirit from me. [12] Restore unto me the joy of thy salvation; and uphold me with thy free spirit. [13] Then will I teach transgressors thy ways; and sinners shall be converted unto thee. [14] Deliver me from bloodguiltiness, O God, thou God of my salvation: and my tongue shall sing aloud of thy righteousness. [15] O Lord, open thou my lips; and my mouth shall shew forth thy praise."

"[16] For thou desirest not sacrifice; else would I give it: thou delightest not in burnt offering. [17] The sacrifices of God are

339

Yashu'a (Jesus) said: "A new commandment I give unto
you, that ye love one another; as I have loved you,
that ye also love one another."

ASSASSINS of DISOBEDIENCE!
Invoking the Power of the Most High Through Obedience, is the Key to Living Your Best Life
as the Supreme Ingredient!
Heaven or Hell?

CHILDREN OF THE MOST HIGH:
PRISTINE YOUTH AND FAMILY SOLUTIONS, LLC.
SONS AND DAUGHTERS OF THE MOST HIGH PUBLISHERS ®

Oh, Gracious Most High Heavenly father, Holy is your name,
Your Will Be Done Now and Forever!
Yashu'a (Jesus) said: "Thou shalt love the Most High Heavenly Father, thy Sustainer with all
thy heart, and with all thy soul, and with all thy mind. Thou shalt love
thy neighbour as thyself."

a broken spirit: a broken and a contrite heart, O God, thou

wilt not despise. ¹⁸ Do good in thy good pleasure unto Zion:

build thou the walls of Jerusalem. ¹⁹ Then shalt thou be

pleased with the sacrifices of righteousness, with burnt

offering and whole burnt offering: then shall they offer

bullocks upon thine altar."

All obedient children of the Most High are seeking the

Kingdom of God and the Messiah Yashu'a (the True Vine,

Yashu'a (Jesus) said: "A new commandment I give unto
you, that ye love one another; as I have loved you,
that ye also love one another."

ASSASSINS of DISOBEDIENCE!
Invoking the Power of the Most High Through Obedience, is the Key to Living Your Best Life
as the Supreme Ingredient!
Heaven or Hell?

CHILDREN OF THE MOST HIGH:
PRISTINE YOUTH AND FAMILY SOLUTIONS, LLC.
SONS AND DAUGHTERS OF THE MOST HIGH PUBLISHERS ®

Oh, Gracious Most High Heavenly father, Holy is your name,
Your Will Be Done Now and Forever!
Yashu'a (Jesus) said: "Thou shalt love the Most High Heavenly Father, thy Sustainer with all
thy heart, and with all thy soul, and with all thy mind. Thou shalt love
thy neighbour as thyself."

Jesus), who will take those who have repented, accepted him as their personal savior, and received the holy spirit, to the Most High Heavenly Father. Once a person has accepted the Messiah Yashu'a (Jesus) as their personal savior, there is a Kingdom of God inside of them, but not there exclusively; and they are always being attacked by the children of the devil. "Love gives naught but itself and takes naught but from itself. Love possesses not nor would it be possessed; For love is sufficient unto love." (Gibran, 1968).

What are the True Vine (Yashu'a, Jesus) Mind Gardening Daily Individual or Family Household Habits of Success?

341

Yashu'a (Jesus) said: "A new commandment I give unto you, that ye love one another; as I have loved you, that ye also love one another."

ASSASSINS of DISOBEDIENCE!
Invoking the Power of the Most High Through Obedience, is the Key to Living Your Best Life
as the Supreme Ingredient!
Heaven or Hell?

CHILDREN OF THE MOST HIGH:
PRISTINE YOUTH AND FAMILY SOLUTIONS, LLC.
SONS AND DAUGHTERS OF THE MOST HIGH PUBLISHERS ®

Oh, Gracious Most High Heavenly father, Holy is your name,
Your Will Be Done Now and Forever!
Yashu'a (Jesus) said: "Thou shalt love the Most High Heavenly Father, thy Sustainer with all
thy heart, and with all thy soul, and with all thy mind. Thou shalt love
thy neighbour as thyself."

The True Vine (Yashu'a, Jesus) Mind Gardening Daily
Individual or Family Household Habits of Success are:

1. Obey the Most High Heavenly Father's will and
   commandments now and forever!

2. Love the Most High Heavenly Father with all of your
   heart, all of your spirit, all of your soul, all of your mind,
   and all of your entire being!

3. Decrease so that the Spirit of the Messiah Yashu'a
   (Jesus) can increase in you!

4. Do unto others as you would want others to do unto you!

5. Always think positive!

6. Always be positive!

Yashu'a (Jesus) said: "A new commandment I give unto
you, that ye love one another; as I have loved you,
that ye also love one another."

ASSASSINS of DISOBEDIENCE!
Invoking the Power of the Most High Through Obedience, is the Key to Living Your Best Life
as the Supreme Ingredient!
Heaven or Hell?

CHILDREN OF THE MOST HIGH:
PRISTINE YOUTH AND FAMILY SOLUTIONS, LLC.
SONS AND DAUGHTERS OF THE MOST HIGH PUBLISHERS ®

Oh, Gracious Most High Heavenly father, Holy is your name,
Your Will Be Done Now and Forever!
Yashu'a (Jesus) said: *"Thou shalt love the Most High Heavenly Father, thy Sustainer with all thy heart, and with all thy soul, and with all thy mind. Thou shalt love thy neighbour as thyself."*

7. Always have a positive attitude!

8. Open your heart before you open your mouth!

9. Remember, words should be soft, not hard!

10. It's nice to be important, but it is more important to be nice!

11. Mine your mind for the jewels of your soul!

12. Pray together daily!

13. Eat together in the same room a minimum of once a week!

14. Observe the Sabbath (Shu-Bat) weekly as a family!

343

Yashu'a (Jesus) said: *"A new commandment I give unto you, that ye love one another; as I have loved you, that ye also love one another."*

ASSASSINS of DISOBEDIENCE!
Invoking the Power of the Most High Through Obedience, is the Key to Living Your Best Life
as the Supreme Ingredient!
Heaven or Hell?

CHILDREN OF THE MOST HIGH:
PRISTINE YOUTH AND FAMILY SOLUTIONS, LLC.
SONS AND DAUGHTERS OF THE MOST HIGH PUBLISHERS ®

Oh, Gracious Most High Heavenly father, Holy is your name,
Your Will Be Done Now and Forever!
Yashu'a (Jesus) said: *"Thou shalt love the Most High Heavenly Father, thy Sustainer with all*
thy heart, and with all thy soul, and with all thy mind. Thou shalt love
thy neighbour as thyself."

15. Study and read the scriptures of the Most High as a family a minimum of once a week!

16. Watch a TV show or movie at home a minimum of once a week!

17. Workout together as a family or ensure that all family members are working out on a weekly basis if their medical physicians have approved of them doing so.

18. Have family meetings once a week to discuss everyone's overall well-being, current events or anything else that is on any family member's mind, without the TV or any other electronic devices being on as a potential conversation distraction. One person speaks at a time, no arguing, no vulgarity, and all family members must respect each other!

344

Yashu'a (Jesus) said: *"A new commandment I give unto you, that ye love one another; as I have loved you, that ye also love one another."*

ASSASSINS of DISOBEDIENCE!
Invoking the Power of the Most High Through Obedience, is the Key to Living Your Best Life
as the Supreme Ingredient!
Heaven or Hell?

CHILDREN OF THE MOST HIGH:
PRISTINE YOUTH AND FAMILY SOLUTIONS, LLC.
SONS AND DAUGHTERS OF THE MOST HIGH PUBLISHERS ®

Oh, Gracious Most High Heavenly father, Holy is your name,
Your Will Be Done Now and Forever!
Yashu'a (Jesus) said: *"Thou shalt love the Most High Heavenly Father, thy Sustainer with all thy heart, and with all thy soul, and with all thy mind. Thou shalt love thy neighbour as thyself."*

19. Do some agreed upon, healthy, fun, and safe family event a minimum of once a month or weekly or bi-weekly together as a family.

345

Yashu'a (Jesus) said: *"A new commandment I give unto you, that ye love one another; as I have loved you, that ye also love one another."*

ASSASSINS of DISOBEDIENCE!
Invoking the Power of the Most High Through Obedience, is the Key to Living Your Best Life
as the Supreme Ingredient!
Heaven or Hell?

CHILDREN OF THE MOST HIGH:
PRISTINE YOUTH AND FAMILY SOLUTIONS, LLC.
SONS AND DAUGHTERS OF THE MOST HIGH PUBLISHERS ®

Oh, Gracious Most High Heavenly father, Holy is your name,
Your Will Be Done Now and Forever!
Yashu'a (Jesus) said: *"Thou shalt love the Most High Heavenly Father, thy Sustainer with all thy heart, and with all thy soul, and with all thy mind. Thou shalt love thy neighbour as thyself."*

In the KJV bible book of Genesis, chapter 14 verse 18; it states: "And Melchizedek (Malkiy-Tsedeq, מַלְכִּי־צֶדֶק) king of Salem brought forth bread and wine: and he was the priest of the <u>Most High</u> (ELYOWN עֶלְיוֹן EL אֵל) God." In the KJV bible book of Psalms chapter 82 verse 6; states: "I have said, Ye are gods; and all of you are children <u>of the Most High</u> (is the KJV bible Hebrew Strong's Concordance#5945 which is the title: <u>ELYOWN</u> עֶלְיוֹן (the God) EL אֵל)." In the KJV bible book of Numbers chapter 23 verse 19; states: "<u>God (EL אֵל) is not a man</u>, that he should lie; neither the <u>son of man, that he should repent</u>: hath he said, and shall he not do it? or hath he spoken, and shall he not make it good?" However, **for clarification it is critical that all children of the Most High know that in the KJV bible book of Genesis Chapter 1 verse 1; the original Aramic (Hebrew) word for "God" is "Elohiym" not the <u>Most High</u> (ELYOWN עֶלְיוֹן EL אֵל), the Sustainer, the Nourisher, the Provider of all Life, and the Omnipotent and the Omnipresent Creator of the boundless universes. So, the children of the Most High: Pristine Youth and Family Solutions, LLC. hopes that all children of the Most High acquire an** overstanding of the differences between "God" ("אֱלֹהִים 'Elohiym") in the KJV bible book of Genesis chapter 1 verse 1, "the LORD, יְהֹוָה Yehovah, (Yahuwa, Yahweh, Jehovah, Yahayyu)" who <u>repented</u> to the <u>Most High</u> (ELYOWN עֶלְיוֹן EL אֵל) in the KJV bible book of Genesis chapter 6 verse 6; who is referred to as: "**the LORD; and the** יְהֹוָה Yehovah "God" "**אֱלֹהִים 'Elohiym**" who gets <u>jealous</u> in the KJV bible book of Exodus chapter 20 verse 5; **ARE NOT TO BE CONFUSED AS BEING the <u>Most High</u> (ELYOWN עֶלְיוֹן EL אֵל), the Sustainer, the Nourisher, the Provider of all Life, and the Omnipotent and the Omnipresent Creator of the boundless universes who they all worship and do the 'Will" of!**

346

Yashu'a (Jesus) said: *"A new commandment I give unto you, that ye love one another; as I have loved you, that ye also love one another."*

ASSASSINS of DISOBEDIENCE!
Invoking the Power of the Most High Through Obedience, is the Key to Living Your Best Life
as the Supreme Ingredient!
Heaven or Hell?

CHILDREN OF THE MOST HIGH:
PRISTINE YOUTH AND FAMILY SOLUTIONS, LLC.
SONS AND DAUGHTERS OF THE MOST HIGH PUBLISHERS ®

Oh, Gracious Most High Heavenly father, Holy is your name,
Your Will Be Done Now and Forever!
Yashu'a (Jesus) said: *"Thou shalt love the Most High Heavenly Father, thy Sustainer with all*
thy heart, and with all thy soul, and with all thy mind. Thou shalt love
thy neighbour as thyself."

Nothing would exist if you Oh Gracious Most High Heavenly Father, The Creator didn't create it. You are alone in Your Greatness; you have no partners that share in your grace. To you all sovereignty is due and you are all powerful over everything. We seek refuge in you, the ever watchful Most High who hears and knows all things! Glory be to you as many times as the number of things you have created! All gratitude is due to you oh gracious Most High Heavenly Father, you are the Creator and Sustainer of all the boundless universes. You are the Yielder, and the most Merciful. The Ruler of the Day of Decision.

347

Yashu'a (Jesus) said: *"A new commandment I give unto you, that ye love one another; as I have loved you, that ye also love one another."*

ASSASSINS of DISOBEDIENCE!
Invoking the Power of the Most High Through Obedience, is the Key to Living Your Best Life
as the Supreme Ingredient!
Heaven or Hell?

CHILDREN OF THE MOST HIGH:
PRISTINE YOUTH AND FAMILY SOLUTIONS, LLC.
SONS AND DAUGHTERS OF THE MOST HIGH PUBLISHERS ®

Oh, Gracious Most High Heavenly father, Holy is your name,
Your Will Be Done Now and Forever!
Yashu'a (Jesus) said: "Thou shalt love the Most High Heavenly Father, thy Sustainer with all
thy heart, and with all thy soul, and with all thy mind. Thou shalt love
thy neighbour as thyself."

It's you whom we worship and it is you alone whom we beseech for help, oh Guide, guide us to the narrow path (which reflects moral integrity and positive character traits in action) of the ones who stand straight, the narrow path of those who earned your grace not inclusive of those who brought an everlasting curse on themselves, those who conceal the facts of that which they know to be true in order to lead the sincere-hearted seekers of your truth astray. Amen

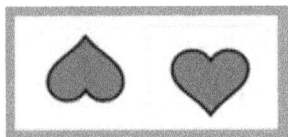

Yashu'a (Jesus) said: "A new commandment I give unto you, that ye love one another; as I have loved you, that ye also love one another."

ASSASSINS of DISOBEDIENCE!
Invoking the Power of the Most High Through Obedience, is the Key to Living Your Best Life
as the Supreme Ingredient!
Heaven or Hell?

CHILDREN OF THE MOST HIGH:
PRISTINE YOUTH AND FAMILY SOLUTIONS, LLC.
SONS AND DAUGHTERS OF THE MOST HIGH PUBLISHERS ®

Oh, Gracious Most High Heavenly father, Holy is your name,
Your Will Be Done Now and Forever!
Yashu'a (Jesus) said: *"Thou shalt love the Most High Heavenly Father, thy Sustainer with all*
thy heart, and with all thy soul, and with all thy mind. Thou shalt love
thy neighbour as thyself."

About the Author

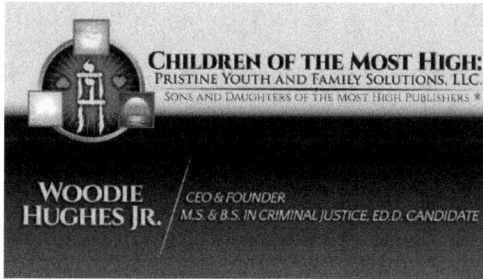

CHILDREN OF THE MOST HIGH:
PRISTINE YOUTH AND FAMILY SOLUTIONS, LLC.
SONS AND DAUGHTERS OF THE MOST HIGH PUBLISHERS ®

WOODIE HUGHES JR. / CEO & FOUNDER
M.S. & B.S. IN CRIMINAL JUSTICE, ED.D. CANDIDATE

Mr. Hughes is a Servant of the Most High, Teacher of the
Most High's Doctrine, and a Youth and Adults Workshop
and Presentation Consultant.

📞 478-538-1918
✉ INFO@CHILDRENOFTHEMOSTHIGH.COM
🌐 CHILDRENOFTHEMOSTHIGH.COM
🐦 @WOODIEHUGHESJR9
f CHILDRENOFTHEMOSTHIGHPRISTINEYOUTHANDFAMSOLUTIONS

349

Yashu'a (Jesus) said: *"A new commandment I give unto*
you, that ye love one another; as I have loved you,
that ye also love one another."

ASSASSINS of DISOBEDIENCE!
Invoking the Power of the Most High Through Obedience, is the Key to Living Your Best Life
as the Supreme Ingredient!
Heaven or Hell?

CHILDREN OF THE MOST HIGH:
PRISTINE YOUTH AND FAMILY SOLUTIONS, LLC.
SONS AND DAUGHTERS OF THE MOST HIGH PUBLISHERS ®

Oh, Gracious Most High Heavenly father, Holy is your name,
Your Will Be Done Now and Forever!
Yashu'a (Jesus) said: *"Thou shalt love the Most High Heavenly Father, thy Sustainer with all*
thy heart, and with all thy soul, and with all thy mind. Thou shalt love
thy neighbour as thyself."

Mr. Woodie Hughes Jr. is the CEO & Founder of the Children of the Most High: Pristine Youth and Families Solutions LLC., Sons and Daughters of the Most High Publishers. Mr. Hughes is a Servant of the Most High and a Teacher of the Most High's Doctrine. Mr. Hughes is an Author who writes books that are being put forth by the will of the Most High Heavenly Father to inspire all youth and all adults **who are children of the Most High** to acquire the **competitive edge** against the children of devil. Mr. Hughes is a career university educator. Mr. Woodie Hughes Jr. and Mrs. Tonya Hughes have been happily married for 20 years and have a son and a daughter. Mr. Hughes is a veteran who has received a United States Army honorable discharge for his 8 years of service with the Illinois Army National Guard.

350

Yashu'a (Jesus) said: *"A new commandment I give unto you, that ye love one another; as I have loved you, that ye also love one another."*

ASSASSINS of DISOBEDIENCE!
Invoking the Power of the Most High Through Obedience, is the Key to Living Your Best Life
as the Supreme Ingredient!
Heaven or Hell?

CHILDREN OF THE MOST HIGH:
PRISTINE YOUTH AND FAMILY SOLUTIONS, LLC.
SONS AND DAUGHTERS OF THE MOST HIGH PUBLISHERS ®

Oh, Gracious Most High Heavenly father, Holy is your name,
Your Will Be Done Now and Forever!
Yashu'a (Jesus) said: *"Thou shalt love the Most High Heavenly Father, thy Sustainer with all thy heart, and with all thy soul, and with all thy mind. Thou shalt love thy neighbour as thyself."*

Mr. Hughes is the son of Mrs. Annette Hughes and Mr. Woodie Hughes Sr. who have been happily married for 50 years (as of 2020)! For over 27 years, Mr. Woodie Hughes Jr. has continued to be a devout student and teacher of the Most High's doctrine who is guided by the will of the Heavenly Father, and the Messiah Yashua's (Jesus) spirit of knowledge, spirit of wisdom, and spirit of true-faith all working as the same spirits (KJV bible book of 1st Corinthians chapter 12 verses 8-9) of the Messiah Yashu'a (Jesus) which has graciously been bestowed upon him. Mr. Hughes has accepted the Messiah Yashu'a (Jesus) as his savior and is in the Body of Christ!

Yashu'a (Jesus) said: "A new commandment I give unto you, that ye love one another; as I have loved you, that ye also love one another."

ASSASSINS of DISOBEDIENCE!
Invoking the Power of the Most High Through Obedience, is the Key to Living Your Best Life
as the Supreme Ingredient!
Heaven or Hell?

CHILDREN OF THE MOST HIGH:
PRISTINE YOUTH AND FAMILY SOLUTIONS, LLC.
SONS AND DAUGHTERS OF THE MOST HIGH PUBLISHERS ®

Oh, Gracious Most High Heavenly father, Holy is your name,
Your Will Be Done Now and Forever!
Yashu'a (Jesus) said: *"Thou shalt love the Most High Heavenly Father, thy Sustainer with all*
thy heart, and with all thy soul, and with all thy mind. Thou shalt love
thy neighbour as thyself."

References

Ambrose, Stephen E., (2002). Smithsonian Magazine article entitled: "Founding Fathers and Slaveholders."

Clarke, J. H. (1992). Christopher Columbus and the Afrikan holocaust: Slavery and the rise of European capitalism (pp. 4-16). Brooklyn: A & B Books.

Carroll, R., & Prickett, S. (Eds.). (2008). The Bible: Authorized King James Version. OUP Oxford.

Gibran, K. (1968). Secrets of the Heart. Hallmark Cards Inc.

Gowan, D. E. (1988). From Eden to Babel: A Commentary on the Book of Genesis 1-11. Wm. B. Eerdmans Publishing.

Greene, R. (1998). The 48 Laws of Power. Penguin.
Hannah-Jones, Nikole Sheri; (2019). A reporter for the New York Times, 1609 Project.

Yashu'a (Jesus) said: "A new commandment I give unto you, that ye love one another; as I have loved you, that ye also love one another."

CHILDREN OF THE MOST HIGH:
PRISTINE YOUTH AND FAMILY SOLUTIONS, LLC.
SONS AND DAUGHTERS OF THE MOST HIGH PUBLISHERS ®

Oh, Gracious Most High Heavenly father, Holy is your name,
Your Will Be Done Now and Forever!
Yashu'a (Jesus) said: "Thou shalt love the Most High Heavenly Father, thy Sustainer with all thy heart, and with all thy soul, and with all thy mind. Thou shalt love thy neighbour as thyself."

References

Hendricks, L., Bore, S., Aslinia, D., & Morriss, G. (2013). The effects of anger on the brain and body. In National forum journal of counseling and addiction (Vol. 2, No. 1, pp. 2-5).

Houghton Mifflin Company. (2020). Online American Heritage Dictionary. Fifth Edition.

Hughes Jr., Woodie. (2019). Spiritual Trillionaire: Cherishing the Breath of Life While Simultaneously Preparing for the Blow of Death!

Lane Arabic/English Lexicon (2003).

Lyubomirsky, S., King, L., & Diener, E. (2005). The benefits of frequent positive affect: Does happiness lead to success? Psychological bulletin, 131(6), 803.

Mchie, Benjamin (2019). African American Registry® (the Registry).

Yashu'a (Jesus) said: "A new commandment I give unto you, that ye love one another; as I have loved you, that ye also love one another."

ASSASSINS of DISOBEDIENCE!
Invoking the Power of the Most High Through Obedience, is the Key to Living Your Best Life
as the Supreme Ingredient!
Heaven or Hell?

CHILDREN OF THE MOST HIGH:
PRISTINE YOUTH AND FAMILY SOLUTIONS, LLC.
SONS AND DAUGHTERS OF THE MOST HIGH PUBLISHERS ®

Oh, Gracious Most High Heavenly father, Holy is your name,
Your Will Be Done Now and Forever!
Yashu'a (Jesus) said: "Thou shalt love the Most High Heavenly Father, thy Sustainer with all thy heart, and with all thy soul, and with all thy mind. Thou shalt love thy neighbour as thyself."

References

Online Gesenius' Hebrew-Chaldee Lexicon (2020).

Online Merriam-Webster Dictionary (2020).

Online Etymology Dictionary (2020).

Palmer, C. (1992). African slave trade: the cruelest commerce. National geographic, 182(3), 62-91.

Safrai, S., Stern, M., Flusser, D., & van Unnik, W. C. (1976). Education and the Study of the Torah. In the Jewish People in the First Century, Volume 2 (pp. 945-970). Brill.

Zodhiates, S. (Ed.). (1991). The Hebrew-Greek Key Word Study Bible: King James Version, Zodhaites' Original and Complete System of Bible Study World Bible Publishers, Incorporated.

Yashu'a (Jesus) said: "A new commandment I give unto you, that ye love one another; as I have loved you, that ye also love one another."

www.ingramcontent.com/pod-product-compliance
Lightning Source LLC
LaVergne TN
LVHW051620080426
835511LV00016B/2095